The Ocean of All Possibilities

The Multiverse, the Eternal
Return... and Your Immortal Self

ANTHONY EAMES

BALBOA.PRESS

A DIVISION OF HAY HOUSE

Balboa Press books may be ordered through booksellers or by contacting:

Balboa Press
A Division of Hay House
1663 Liberty Drive
Bloomington, IN 47403
www.balboapress.com.au
AU TFN: 1 800 844 925 (Toll Free inside Australia)
AU Local: 0283 107 086 (+61 2 8310 7086 from outside Australia)

Print information available on the last page.

ISBN: 978-1-5043-2366-6 (sc)
ISBN: 978-1-5043-2367-3 (e)

Balboa Press rev. date: 05/13/2021

I thank everyone who helped me with this project, especially Terry, Joanna and Damien for your invaluable inputs.

Above all, I acknowledge the care and encouragement of Dr. Fujiko Watt - the gifted lady I am proud to call my wife.

Anthony Eames

Contents

'Of course,

the limitless universe

is incomprehensible,

but the limited universe

is absurd.'

AUGUSTE BLANQUI (1805 – 1881)

Preface

Parallel universes... eternal recurrence... the Multiverse... Block Time...

Not so long ago the exclusive preoccupation of science fiction fantasy, these mind-stretching concepts have become the focus of serious debate among physicists and cosmologists and are now staple fare in the most respected science journals.

Thus far, these radically new perspectives on our universe and our place in it have had little impact on how most people outside the scientific community relate to the world and order their lives. But this could be about to change

Just as Einstein's General Theory of Relativity eventually moved beyond a small circle of theoretical physicists to become a subject of wide public interest in the 1920s (it inspired Picasso's Cubist art, amongst other things), quantum mechanics' startling insights are today capturing the attention of an ever-widening audience. But if Einstein's relativity taxed our great-grandparents' brains, the task we face today is even harder, given that physicists themselves admit to being baffled by much of what appears to happen in the shadowy world of the quantum.

While the topic of parallel universes, or the Multiverse, is regularly aired in popular science magazines and on serious television programs, inevitably it comes across as something so bizarre that it is hard to think of it having any real connection with ordinary people living ordinary lives. Confronted by concepts so counter-intuitive and at odds with our trusted sense of reality, it is easy to understand why few can connect these speculations to the 'real' world we know.

The purpose of this book is to help connect these astonishing ideas with popular discourse. With a particular focus on the Multiverse concept and what Friedrich Nietzsche called 'The Eternal Return', it looks at how these emerging insights could open a wholly new understanding of the cosmos and where we fit into it. Along the way, the reader will be offered a different perspective on life and death that is explicable, plausible and enriching.

'The Ocean of All Possibilities' looks not only at current scientific inquiries but also at how seeking individuals over the ages have approached the questions of time and of eternal recurrence, for example, and has tried to pull these threads together to create a clearer, overall theme.

Accordingly, this exploration is informed by the rich and dense tapestry of ideas drawn from pre-Socratic philosophers, St Augustine, Zen teachers, Nietzsche (of course), poets living and dead, modern philosophers, and contemporary films and novels.

It is a net cast very wide...

Author's Note

Lately, there has been a surge of material seeking to legitimise certain New Age ideas with the help of insights based, it is claimed, on quantum science.

Granted, to many lay people even slightly acquainted with the new physics, the world of the quantum could appear so at odds with the clarity and logic of Newtonian physics, so improbable and 'magic', that it may seem to provide a half-way plausible underlay for all sorts of esoteric beliefs.

Nonetheless, the reality is that physicists look upon these misinterpreted or wildly speculative claims with great unease - and so should you. There is much about the new physics that seems disconcertingly counter-intuitive and very hard to understand, but it is still *science* and it is not a tool for occultists and spell-weavers.

Indeed, as we shall see, the rigorously scientific exploration of our quantum domain reveals more than enough magic of its own to excite anyone's imagination!

Anthony Eames
Sydney, Australia
March 2021

• <u>THE GREAT INTERROGATION</u>

Time… What is this most familiar, and most elusive,

of all mysteries? And how are we – mayfly creatures

of a moment – to find any slight

purchase on eternity?

And when we read the great

rhythms and cycles of life,

how can we not ask: 'have I been here before –

and am I yet fated to come this way again?'

To be human is to think, to wonder … and to

be ever tormented by this riddle!

1. The Most Intractable of Riddles

Fundamental Questions About Time, Human Destiny and Self

As a boarder in an Irish Catholic school in the nineteen-fifties, I was constantly directed to reflect on eternity. The recurring theme in religious talks, sermons and in the classroom was that this life was but a short, preparatory trial whose real purpose was to settle whether we would spend the rest of time enjoying heavenly bliss or, instead, would suffer the unending torments of hellfire. The afterlife, we were instructed, was where the real game would take place!

This was reinforced each year when the college president would treat us to his favourite sermon. It took the form of an imagined discussion in which a priest questioned a young man about his life plans.

'I intend studying law and qualifying as a solicitor.'

'And what then?'

'I suppose I'll get married and raise a family.'

'And what then?'

This interrogation went on until the youngster was, by degrees, forced to see himself as an old man on his deathbed and ready to breathe his last.

'And what then?', the priest would ask triumphantly.

None of the clergy who taught us could say much about the celestial option. Standing for all time in the presence of God, we were confidently assured, we would be endlessly transfixed by radiant happiness. To a schoolboy for whom half an hour kneeling at a pew during morning mass was an arduous enough test of piety, the allure of countless centuries singing God's praises seemed less than enticing.

The picture of Hell was altogether much more specific. Drawing upon Biblical warnings and the writings of various saints and others who had been granted a preview of Lucifer's domain, our religious instructors graphically described what awaited the unrepentant sinner.

In a stygian underworld of fire, boiling smoke and sulphurous lakes, hordes of leather-skinned demons would torment the damned, whose shrieks and plangent cries to Heaven would remain forever unanswered. And worst of all, would be the crushing realisation that all this unspeakable pain, anguish and loss was to last forever and ever. *Per saecula saeculorum.*

I once saw the famous *'Doom'* painting in the early medieval Church of Saints Peter and Paul in the Surrey village of Chaldon in England, which shows the horrifying threat that would have oppressed a mostly illiterate congregation. Dating from around 1170 and rediscovered during renovations in 1870, the large mural had monstrous demons ministering various infernal torments to the damned: boiling in pots, roasting over hot grills, amongst a few other exquisite tortures. For their part, the lucky souls who had made it to Paradise hung around in a desultory group looking down upon this mayhem with slightly bored expressions. Nonetheless, this lurid spectacle must have worked powerfully to dissuade at least a few of Chaldon's parishioners from drunkenness, gluttony and lewdness!

Precisely as was intended, all our priests' talk of a never-ending afterlife set me to thinking much about time and eternity. Probably not what they had intended was that this led me to read about eastern religions, metaphysics and, later, popular writings on Einsteinian physics and quantum mechanics.

It seemed at that time that we were offered two possibilities. One was that the physical universe was eternal, possibly in the form of a constantly regenerating cosmos, the 'Steady State' option proposed in 1948 by Fred Hoyle, Thomas Gold, Hermann Bondi and others. Alternatively, there was the more widely accepted 'Big Bang' theory (Sir Fred Hoyle's own dismissive epithet) which sees the universe exploding from a single point and, over billions of years, transforming from an inchoate sea of particles and energy into the stars and galaxies we live among today.

Within the Big Bang fraternity, some believed that over unimaginable eons this expansion would slow down and eventually all matter would then fall back into a 'Big Crunch'

3

and, possibly, then explode once more into another cycle of existence (the 'Pulsating Universe' model).

Others speculated that, having exploded out of nowhere, the universe will collapse and disappear forever into a singularity. The majority today, by contrast, imagine that our universe will expand forever. One by one, the stars will finally exhaust their fuel and, like dead cinders, drift ever farther apart into an eternal night, far outside the observable limits of the cosmos. Either way, as a fiery death or as a frozen death, it would be the end of this universe we know and everything and everyone in it.

For me, the question was how could our universe summon itself out of nothingness as a once-only, single event in all eternity unless bidden by an outside agency? After all, no philosophy or religion had ever challenged the observation made by Melissus of Samos in the fifth century BC that 'nothing can come from nothing' (εἴη γὰρ ἂν οὕτω καὶ οὐ γένοιτο or, more usually given in Latin as *nihil ex nihilo fit*).

The answer supplied by many religions, of course, is that it was God who performed this genesis miracle. But then would not God himself (or herself) be eternal, an unchanging Prime Mover? Yes, would be the religionists' response. So, why would an eternal God, all-powerful and self-sufficient, decide at one instant in all eternity that there was a need to create a single universe? Would not this need and intent have coexisted with God through all time? Or would God, the Supreme Being or whatever name one might choose to describe this entity, be forever creating and, possibly, destroying universes?

However I looked at it, it seemed certain to me that *something* was eternal, whether a single undying cosmos or an unending succession of single universes or a multiplicity of universes.

From this starting point, at some time in my twenties I came up with an idea that seemed to me inescapably logical and yet loaded with mind-boggling implications.

Endless Revisitations
If in one form or another the universe is eternal, I reasoned, then it must follow that the precise conjunction of the elements that make up this world and this instant would reassemble itself again and again, endlessly over incalculable ages. Thus, every event in our world would be revisited, not only in a way exactly identical to what we are experiencing, but also in numberless variations.

Some of these mirror worlds would be different only in the subtlest way; for example, in one my favourite eggcup might reappear in a different shade or colour. In another, one might be born with red hair – or find that one's mirror self had inherited great wealth.

For some years I mused over the rich implications stirred up by this thought.

Eventually, of course, I found that I was far from being the first to be struck by this idea. I read that the great French mathematician, Henri Poincaré (1854-1912), had himself speculated along these very lines. Then I discovered that the Eternal Return was a central element of the philosopher Nietzsche's thinking; and, indeed, that the idea had been posited in Hellenic times and was an article of faith of many venerable religions and philosophies.

I must confess that at first I was a little piqued at being robbed of exclusive title to this interesting notion. However, that quickly gave way to satisfaction that at least this idea had been taken seriously – and endorsed – by such august thinkers.

Best-sellers like Fritjof Capra's *'The Tao of Physics'*, Gary Zukav's *'The Dancing Wu Li Masters'*, highlighted a big appetite for books promising to explain the new physics and cosmology in straightforward language. That demand continues to this day.

Many readers were drawn in by the prospect that this bizarre, hobgoblin world of quantum physics might unlock centuries of debate over all sorts of fundamental questions. But surely it would be almost impossible to persuade ordinary people to accept, or even understand, anything so improbable?

Against this, I can only say that when Nicolaus Copernicus presented his case that the planets, including our own, circled the Sun, and that the Earth no longer sat in majestic splendour at the centre of all creation, he was ridiculed for challenging not only the authority of Ptolemy, but the clear evidence available to anyone who lifted their eyes heavenwards. Little wonder that he wisely withheld publication of his book, *'De revolutionibus orbium coelestium'* (On the Revolutions of the Celestial Spheres) until just before his death in 1543.

Thanks to the discoveries of the mighty Galileo Galilei and Johannes Kepler, amongst others, Europe's intellectuals eventually recognised that Copernicus had been right after all. Indeed, Galileo's observations of Jupiter through his *telescopi* showed that the gas giant was itself encircled by a retinue of moons that formed its own 'mini-solar system'.

Opening the Mind's Door

Whatever the intellectual ferment created by these discoveries, did they really affect the lives of ordinary people? I believe the answer is that, in time, they did. By asserting the primacy of observable, verifiable facts linked with objective reasoning, they showed the poverty of relying blindly upon rigid church authority and unchallengeable verdicts of Hellenic times. Despite facing many hurdles, courageous questors for the truth could see a way ahead - and that this search would be illumined by science. In time, this became the accepted way to understand and change our world, and so humanity passed through the portal into the modern era.

With the seventeenth century came a surge of enquiry and discovery that put many medieval certainties to rout. Observation, measurement and calculation, rather than a reverential and unquestioning deference to hoary wisdom, delivered more and better answers to old and new questions.

In just this way, by sifting through the greatest mass of sidereal observational data ever recorded up to that time, Johannes Kepler deduced his three laws of planetary motion: i.) all solar bodies circle the sun in ellipses; ii.) the area swept out by the line from the orbiting planet to the sun remains constant over a given time, regardless of its varying distance from the sun; and iii.) the square of a planet's orbital period is proportional to the cube of the semi-major axis of its orbit. With no exaggeration, we can say that this was when the *science* of astronomy was born.

And then came Newton. If Copernicus, Galileo, Kepler and the others had begun to open our eyes to how the universe was conducting itself, it was Isaac Newton who explained *why* the bodies moved about so. A strange individual who invented modern physics while also enthusiastically immersed in alchemy and astrology, he could be said to have created the intellectual bridge between the medieval and modern worlds. Single-handedly, Newton described a clockwork universe in which everything moved according to immutable, universal laws that, in turn, could predict precisely where the celestial bodies would be at any future time.

Quite apart from his many other achievements (co-inventing calculus, for example, and greatly advancing optics), this was an intellectual feat that is still without parallel in history. In a real sense, it is Newton who steers our spacecraft towards the farthest reaches of the planetary system.

Our continuing journey from medieval certainties has entailed a progressive dispossession of humankind. Once the darlings of God's creation, we have been nudged from centre-stage and with each new revelation we find ourselves shrinking ever further into physical insignificance.

Challenging the Ptolemaic vision, Copernicus had relocated our planet from the axis of the solar system - and everything else - to a subsidiary position amidst a planetary entourage that was still thought to be the centrepiece of the universe. Then we came to realise that our sun was but one inconsequential body in the dormitory suburbs of the Milky Way - itself a vast agglomeration of 100-400 billion suns. Next, Hubble's discoveries were to reveal that our mighty Milky Way is but one of what was thought to be 170-200 billion similar galaxies.

All the while, of course, the boundaries of our observable universe were pressing ever-outwards and are now calculated to reach some 46 billion light years from the earth and with a diameter of twice that. Bearing in mind that a light year at the currently calculated speed of light (almost 300,000 kilometres a second) measures out a full 9 trillion kilometres, we are talking about distances beyond any human imagining. This gigantic universe, thought to have emerged from a 'Big Bang' instant of creation some 13.7 billion years ago, might be home to at least 10^{24} stars.

Beyond All Numbers

Now, we are being told, our entire universe, which the late Carl Sagan memorably explained encompasses more stars than there are grains of sand on all the beaches on Earth, may itself be but one of an infinite ensemble of universes - the Multiverse - that come into being and die in a process that has neither beginning nor end!

To any person who gives it the slightest reflection, this revelation cannot be anything less than shocking. For one thing, some will find it hard to believe that any Creator-God could maintain a personal special interest in mankind's fortunes, much less in the fate of any single individual eking out their brief moment on this drifting dust-mote we call the Earth. And for the unbelievers themselves, the insignificance of all human endeavour within this cosmic vastness must surely make our grand pretensions utterly risible.

So, one can begin to understand the church prelates who declined Galileo's invitation to look through his telescope and see the Ptolemaic universe refuted by their own eyes. They could not bear their entire world and all their scripture-vouched doctrines and explanations being reduced to nonsense. In our own time we also stand at such a crossroads where our intuitive sense of the world and our place in it are being shaken profoundly.

2. Eternity

The Nature of Eternity and Infinity

If there is one place that really knows how to put on a good party, it is Sydney, Australia's largest city. So, it was no surprise that, as host of the 2000 Olympic Games and one of the first cities to herald in the millennial year, Sydney should open the festivities with the biggest fireworks spectacular ever seen over its beautiful Harbour. As this pyrotechnic extravaganza at last reached its end, the iconic Harbour Bridge was dramatically enveloped in curtains and cascades of light that drew an amazed roar from hundreds of thousands ringing the shoreline. Suddenly, this display darkened and across the giant spans of the bridge was traced a single, shimmering word...

'Eternity'.

To billions of television viewers around the world this must have seemed a mystifying endnote for such relentlessly upbeat and boisterous opening ceremonies. But most Sydneysiders instantly recognised this word, with its distinctive italic script, as a motif strongly embedded in the city's folklore.

In the 1930s, people walking the city's downtown streets first noticed the single word, *Eternity*, neatly inscribed on the pavement in chalk. The same word, written in a stylised copperplate hand, was then to appear all over the city for several decades, prompting much speculation as to the identity of the mysterious nocturnal scribe, soon known by all as 'The Eternity Man'.

Eventually, after some 30 years' speculation, one night he was photographed in the act and identified as one Arthur Stace. The story emerged that Stace, a former thief and alcoholic addicted to drinking methylated spirits, had found God and turned his life around. Overwhelmingly grateful for his redemption, he had taken to writing 'Eternity' on Sydney's walkways some half-million times, always on his hands and knees, and in all weather. His gentle hope was to inspire the folk of this robustly secular city to look to the hereafter.

Once the mystery of the Eternity Man's identity was resolved, the city was fascinated by the simple and dedicated piety of this solitary, former derelict. Long after his death in 1967, Arthur Stace still remains a key figure in local folklore and, indeed, was the subject of a film documentary and of an opera performed at the iconic Sydney Opera House in 2005. Fittingly, there is a reproduction of his 'Eternity' embossed in brass in the pavement of Sydney Square outside St Andrew's Cathedral.

The Persistent Mystery

Arthur Stace chose his one-word sermon very well. The idea of eternity is certain to compel the attention of devout believer and cheerful pagan alike because it is the ever-present backdrop behind each individual existence. It is a concept that is inevitably humbling, for it makes all our pretensions and strivings seem very small indeed. And for some, just the very thought itself is terrifying - and that fear of the eternal or the infinite even has its own name: *apeirophobia*.

Eternity is a daunting mystery that has long exercised the minds of philosophers and metaphysicians, prophets and saints, scientists and lay people for as long as we marvelled at the great arc of timeless stars above.

The enquiring Greeks thought eternity such a powerful concept that they allocated to it its own deity. *Aion* (Greek - Αιών) was the god who presided over unbounded time: a domain different to the linear time of past, present and future that was the fiefdom of the god *Chronos* (Χρόνος - Time). Usually portrayed as a youth, Aion was also rendered as an old man, in this way indicating that he represented the unending cycles of time. Aion became an important figure in the esoteric Roman-era cults of Dionysius, Mithraism, Gnosticism and others - and the god was also identified with the Eternal City of Rome itself. From that god's name, we derive the modern word, 'eon' - a very long period of time.

While the Romans created *Aevum* as the equivalent of Aion, this deity was represented in female form as the goddess *Aeternitas* (Eternity) and as such was much more prominent and more widely revered; even appearing on the coinage issued in the reigns of six emperors.

Then and now, almost everyone has had to confront the challenge of eternity – and, like the great 18th century lexicographer Dr Samuel Johnson, usually found the task daunting.

It was recorded that one of his future biographers, Hester Thrale Piozzi, once sought his thoughts on the subject of eternity. For a man famous for his decisive pronouncements across a vast range of topics, his reply was uncharacteristically muted:

'Such a notion, indeed, can scarcely find room in the human mind'.

Very much the same was said by the American writer, Edgar Allen Poe, in his essay, *'Eureka'* (1848):

'…As an individual, I may be permitted to say that I cannot conceive Infinity, and am convinced that no human being can.'

In my youth, as I said, I had every opportunity to meditate upon the mind-numbing significance of eternity. At my boarding school almost every religious retreat ended on a sermon that described most graphically the horror of eternal hellfire.

The Australian film, *'Devil's Playground'* featured something very close to this very sermon, when a priest – played by the author Thomas Keneally - addressed a group of young seminarians.

Likewise, the following excerpt from James Joyce's *'Portrait of the Artist as a Young Man'* also paraphrases almost exactly the chastening sermon that I had heard so often, and which was confidently relied upon to silence both boisterous young tearaways and pious altar boys:

'Forever! For all eternity! Not for a year or for an age but forever. Try to imagine the awful meaning of this. You have

often seen the sand on the seashore. How fine are its tiny grains! And how many of those tiny little grains go to make up the small handful which a child grasps in its play. Now imagine a mountain of that sand, a million miles high, reaching from the earth to the farthest heavens, and a million miles broad, extending to remotest space, and a million miles in thickness; and imagine such an enormous mass of countless particles of sand multiplied as often as there are leaves in the forest, drops of water in the mighty ocean, feathers on birds, scales on fish, hairs on animals, atoms in the vast expanse of the air: and imagine that at the end of every million years a little bird came to that mountain and carried away in its beak a tiny grain of that sand. How many millions upon millions of centuries would pass before that bird had carried away even a square foot of that mountain, how many eons upon eons of ages before it had carried away all? Yet at the end of that immense stretch of time not even one instant of eternity could be said to have ended. At the end of all those billions and trillions of years eternity would have scarcely begun.'

This is only part of the priest's grim sermon, but the point had already been made. And had anyone managed to push this unthinkable thought from their minds, there was still the grim reminder on countless gravestones in old country cemeteries that urged:

'Pause, Stranger as you pass by.
As you are, so once was I;
As I am so must you be.
Therefore fix your thoughts on Eternity!'

Myths of Endless Atonement

Twenty-five centuries or more ago, the Greeks also well understood that nothing would work deeper into an audience's imagination than the telling of a dire torment inflicted, and endured, without remission *for all time*. Of such morality myths, the most enduring are the stories of Prometheus, Sisyphus and Tantalus.

Sisyphus was a king, avaricious and deceitful, who violated the laws of hospitality by killing travellers and guests. The gods' punishment was to force him to push a heavy rock up a steep hill. Each time his labours finally brought the peak within touching distance, the rock would suddenly roll all the way back to his starting point. Again and again, he strained at this bootless task through all eternity, ever mindful of its unavailing futility. (In his essay, *'The Myth of Sisyphus',* the philosopher Albert Camus holds up the story of Sisyphus as an example of how we might endure the eternal return with an unbroken spirit!)

Prometheus was a Titan, a god-like giant, with a deep affection for humanity. To aid us, he stole fire from Zeus, the king of the gods, and passed this inestimable gift on to mortals. For this impious crime, Zeus had Prometheus chained to a rock to be visited every day by a large eagle that ate his liver. This organ would then grow back again in time to be devoured yet again by the same eagle the following day, and every day after that.

One legend says that Tantalus was punished for stealing ambrosia and nectar (the food and drink of the gods) from Zeus' table to bring back to his people, an act of promethean beneficence. The other account is that he had sacrificed his son, chopped him up and served him up in a banquet to the unsuspecting gods! In any case, his punishment was to stand locked in a pool of water, underneath a tree with low-hanging branches. Racked with thirst, he found the water receding out of reach whenever he tried to take a quenching sip, and when he reached up to sate his hunger with a piece of fruit, the branches would rise up just out of his grasp. Thus, anything that we desire obsessively, yet remains unobtainable, is said to be 'tantalising'.

The horror of these accounts was threefold: the agony of the punishment itself, the fact that it was unremitting for all time and that Prometheus, Sisyphus and Tantalus understood that this was to be so.

Later, in the Christian world, there arose another myth built around the idea of unceasing earthly punishment and this became known across Europe as the Legend of the Wandering Jew. The story was that, as Christ was dragging his cross to the place of his crucifixion, a man in the crowd, a certain Ahasverus, mocked him and struck him for making such slow progress. Christ then told Ahasverus (also known as Buttadaeus) that he would be doomed to walk the face of the earth until Jesus' return at the Second Coming. According to the myth, Ahasverus soon repented of his sin and became a baptised convert – but was still not spared his long wait. In the meantime, he aged normally up until the age of 100, at which time his skin peeled off and he emerged once more as a young man of 30.

In this fashion, Ahasverus wandered endlessly backwards and forwards across Europe, earning food by recounting his pitiful tale to everyone, from simple villagers up to the courts of religious prelates, learned men and princes. There were reported sightings of this pathetic individual all over Christendom, from Spain to Russia, throughout the Middle Ages, and up until the 19th century. This world-weary penitent, longing for respite from deathlessness, it was said, had even been encountered in North America.

'As Far from Infinitude as Ever'
How can we conceive of eternity?

Let us begin with numbers. Acting upon a need only another mathematician could fully appreciate, Edward Kasner decided to fix an extremely large, all-purpose number whose value would be easily remembered. It needed a name and for this he turned to his 9-year-old nephew, Milton, who in 1920 decided that such an improbably huge number begged an equally improbable name... and so the term *googol* was coined.

A googol is 10 to the 100th power, that is 1 followed by 100 zeros. This is a number so huge that none but those who soar in the airy realms of higher mathematics could possibly find any use for it.

Clearly then, a googol is quite a hefty number, as this example will illustrate. Our universe, it is conservatively estimated, contains up to 400 billion galaxies, each containing roughly 100 billion stars - and no one can yet guess how many planets and other bodies. On top of that, there is a prodigious amount of 'dark matter' that, many believe, may dwarf the mass of all the stars and their planets. Add up all the elementary particles of all this material in our cosmos and, with a total of only 10 to the 80th power, we would still fall well short of a googol.

Yet a googol of years might elapse and we would still not even have accounted for the merest slice of eternity. Turn to a googolplex (10 to the power of googol) and the result would still be no more impressive. As the sermonising priest told his awestruck young listeners all those years ago, our journey through eternity would not even have begun.

Again, as Dr Johnson explained to Mrs Thrale:

'We must settle the matter thus: numeration is certainly infinite, for eternity might be employed in adding unit to unit; but every number is in itself finite, as the possibility of doubling it easily proves; besides, stop at what point you will, you find yourself as far from infinitude as ever.'

Obviously, when grappling with the idea of eternity we have to dispense with mere numbers for, like its twin, infinity, it is quite literally beyond counting. Here we encounter paradoxes and anomalies that profoundly challenge our intuitive grasp of the everyday world.

For example, an eternity multiplied by itself still remains... an eternity. Again, something that happens daily throughout eternity cannot be said to happen any more times than that which only happens every year.

Were I to buy a lottery ticket every week, year in and year out, it might be realistic under the odds to expect the big prize on average once in a thousand lifetimes. Within eternity the number of tickets bought and the big prizes won would both occur an infinite number of times – and you cannot have one infinity greater than another, just as you cannot have one eternity longer or shorter than another! However, what we can say is that one event would occur through eternity more or less *frequently* than another.

Another thing to remember is the circularity of eternity.

Let me explain. For some 20 years I used an ancient computer game of draughts (or checkers, as it is known in North America) as a form of mental callisthenics first thing in the morning, with the emphasis upon speed rather than slow, chess-like deliberation. With practise I could spot recurring set pieces and reliably guess where I might be in half a dozen or more moves. Playing against such a simple algorithm meant I would only rarely encounter an unfamiliar course of play!

Likewise, if you had a group of poker players shuffling, dealing and playing cards long enough, they too would reach the position where they would have encountered just about every possible game variation and would henceforth be merely repeating earlier plays.

On a cosmic scale, the same thing would also happen over eternity. Every possibility, no matter how remote, would be acted out over time so that all that could ever happen would be no more than an encore of what had already occurred an infinite number of times previously. Not only that, but the very sequence of events would be replayed repeatedly in the same order, no matter how prodigiously long that sequence might be.

In this way, one cannot see eternity as an open-ended run of always-unique phenomena and events: it must be a replay of what has happened and what will happen. Chaos theory, which challenges the precise replicability of complex, random systems incorporating a sufficient range of permitted variations, can only stand within the context of a single universe's lifetime. It must break down when confronted by eternity for the simple reason that eternity encompasses every possibility, no matter how fragile and rare, and duplicates it endlessly, like an inconceivably huge fractal. If it could not, then it would not be eternity.

Appropriately, the idea of eternity has been symbolised since the time of the Ancient Greeks as a snake swallowing its own tail. *Ouroboros* (ουροβόρος), as this symbol is known, clearly refers to the cyclicality of time, incorporating an endless repetition of all events through eternity. The same concept is also shown in the mathematical symbol for infinity – ∞ – known as *lemniscus*, from the Latin for 'pendant ribbon'.

$$\infty = \text{INFINTY}$$

Very graphically, this symbol reminds us that it is as futile to look for a beginning or an end to eternity as it is to try to locate a starting or ending point on a circle or closed loop.

In Summary

So, we may say that eternity encompasses these characteristics:

1. Eternity is not simply an inconceivably vast number of years or events. Even the mind-numbing stretch of time described by Joyce's priest still deals with numbers and imaginable intervals, but the reality is that eternity is *all* numbers and *all* time.

2. Eternity and infinity share key characteristics: one describes endless time and the other refers to endless space or numbers. Both must encompass all possible phenomena and all possible events.

3. Eternity and infinity are immutable. An inconceivably large number may be added to or subtracted from them, or used to divide or multiply them, and the result is always exactly the same: you are still left with eternity and infinity.

4. If the range of possible sets of physical laws in the Multiverse is not unlimited, we must accept that every universe will be re-enacted over and over again. This makes the Multiverse the arena in which an enormous, but theoretically limited, range of possibilities is being forever rediscovered in a great, unending cycle.

5. There can be no unique event within eternity. Consider this: any single event must have been preceded by eternity – and will be followed by eternity. Accordingly, it

would be quite impossible to fix a time when this singular event could fall or could have fallen. Whatever time you choose will be either an eternity before or after this unique event. An event of fixed duration, no matter how long it may last, will be a singularity of no duration in relation to the overall span of infinite time.

6. The corollary is that any event that could ever have happened will have to have been acted out an infinite number of times. The rarest, once-in-the-duration-of-a-universe happening will be revisited just as many times as a commonplace occurrence – that is, by an infinite number. Again, what will vary, of course, is the regularity or periodicity of a particular event.

Truly, eternity is a very weighty thing to contemplate, as both Dr Johnson and the pavement evangelist Arthur Stace recognised - and, no philosophical and scientific enquiry into the fundamental nature of reality can succeed without taking it into account.

3. A Question of Time

The New – and Not So New – Insights
into the Nature of Time

What is time? This question is as old as philosophy itself.

Our everyday sense of time is simple enough. It moves in one direction. There is a past, a future and a line that intersects the two that we call the present - and this is where *we* live. This intuitive or subjective sense of time is supported by the fact that we (more or less successfully) order our lives by it.

So, we happily accept Aristotle's view that the 'now' is both an end of what has passed and a beginning of time yet unfolding.

Yet the exasperated plaint of St Augustine (354 - 430 A.D.) still has the same familiar ring today as it surely had all those centuries ago. In his *'The City of God'*, the great philosopher and theologian asked:

'For what is time? Who can easily and briefly explain it? Who can even comprehend it in thought or put the answer into words? Yet is it not true that in conversation we refer to nothing more familiarly of knowingly than time? And surely we understand it when we speak of it; we understand it also when we hear another speak of it.'

After much reflection, St Augustine, the Bishop of Hippo in North Africa, came to the perceptive view that our sense of the present is the creation of an 'intellective memory' in which the mind fuses the just-happened with the anticipated 'just-about-to-happen'. We can understand that this sense of the 'now' is dynamic, being constantly updated with fresh information at a rate fast enough to sustain the illusion of continuity – and what we describe as the 'passage of time'.

As beings capable of reflection, humans are ever mindful of time. A sense of time is the starting point for drawing a connection between cause and effect, for predicting outcomes and deducing probabilities, for imagining and planning, for drawing conclusions and learning: all the hallmarks of a mind that is not completely instinctual and reflexive, but instead is aware of itself and can think in the abstract. It would be impossible to imagine any type of self-awareness that is not anchored to a sense of temporality.

Inevitably, too, this sense of time and self connects to the notion of personal mortality and to speculation about The Great Beyond.

The River of Time
We often hear and read, too, of 'the arrow of time', as in Groucho Marx's much-quoted dictum, *'time flies like an arrow... fruit flies like a banana!'*. The 'arrow' is a favourite metaphor for suggesting the unidirectional and swift procession of events.

However, the other familiar metaphor for time describes it as a river, eternal and unstoppable. Indeed, we do experience time as something that *flows*. An unbroken procession of events glide past that fixity that we call the self, emerging from the future, falling into the purview of the present and then disappearing into the past.

The Emperor-Stoic Philosopher Marcus Aurelius writes in his *'Meditations'* (Book IV): *'Time is like a river made up of the events which happen, and a violent stream; for as soon as a thing has been seen, it is carried away, and another comes in its place, and this will be carried away too.'*

Many centuries later, Herman Hesse wrote in his novel, *'Siddhartha'*, of the young man, Govinda, trekking across India in a fruitless quest to gain insight and serenity, only to find his answer at last on the bank of a great river whose paradoxical character, as a fixed body that is yet ever-moving, presented a mind-opening insight into the transience of all existence.

'He no longer saw the face of his friend Siddhartha, instead he saw other faces, many, a long sequence, a flowing river of faces, of hundreds, of thousands, which all came and disappeared, and yet all seemed to be there simultaneously, which all constantly changed and renewed themselves, and which were still all Siddhartha.'

In this vision Govinda saw the faces of a dying fish, a new-born baby, an act of murder, couples making love, corpses and gods: the whole procession and panoply of life in its myriad manifestations and interactions.

'...He saw all of these figures and faces in a thousand relationships with one another, each one helping the other, loving it, hating it, destroying it, giving re-birth to it, each one has a will to die, a passionately painful confession of transitoriness, and yet none of them died, each one only transformed, was always re-born, received evermore a new face, without any time having passed between the one and the other face - and all of these figures and faces rested, flowed, generated themselves, floated along and merged with each other...'

The Argentinian writer, Jorge Luis Borges, whose fascination with temporality weaves through many of his short stories, believed that time, flowing time, was the essence of his being.

'Time is a river that carries me away, but I am the river.' (*Other Inquisitions*, 1952)

Newton's view was that time not only flowed, but was a universal, absolute constant. Wherever one might live in the universe, time there would be exactly the same and would process at exactly the same, stately pace as it would in a far-distant galaxy. As he put it, 'time flows equably without reference to anything external...'

On this assumption, two precisely accurate clocks, set to exactly the same time, would always remain in perfect synchronicity, no matter how far distantly you then separated them.

The Paradox of Time

Possibly the most famous poser about time was presented by the Greek philosopher Zeno in the 5th century BC. A pupil and friend of Parmenides, he was a prominent member of the pre-Socratic philosophical movement, the Eleatic School, founded by Parmenides in Elea in southern Italy. For his part, Zeno was a monist, that is, one who believed that all things are, in essence, simply aspects of a single eternal reality which he called 'Being'. Maintaining that 'all is one', Zeno said that, at the most fundamental level, both change and a state of non-being are impossible.

Zeno asked us to imagine a race between a hare and a tortoise, with the tortoise given a several metre start. Naturally, his audience's common-sense experience of the world would have told them that this was a no-contest, no matter how lazy the hare or competitive the tortoise. The hare would very quickly overtake the tortoise to win the race.

Then, Zeno declared, how do you answer this? Each time the hare leaps forward it closes the gap between itself and the tortoise. However, no matter how much slower, the tortoise also nudges forward. So, even as the hare is within a millimetre of surging ahead of the tortoise, the tortoise would have moved that tiny fraction further forward. While the gap between the two would get smaller and smaller, the tortoise's constant progress would ensure that the gap would never close completely - and so the hare would never outpace the tortoise.

In the real world, we know very well that the hare would have bounded confidently past the lumbering tortoise, but for centuries thinkers battled to resolve Zeno's Paradox.

And this is only one of the riddles that attach themselves to the notion of a fluid, linear time and our definition of the present as the narrow line that separates the past from the future.

How about this? We believe that, by definition, the past, obviously no longer exists: it did; but does no more. At the same time, the future, by definition, will sometime exist, but right now does not.

So what exactly does exist? Is it the 'present'? As a hairline division between the two apparently non-existent states, it cannot logically have any duration in itself because such an interval could still be cleaved into the no-longer-existing past and the yet-to-exist future. Since we living beings are alive and aware of the fact, we exist - but where? Answer that and you have taken a big step towards explaining both time and the nature of individual consciousness.

And another one... Assuming that eternity exists (and how could it not! many would say), then it follows that one's life was preceded by an eternity, a period of infinite span and with no beginning - and just as certainly, it will be followed by an eternity with no end, regardless of what happens to our local universe. How then, can it be that your existence is a unique event happening *now* - and not at some time in the eternal past or eternal future?

And this is just a sampling of the baffling paradoxes that are delivered gift-wrapped, courtesy of our notion of linear time!

Inconstant Time

A century ago, Albert Einstein challenged Newton's assertion that time was universally constant: an uncontested axiom for more than two hundred years. First, Einstein declared that time and space both were inextricably linked. Furthermore, time was a purely local affair, with the hands of a fast-traveling clock rotating slower relative to those of another, stationary clock.

Seeming to contradict observed reality, the Special Theory of Relativity appeared to do violence to both common experience and generations of science. Luckily for Einstein, his ideas arrived when science and technology could soon put them to the test, and in due course he was proven right. (It should be mentioned that in 1898, the French mathematician, Henri Poincaré had also described a version of time relativity).

According to Einstein, the two clocks mentioned earlier would, even if perfectly accurate, show different times if one of them was made to accelerate to a very great speed relative to the other - or, alternatively, if it entered a very powerful gravitational field.

The faster one travels up to, but not past, the speed of light, the more time slows down for the traveller relative to the rate that time passes for those he had left behind. On this basis, astronauts who travelled to the Moon and back were fractionally younger (300 millionths of a second) than if they had stayed at home. Because of this time dilation they had not only travelled to the Moon, but also had made a very small, but real, excursion into their Earth-bound colleagues' future! (The time travel record is held by Cosmonaut Sergei Avdeyev. After some two years on the space station Mir rotating around the Earth, he is all of 0.02 seconds younger than he should be had he remained earth-bound.)

From this, we can say that time can be conceived of, not as an arrow flying at a fixed speed, but more like a broad current in which the water flows in one direction, but processes at varying speeds from place to place along its course, faster in the middle and slower along the banks, affected at different points by channel width, the undulations of the underwater topography, obstacles, winds, cross-currents and other variables.

It should be declared that, while time travel into the future is real and demonstrable, time travel into the past for anything above a sub-atomic particle, at least, is not at all a certain prospect, even theoretically.

As explained, human-engineered, forward time travel is already here and is quite a routine operation. High-energy particle accelerators push electrons, protons and other sub-atomic particles to speeds approaching that of light and this slows their time relative to that of the scientists conducting their experiments. In this way, these fast-moving particles have been propelled into our future and, if these particles were conscious entities, they would be seeing the scientists slipping into their past!

At the level of our everyday experience, relativity's mechanism still operates, even if the time slippage between someone in a jet aircraft and a person waiting to greet them at the airport is so minute as to seem immeasurable (but not quite, for it has been done!). Nonetheless, the fact is that everything relative to everything else is slipping forwards or backwards in time: quite simply, in absolute terms there is no universal 'now'.

This is the very point presented in what philosophers call the 'Rietdijk-Putnam Argument', so named after the theoretical physicist C.W. Rietdijk and philosopher Hilary Putnam, which draws upon special relativity to support the position known as 'four-dimensionalism'. As Einstein showed, each observer moving around at different velocities relative to others and other things must occupy their own time-frame, or 'plane of simultaneity'. In other words, every one of us lives within our own 'now' - even if it is only imperceptibly different to the 'nows' of others. The fact that all these 'nows' can exist within the same universe proves, argued Rietdijk and Putnam, that time itself has the qualities of a dimension, just like the three spatial dimensions. In this, they echoed the leading 20th-century philosopher Martin Heidegger, who stated emphatically that 'true time is four-dimensional'. (This idea will be explored in more detail later.)

On top of this, the quantum world's uncertainty principle means that sub-atomic particles are very hard to pin down in terms of location and velocity: the more accurately one tries to gauge the velocity, the less accurately one can fix the position - and vice versa. Amongst other things, time itself becomes quite topsy-turvy in the sub-atomic domain, with a particle able to pop backwards and forwards between the future, present and past of those doing the measuring.

How unrelentingly unidirectional is time? A persuasive case has been presented that electromagnetic waves, including radio waves, seem to travel in *both* directions at once! Physicists talk of 'advanced' waves, which arrive before they are sent, and 'retarded' waves which arrive after they have been sent.

Another indication of backwards time travel has been described by Caslav Brukner of the University of Vienna and his collaborators who suggest that backwards time travel is possible at the sub-atomic level when moments of time, like particles, can become quantum entangled.

Their thought experiment that sought to examine how quantum theory links successive measurements of a single quantum system.

When measuring a proton's polarisation, for example, a particular result is obtained. Yet when it is measured again later, there is a second result, they reported. Apparently, the very act of measuring the photon polarisation a second time affects how it was polarised earlier on, suggesting a continuing connection between the past and the future.

Here then are some of the counter-intuitive challenges that suggest that, for the layperson at least, if one is not confused by all this, it is only because one has not been paying sufficient attention!

The idea has even been put that we might be living in a universe where time is running backwards - and not know it! The reason would be that, with the passing of each second back in time from the future through the present and to the past, our minds would be progressively stripped of our memories and awareness of the 'future'. We would only be conscious of the memories of the diminishing, residual 'past' that had not yet been removed and, at each moment, we would blithely assume that everything was proceeding forward in a state of constant unfolding and becoming. This raises the bizarre thought that we are in what could be called a 'palindromic cosmos' in which events start at a genesis launching point and proceed all the way through to the end of our universe's life span - whereupon things slip into reverse gear and, at the same pace, rewind all the way back to the beginning, ready to start all over again. And we, of course, not one whit the wiser about this endless see-sawing!

For all this speculation, the fact remains that we know of no handy way to foretell future events and have to patiently wait for time to advance at its own speed. Despite extensive studies and tests, there has yet to be any scientific verification of the claims for precognition. However, if it were ever found to be a fact, then one could be confident that it had something to do with an as yet unknown physical action, rather than a supernatural endowment or intervention.

Here we should attend to what the Roman poet Horace observed about clairvoyance in his work, *'Carmina' (III, 29, 29)*, some two millennia ago:

'A wise God shrouds the future in obscure darkness.'
(Prudens futuri temporis exitum Caliginosa nocte premit deus.)

Time as a Dimension

Some theoretical physicists are now talking about the Multiverse hosting up to eleven dimensions, most of which may be self-contained, extremely small and quite outside the reach of our senses. Describing many of these 'additional' dimensions is clearly beyond any analogy that would be useful to the layperson; this is strictly the domain of very complex higher mathematics and those few who understand and speak its language.

Thus chastened, let us now take another look at the four-dimensional world everyone is familiar with, even if they do not fully understand it. This 'temporospatial' sphere is made up of the three spatial dimensions of length, height and depth plus the dimension of time. This description clearly assumes that time is *not* a spatial dimension, but something flowing and dynamic that works alongside the three spatial dimensions.

I have long felt uncomfortable with making time a special case in this way, except as a pragmatic distinction in our everyday life. To me, time is as much a spatial dimension as the preceding three dimensions. Over the centuries, others came to the same conclusion, for example, the Chinese philosopher and logician, Kung-sun Lung (c. 325–250 BC), was convinced of the essential unity of time and the material universe.

Look at it like this. Supposing we start with a point, which has existence, but no dimension. Could there ever be such an entity? The answer is yes, it might be able exist - and in this universe it could have been the singularity that was for an infinitesimal instant the start of the Big Bang that is said to have launched the cosmos we live in!

The singularity presumed to lie at the heart of each of the countless black holes in our universe likewise may have no dimension in itself, but its forces, such as its gravity, its event horizon (where gravity's power prevents light or other information reaching outside observers) and the leakage of particles known as the Hawking Effect, do operate within our multidimensional universe. The primordial singularity that heralded the Big Bang did not pop up in black space: it was *all* the space and all the time that was to be our universe. In other words, there was nothing in our universe that was outside this singularity or the expanding heat ball that it became.

Getting back to our hypothetical non-dimensional point, we find that if we collect a number of such points, one beside the other, and extend them into a line this then introduces the dimension of length. This line, if the universe were boundless, could be made up of an infinite number of points in a line.

Our next step is to introduce the second dimension. Here we create a flat area that, once again, is made up of an infinite number of lines, placed side by side. The third dimension - depth - now requires us to stack up an infinite number of salami-sliced flat panels. So far, so good. With time added to the mix we (theoretically) multiply infinitely the possible configurations of the three-dimensional volume by introducing movement and changing relationships. I suggest that we can go one step farther yet in this dimensional sequence: the fifth dimension.

Now we would see the time dimension being multiplied to create an infinite number of separate 'time silos'. This, I suggest, may possibly be the vessel that contains the countless universes within the Multiverse - as shown by these images

1. We start with a point or singularity, which has no dimension…

2. Then we introduce the first dimension, represented by a line (which can contain an infinite number of points (singularities) along its length)…

3. When the second dimension is added the result is a flat plane whose area can encompass an infinite number of two-dimensional lines...

4. Entering the third dimension, we create a solid volume housing an infinite number of planes, represented here by a 'wire-frame' box...

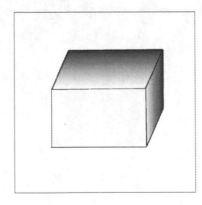

5. Continuing this progression, the fourth dimension, time, multiplies infinitely these static wire-frame boxes, so that this illustration is completely inked out. We have a seamless continuum of all possible wire-frame boxes or instants within our universe.

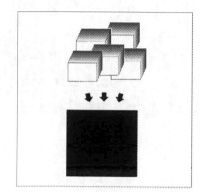

6. For the fifth dimension we picture *an infinity* of these individual, closed space-time entities or universes. We have now arrived at the Multiverse!

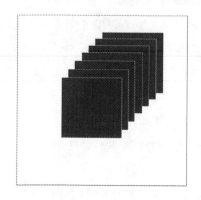

Frozen 'Snapshots'

So, is time really a flowing continuum, the 'river of time' as we perceive it in our everyday lives, or is it made up of discrete, irreducible instants?

A new view is gaining currency, which apparently offers to put to rest some of the dilemmas previously described, including Zeno's Paradox. Along with the emergence of, and growing support for, the Multiverse theory, there has been some interesting speculation about the very nature of time itself.

Put very simply, this new thinking postulates that time is not a flowing river at all, but is made up of absolutely minute frozen 'snapshots'.

Most theoretical physicists now accept that String Theory represents a very plausible account of how the most fundamental building blocks of matter are constructed and behave. True, String Theory embraces various contending views and interpretations (including such versions as M-Theory, D-Theory, and so on), but there is a general consensus about the theory's basic assumptions. Among these is that there is nothing, and can be nothing, smaller than a 'string', which, incidentally, is described as existing in one dimension only.

If the size of the components of matter is not infinitely reducible, then it is very difficult to see that time itself does not also meet an ultimate barrier where it is no longer capable of being further reduced. If we excuse time from any such limitation and insist that it can sustain infinite regression, then we introduce all sorts of problems and anomalies regarding strings themselves.

What, then, is the smallest interval of time? Is there a particle of time so irreducible that there can be no shorter duration - just as the string itself is thought to be the smallest particle of matter?

Physicists working at the nuclear level have been coining ever-smaller units of time, so that to the nanosecond (a billionth of a second) has been added a retinue of increasingly shorter intervals, including the picosecond, the femtosecond, the attosecond, the zeptosecond - and least, but probably not last, the yoctosecond (10 to the power of -24 of a second).

Beyond that, we have 'Planck Time' at 10 to -44 (or 0.0000 0000000000000000000000000000000000001 second). This is the shortest meaningful interval of time that theoretical physics can describe, and so is the earliest point at which our universe can be measured after the Big Bang!

According to Dr Julian Barbour, a leading proponent of the 'snapshot' theory, all these instants covering what we perceive as events past, present and future are co-existent - and equally real.

As he once said in an interview:

'My basic idea is that time as such does not exist. There is no invisible river of time. But there are things that you could call instants of time, or "Nows". As we live, we seem to move

through a succession of Nows, and the question is, what are they? They are arrangements of everything in the universe relative to each other in any moment, for example, now.'

Indeed, the current thinking accepted by most physicists is that time is not a linear, one-way progression at all, despite what our everyday experience may suggest. Theoretical physicists like Dr Julian Barbour describe a universe - or more properly speaking, a Multiverse which includes all universes - where time and space are frozen in a single entity which encompasses everything we think of as being past, present and future. In this space-time realm every event that can possibly occur (i.e., what does not violate a range of physical and logical possibilities), co-exists with all others with equal validity.

Dr Barbour writes that physicists trying to unify Einstein's general theory of relativity and quantum mechanics keep discovering indications that the 'arrow of time' is, indeed, an illusion.

What we see as the 'flow of time' is simply the impression we sentient beings gain from passing from one of these co-existent instants to another. The way our perception and consciousness interpret the immeasurably rapid sequence of frozen instants persuades us that time is different in nature to the first three spatial dimensions.

In his book, *'The End of Time'*, Barbour describes a state that he calls 'Platonia' as an eternity that simultaneously contains all matter and all possible arrangements and positions of matter. He writes:

'In this picture, there are no definite paths. We are not beings progressing from one instant to another. Rather, there are many "Nows" in which a version of us exists - not in any past or future, but scattered in our region of Platonia.'

He added that:

'if some Nows in Platonia have much higher probabilities than others, they are the ones that are actually experienced. This is like ordinary statistical physics: a glass of water could boil spontaneously, but the probability is so low that we never see it happen.'

Physicist Brian Greene, the author of *'The Fabric of the Universe: Space, Time, and the Texture of Reality'* and presenter of the *'The Elegant Universe'* TV series, also believes that our sense of 'now' is simply a construct of the human brain.

He explains that we might be certain that this very moment is the one, authentic *now*, but did we not assume the same for the 'now' that happened 10 minutes ago? And, he reminds us, will we not believe the same of the 'now' that will fall due 10 minutes from this very moment?

Again, I believe a very useful analogy for the way we perceive the flow of time is shown by how a succession of still images flickering past the eye on the cinema screen at 24 frames a second (25 frames a second in video) is interpreted by the brain as smooth, continuous movement.

Before 1830, there was no way of creating a moving image other than by making an actual working model, or toy theatre. However, the introduction of the zoetrope proved that a rapid enough succession of individual images could create an illusion of continuous motion - and so the path was opened for the eventual invention of the cinema.

Increasingly, research suggests that the brain's tendency to 'smear' these still images in this way is not simply because of an inability to keep up with a rapid succession of events. It is actually an essential device necessary to create a sense of both continuity and of the present; and it may well underlie our experience of consciousness. It certainly seems to be present in the higher orders of creatures, including mammals, birds and reptiles. On the other hand, it is certainly possible to exist without this sense of a 'present' in which instants run together to create the illusion of flowing continuity. It is thought that many creatures lack this ability or, at best, have only a vestigial version of it.

This deficiency can be found among some individuals, too. For example, in his book, *'In the River of Consciousness'*, the late British neurologist Dr Oliver Sachs referred to an unfortunate woman who had developed just such 'motion blindness' following a stroke. Instead of the normal sense of smooth continuity one normally observes:

'There were "freeze frames" lasting several seconds, during which Mrs. M. would see a prolonged, motionless image and be visually unaware of any movement around her, though her flow of thought and perception was otherwise normal'.

44

It was reported that Dr James Hartle of the University of California, Santa Barbara had proposed that nature has equipped us with a sense of flowing time because it has vital survival value. He stated:

'A frog that calculates the trajectory of a fly from the most recent data, eats; one that doesn't, starves.

Our powerful sense that there is a "now" and that time "flows" from the past, through the present, to the future, has survival value.

It is the only plausible explanation, since none of these concepts actually appear in Einstein's special theory of relativity, our most fundamental physical description of space and time.

In Einstein's universe, there can be no such thing as a universally agreed past, present and future.'

Within the context of space-time, the very concepts are meaningless.'

Here I draw upon an analogy intimately familiar to anyone who has worked with movie material shot on celluloid film. A two-hour film reel contains a little under two hundred thousand still frames – and each of these frozen images co-exists with, and is equally as valid as, all the others. Now try to imagine that the data from the sensory world around you is the film, that your brain is the projector, and what you consciously perceive is the moving image on the screen. Naturally, you easily assume that only the ever-moving slice of the present is what is real at that very moment - and not those other still frames that have either gone through the shutter gate, or are yet to do so.

But the truth is that all those other still frames are just as real as, and co-exist with, the frames thrown onto the screen by the projector's lens.

The series-of-snapshots idea is not at all a totally new concept - and it was certainly an idea understood by most Greek philosophers, whether or not they agreed with it.

As well, the great 18th century Scottish philosopher David Hume took a similar view, describing our sense of time as 'nothing but a bundle or collection of different perceptions, which succeed each other with an inconceivable rapidity, and are in a perpetual flux and movement'.

Einstein said that his own thinking had been influenced by Hume's *'A Treatise of Human Nature'*, which stated that time did not exist separately from the movement of objects, and that scientific concepts must be based on experience and evidence, not just on reason alone.

Do we go along with the new - or rather, revisited? - concept of time as being something that, aside from our own eccentric way of perceiving it, does not flow as a succession of events, but exists as a compendium of possible events, all existing contemporaneously (the frozen snapshots we looked at earlier)? If so then, I believe, we are not far from conceiving of time as just another spatial dimension, and a logical and obvious progression from the third dimension.

The Stillness of Time

That our sense of ever-moving time is illusory is a view shared by many thinkers, both modern and ancient, including scientists, philosophers, religious teachers and mystics. Buddhism, particularly, sees our notions of 'time', 'the past' and 'the future' as merely human constructs; as superficial realities they are all part of *Maya*, the deceptive world of ever-changing discrete phenomena. All of these chimerical notions vanish once confronted by the timeless, undifferentiated void that is *Nirvana*.

Some eight centuries ago, the great Japanese Zen teacher, Master Dogen Zenji (1200-1253), showed remarkable insight with an observation that few modern physicists would argue with:

'It is believed by most that time passes; in actual fact it stays where it is. This idea of passing may be called time, but it is an incorrect idea, for since one sees it only as passing, one cannot understand that it just stays where it is.'

I would illustrate this idea with an analogy that we would all recognise. Looking out the window of a speeding train, we have the impression that *we* are stationary - and that it is the countryside that is speeding past us. Of course we know very well that it is the fields and houses that are stationery, while the train and its passengers are moving: but as we sit holding an unshaken cup of coffee and reading an unruffled newspaper, there is no denying the powerful sensation that it is the outside panorama that is rocketing past *us*.

Think of the panorama outside our train window as the physical world we live in and that the train is our physical self and that the passenger looking out the window is our consciousness. Now reflect on the possibility that it is we sentient beings who are moving through a static set of linked timeframes – and that there is no 'river of time'.

Master Dogen made this very same argument, using a metaphor familiar to his contemporaries, in his book, '*Shobo Genzo*' (Treasury of the True Dharma Eye):

'*When you go out on a boat and look around, you feel as if the shore were moving. But if you fix your eyes on the rim of the boat, you become aware that the boat is moving. It is exactly the same when you try to know the objective world while still in a state of confusion in regard to your own body and mind; you are under the misapprehension that your own mind, your own nature, is something real and enduring [while the external world is transitory]. Only when you sit straight and look into yourself, does it become clear that the objective world has a reality apart from you.*'

Two centuries after Christ, St Augustine of Hippo saw the question of time as a central philosophical issue intimately linked with any understanding of God. In Book XI of his '*Confessions*', he sees God as existing outside linear time and, indeed, that time as we experience it is something created as part of, and in the same instant as, the material universe we inhabit: an impressively modern insight.

Augustine believed that God occupied a realm where all time was coexistent, hence his statement that 'before time was, time is'.

In our own era, as I said, many scientists, and possibly the great majority of leading theoretical physicists, do not accept that time, as we commonly experience it, is real.

As Poincaré wrote in his *'The Value of Science' (1958)*, 'It is not nature which imposes [time and space] upon us, it is we who impose them upon nature because we find them convenient.' Albert Einstein maintained an identical view, which he expressed as no mere conjecture, but a deep conviction. Writing to console the widow of his recently deceased friend, the physicist Michele Besso, he said:

'In quitting this strange world he has once again preceded me by just a little. That doesn't mean anything. For we convinced physicists the distinction between past, present, and future is only an illusion, however persistent.'

The other towering 20th century theoretical physicist, Einstein's friend and fellow German, Kurt Gödel (1906-1978), concurred. Gödel, who shared wartime exile with Einstein at Princeton in the USA, believed that the nature of time was the foremost question confronting philosophers: for his part he was convinced that time as intuitively experienced simply did not exist at all.

Similar views go back at least to the time of Parmenides and were shared by the giant of modern philosophy, Immanuel Kant and by others all the way up to our own age.

To take but one example, the leading British Hegelian philosopher J. M. E. McTaggart (1866-1925) argued in his widely discussed paper of 1908, *'The Unreality of Time'*, that the temporal order of things was no more than an illusion. What we intuitively experience - the 'A-Series model', he called it - is an ever moving 'now' (the present) which assumes the existence of a 'before-now' (the past) and a 'not-yet-now' (the future). In fact, he believed, the present does not exist as a temporal state at all: only the past and the future are real, and what we are pleased to call 'the present' is simply the intersection between the two. This viewpoint has been endorsed by many other renowned thinkers, including the philosopher, F.H. Bradley.

'Block Time' or 'Eternalism' are terms applied by philosophers to the idea that the past, present and future - in all, possible versions of events - coexist in a static block. Rather than time flowing past conscious entities like us, it is *we* who move through Block Time. A topic to be explored later, this is a view of reality that accords with that held by both eastern philosophers and modern theoretical physicists, amongst others. Buddhist scholars employ a word, *dharmadhatu* to describe 'the space of all phenomena and meanings', a concept similar to the 'Block Universe'.

There is an old Zen koan that illustrates this insight thus:

Two Zen monks were captivated by the sight of a flag flapping in a brisk wind.

'Look,' said one. 'See how that flag is moving!'

'No, replied the other. 'It is the wind that is moving.'

A Zen master overheard them and interjected, 'Neither the flag nor the wind is moving, only your minds!'

Much more recently, the physicist Werner Heisenberg (1901 - 1976) made the same point about the illusory nature of what we choose to regard as 'time' and 'reality'.

'A path comes into existence only when you observe it,' he said, reminding us that time and reality exists, not 'out there', but only as a construct of our own brains. In truth, as most physicists accept, what we deem to be 'reality' has no independent existence until it is perceived.

Feynman's 'Sum Over Histories' Idea

One of the most brilliant scientists of his generation, Richard Feynman (1918-1988), developed a 'Sum Over Histories' theory that suggested that 'time' is simply a direction in space. An interpretation of quantum mechanics, this theory says that the probability of an event is determined by summing together all the possible histories of that event. For example, traveling between two points, a particle might explore all possible pathways, straight and curved, direct and indirect, forwards as well as backwards in time. In the great majority of cases, these various paths' amplitudes add up to a zero and so what we are left to experience are those paths that fit in with the prevalent physical forces and the laws of nature in our particular universe.

According to Feynman's theory, our 'reality' simply backs the most likely horse in the race, but as we know, that does not always turn out to be the predicted winner, because all these histories are simultaneously real. So we should remember that in a timeless world every also-ran galloper must occasionally be as lucky as today's first-placed horse!

For Stephen Hawking and others, Feynman's Sum Over Histories theory opens a way to view the limitless, eternal plurality of worlds. In his paper *'Cosmology From the Top Down'*, Hawking observed, 'Some people make a great mystery of the multi-universe, or the Many Worlds interpretation of quantum theory, but to me, these are just different expressions of the Feynman path integral.'

These are mind-stretching concepts, to be sure. But however hard they may be to intuit as we move through our everyday world, at the very least - according to some - they offer a neat resolution of Zeno's Paradox!

However one might take the arguments for and against the Block Time or Eternalist model as a mechanism operating in this universe (as espoused by Einstein and others, including Dr Julian Barbour), the fact is that within the infinitely larger context of a Multiverse, there is a very strong case for it.

All the physical laws at work within each universe are particular to it and must be contained within that universe. Thus, what we perceive as our past, present and future could not appear as such discrete states if anyone in another universe could somehow peer into our own universe. Relative to an outside observer, all happenings in this universe could only be coexistent: what we deem to be variously our past, present and future states could not be seen as such. In other words, to that outsider we, and the entire history of our universe, both what has been revealed to us and is yet to be revealed, are utterly frozen and intact within our local version of Block Time.

Metaphysical Insights

Besides the philosophers, theologians and mystics who have pondered over it, the idea that all moments coexist also resonates in the lines of many metaphysical poets. Among these was the American-born English poet T.S. Eliot (1888-1965) who was familiar with both Eastern and Western thinking on time, having studied Western philosophy at the Sorbonne in Paris and, later, Indian philosophy and Sanskrit at Harvard. In his poem, *'Burnt Norton'*, he looked at an abandoned house and mused about all the possibilities that might have been - and whether, somewhere, these might have another existence as real as what we are encountering in this life of ours.

'Time present and time past
Are both perhaps present in time future
And time future contained in time past'

And, similarly, the distinguished British poet Henry Austin Dobson (1840-1921) in his poem *'The Paradox of Time'* penned one of his most often-quoted verses:

'Time goes, you say? Ah no!
Alas, Time stays, we go;
Or else, were this not so,
What need to chain the hours,
For Youth were always ours?
Time goes, you say? - ah no!'

And English Romanticism's exemplar of metaphysical poetry, the poet-artist William Blake (1757-1827), put his revelation as simply as this:

'I see the Past, Present and Future, existing all at once
Before me.'

Again, we come back to the question about the direction of time: why do we move 'forward', with cause followed by effect - and not the other way around? One strong argument as to why this should be so is that we, and everything in our universe, are subject to the Second Law of Thermodynamics which dictates that everything moves towards a state of ever-greater entropy, i.e., *forward* in time. Perhaps this is just as well for us. It would be hard to imagine a world in which one started out by already knowing all the events in our life, only to see these memories disappear, one by one, in a life-long process of cumulative forgetting.

Nonetheless, as the physicist Professor Paul Davies put it in his article *'That Mysterious Flow'* (*'Scientific American'*, Sept. 2002):

'By convention, the arrow of time points toward the future. This does not imply, however, that the arrow is moving toward the future, any more than a compass needle pointing north indicates that the compass is traveling north. Both arrows symbolize an asymmetry, not a movement. The arrow of time denotes an asymmetry of the world in time, not an asymmetry or flux of time.

The labels "past" and "future" may legitimately be applied to temporal directions, just as "up" and "down" may be applied to spatial directions, but talk of the past or the future is as meaningless as referring to the up or the down.'

In any case, the question as to the nature of time, including whether it is 'block' or 'linear', still remains one of the fundamental posers for philosophers and physicists.

Seeing a Different Time-Scape

We are so accustomed to the idea of the forward-flying 'arrow of time' that its obvious reality can hardly be challenged. Simply, it is how things go in our world, we would say. Yet, it is not a universally accepted way of experiencing the world and if most physicists see past, present and future as equally valid and coexistent realities, they are not alone.

Sixteenth century records tell us that Jesuit missionaries accompanying the conquistadors to Peru were greatly exasperated to find that the pagan Inca had a very different take on the linearity of time. For these native people, what we regard as past, present and future are deemed by them to all run parallel to one another, meaning that the past *and* the future can both affect what is happening now in the present moment and in our universe. To this very day, the Aymara indigenes in the Andes appear to experience passing time in a way that is exactly opposite to the way we do. For them, the past lies in front of them - and the future is behind them.

This is certainly baffling for most of the rest of us. However, I offer one possibly useful analogy that occurred to me. Imagine you are a passenger in a moving car. You are looking ahead and see the constantly changing scenery coming towards you, the ever-unfurling future, if you like. This is how we in the industrialised world, particularly, apprehend events: we focus on the new possibilities that change our present, knowing that they *will* change - and that we can be significant agents of that change.

Now swivel around in your seat so that your gaze through the rear window takes in the ever-receding scene behind you. What you now see is the past being constantly enlarged and added to by what is sliding past the present, with the new only making sense in the context of what has already happened. That, I suggest, is how the temporal world might have appeared to, and been interpreted by, the Inca!

The Christian missionaries could not grapple with such a violently contrary interpretation of time. And was it not arch-heresy to say that a world still unredeemed by the Saviour's blood should coexist within our own age, one already liberated by Christ's salvation of humanity?

Yet, I suspect, that may not be so far from how most pre-modern societies apprehended the world. For them, a fixed past was simply repeating its ancient themes, and this was exactly how the Romanian mythologist Mercea Eliade (1907-1986) would describe it in his study of ancient mythologies, *'Myth of the Eternal Return'*. How, then, might these two powerfully different ways of seeing time affect one's thinking and behavior? Perhaps forward time sensing would make us innovative, better able to imagine novel, but malleable, futures; impatient of delay, but also less contextual in our thinking, too. On the other hand, 'rear-vision' people of past ages saw all around them only what re-affirmed that they lived in an essentially static world, lightly stirred by predictable rhythms. They saw no reason not to fatalistically accept things as they were, with the one aspiration being to return again one distant day to an idealised past.

Two thousand years ago, Rome was a vast, complex and sophisticated society, surprisingly modern and innovative in so many ways. Technologically, it was not to be overhauled until a few centuries ago, although Ancient China might be considered a close contender. Yet, as adaptable as they were, the Romans seem to have had no concept of the future as being transformative. In fact, quite the opposite. Their rear-vision time sense burdened them with an awed respect for precedent, what the Romans revered as the *mos maiorum* or 'the ways of the elders'. Indeed, novelty, or any attempt to bring it about was openly regarded as un-Roman. Thus, a charge synonymous with high treason was that one had tried to introduce a *'res nova'* ('a new thing'), a sure precursor to revolution and disorder. Like so many old and new societies, they saw their age as a flawed version of a long-past golden age, and many aspired to recreate that imagined halcyon era.

How deeply disturbing would it be for them to be transported into our present time, here to confront a ceaseless vortex of disruptive change, technological and cultural, and to see grandparents and grandchildren struggling to communicate in a shared language?

Looking rearward, it is retained effect that predominates, fixed and unmodified but for the accretion of additional detail which simply enlarges the causational narrative. By contrast, looking ahead, we see an oncoming succession of causative triggers, loaded with unpredictable consequences, but rich with the promise of all sorts of outcomes.

Which of those two ways of interpreting time is right or wrong? As the mythologist Mircea Eliade observed:

'Like the mystic, like a religious man in general, the primitive lives in a continual present. (And it is in this sense that the religious man may be said to be a "primitive"; he repeats the gestures of another and, through this repetition, lives in an a temporal present.)'

Yet most of us pay scant attention to the present, as the good Doctor Samuel Johnson observed in his short novel, *'Rasselas'* (1759):

'The truth is that no mind is much employed upon the present: recollection and anticipation fill up almost all our moments.'

Clearly, our preferred way to track time and motion depends on what offers the best survival advantage - it has been so since a frog first knocked an inattentive beetle off an overhead leaf and into the water!

4. The Great Circle of Life

Creation Myths and Early Cosmologies

Long before I came to Australia, I had dreamt of standing in the Red Centre of this vast island-continent to witness a starry parade more majestic, I had been told, than could ever be seen in a Northern European sky dimmed by clouds, haze and the glow of crowded towns and cities.

Several years after arriving in Australia, I was ready to make that wish a reality. A group of young people in an ancient bus, we ventured deep into what Australians call the *'Never-Never'*. After grueling days crossing a vast land-ocean, we finally reached the Red Centre and at last stood at the base of Uluru, the largest rock in the world. With one glimpse of this massive monolith, soaring above an otherwise flat and featureless desert plain, I understood immediately why untold generations of Aborigines had revered Uluru as their most sacred site.

Throughout that day's drive of several hundred kilometres, the oven-like heat and the incessant drumming of the dusty, corrugated 'road' (since sealed) had reduced us to a wordless, lazy-eyed torpor. But now the air was beginning to chill, as happens in the desert, and we quickly woke up to the magnificent vision unfolding before us.

With the desert darkening rapidly, Uluru was lit up by the setting sun's lengthening rays to reveal a succession of tones - orange, pink, vermillion, blue-grey and then black. Finally, the sun sank below the far-distant, ruler-straight horizon and with that the display came to a sudden end. Almost immediately, my gaze was lifted upwards. The blue-velvet sky was already spangled with brilliant points of intense light; the familiar planets and the brightest stars. Then, as the last glow of day faded, this panorama morphed into a silver-dusted canopy set against an inky backdrop.

To fully take in this vista, I lay on my back and gazed directly upwards. With the low horizon well outside my field of vision, I lay softly cradled by the still warm sand, with little sense of bodily contact, and soon began to feel quite untethered from this world. After a few minutes, I imagined that I was no longer looking upwards, but was free-floating in infinite space, peering *down* into a fathomless cosmic diorama. What I saw was wondrous; almost hallucinogenic. And I became as close, I am convinced, as anyone could come, to *experiencing* deep space while still remaining a groundling. Exhilarating and awesome, this vision remains fresh in my mind to this day.

I have sometimes thought how sad it is that few people today ever get to see the beauty and sheer scale of the cosmos in this way. Locked off in our cities, amid tall buildings, we hardly notice the ever-changing face of the Moon; and even rural communities, increasingly electrified, are denied a glimpse of the full celestial splendour. Apart from the marvel of this spectacle, we are also denying ourselves a powerful reminder of our true place in the bigger scheme of things, and the insight that all our petty worries and desires, our quotidian fretting and self-concern, count for so little in the face of infinity.

But, this existential myopia was not always so. Against mankind's history of 200,000 years or more, artificial lighting came only yesterday: gaslight appeared less than two centuries ago and electric light barely a century ago. Before that, the weak light of a candle or oil lamp pushed back the dark only by an arm's-length or so and did little to alleviate the impenetrable darkness that claimed the world once the sun had set and when the Moon's thin light was on hold.

For generation after generation, humans looked up with curiosity, awe and even terror at this majestic immensity. They had their stories and explanations, of course, but surely some individuals must have wondered whether the shaman's myths really could account for the ineffable spectacle arcing high above them?

But, along with this mystery, our ancestors also saw something of immediate utility in the stately stellar procession wheeling overhead: the erratic dance of the planets and the Moon's ceaseless waxing and waning. Here were measured out the rhythms of their kind's short and uncertain lives: the days of the month; the passing seasons of warmth, cold, rain and drought; the bountiful weeks when the great herds began their thundering migrations; the short periods of plenty and the long times of hardship.

Inevitably, there was the thought that if the stars could tell that much about the wider world, could they not also reveal something about one's own fate, if we only knew how to read their signs? But above any such unreliable portents, early man would have learnt one certain truth: that everything approaches, passes and returns in sure and predictable cycles. And that this ever was so, and always would be.

This is why we move from our previous speculations on eternity and time to where we will now consider the great cycles that have always guided human destiny. By and large, with the exception of the Abrahamic faiths and most modern cosmologists, we shall see that people everywhere and in all ages have tended to see time as processing in large cycles, rather than in a relentlessly unidirectional direction from a distinct beginning to an end of creation.

Indeed, the idea of a great wheel of creation, turning endlessly, is one of the oldest of all human thoughts. Palaeolithic man, staring anxiously at the celestial parade, would have well understood the great circularity of existence. And so, too, did the Sumerians who first recorded their calendar of yearly labours - including harvesting, planting, managing precious rainwater - in a cuneiform script that was already ancient when Pharaoh Djoser built Egypt's first pyramid, all of forty-seven centuries ago.

Thus, millennia before the astonishing revelations of our modern physicists, even millennia before the great Greek thinkers applied their restless intellects to the matter, the mystery of time and eternity surely weighed on the minds of humans everywhere. It was the starting point, and, often, the central reality, of their belief systems. Indeed, there is hardly a religion, past or present, whose revelations do not begin with an account of how we got to be here and where we may be going. Time, transience, mortality, rebirth, eternity: these hefty themes seasoned the discourse and writings of prophets and holy men, theologians and mystics, for the very good reason that they are pivotal to any account of Gods or creation.

In this age of science and rationalism, the question is can transcendental insights help us grasp, at an intuitive level, such unfamiliar concepts as the Multiverse and the Eternal Return? Of course, the fact that circularity or recurrence is such a widely held idea in prescientific societies proves nothing about the objective validity of this concept. But surely these legends and myths tell us that human beings in all ages have been much more comfortable with the idea of the eternal return, than with the linear, beginning-and-end, story of the cosmos. Whatever our own beliefs, those ancient insights surely have something to tell us today, even if only about *ourselves*?

Here we should begin with the fact that religions, typically, address time and eternity from two directions: as central elements of their cosmological narratives and as subjects whose contemplation may lead to an intuitive experience of the ineffable reality that lies behind our familiar world.

Accordingly, this chapter will focus on the creation myths and cosmologies of different cultures, noting that, while widely separated by time, place and traditions, their stories have so many recurring themes.

Sumerian Mythology

Essentially, 'civilisation' describes a settled and ordered community based on managed food production and living by agreed rules. This level of organisation, in turn, generates sufficient surplus labour and wealth to support specialised crafts, set roles and hierarchies and, in most instances, a system of writing.

Settled agrarian communities first appeared in Mesopotamia ('between the rivers' of the Euphrates and the Tigris) in the Middle East. Regarded as the cradle of civilisation, this once-fertile region was inhabited at various times by the Sumerians, Akkadians, Babylonians, and Assyrians. With their lives so closely directed by the diurnal and seasonal changes linked to the precise orbits of the stars and planets, these peoples naturally saw all existence as being governed by great and small cycles. As the source of life, the sun's motion was watched and noted with intense interest, both in its daily rising and setting and its shifting higher or lower in the sky, as a way of calculating the arrival of the seasons. Likewise, the moon's monthly waxing and waning was a perfect metaphor for life, death and rebirth. This cycle of life, the eternal return, was read as an immediate reality that imposed itself not only upon nature, but also upon human affairs.

It was essential for the wellbeing of these kingdoms that these cycles' predictors were carefully recorded. So, it is easy to imagine that the possession and interpretation of this data endowed priests and astrologers with a seemingly magical ability to foresee events - and thus gave them great power and authority. From there it was a short step for those priests to take credit for ensuring that things turned out well, thanks to the timely and necessary intercession of their rituals, prayers and sacrifices.

More than 6,000 years ago, the Sumerians devised a 12-month calendar - essential for plotting and predicting annual cycles. Adapted by the Assyrians and others in the region, this would have been seen as a powerful and practical tool for harnessing the natural cycles.

Not surprisingly, some Sumerian texts suggest a widespread belief in the eternal return and reincarnation. With the cycles of life, death and regrowth evident everywhere, then why, they asked, should we not also see human existence itself passing through similar cycles of birth, death and rebirth?

Egyptian Mythology

Like the Sumerians before them, the Ancient Egyptians were an agrarian people who lived with endless circularity, and this was personified in the female deity, Ma'at. Representing order and continuity, Ma'at travelled with the Sun-God, Re, to ensure he continued his smooth voyage across the heavens by day and through the unseen underworld by night. Consequently, Ma'at was associated with all the cycles of birth, growth and death in the cosmos whereby everything ultimately returned to its origin, only to renew its journey once more.

Viewing all existence as eternal and circular, the Egyptians believed that even the first moment of creation (*Zep Tepy* - 'The

First Time'), would itself be repeated over and over again, just as the parched and cracked soil would every year be replenished and made fertile once again by the beneficent floodwaters of the Nile. The scarab or dung beetle was regarded as a symbol of this eternal process of renewal and rebirth in which all things would faithfully retrace their pathways, again and yet again.

Dharmic Religions

The reality of eternity and unceasing cycles of existence are essential truths in Hinduism and its offshoots of Buddhism, Jainism and Sikhism. Collectively, these are known as the Dharmic religions, from the Sanskrit *'dharma'*, meaning 'the universal law' or 'path of righteousness'. These faiths proclaim that the myriad of all living things must endure the burden of rebirth, again and again throughout the span of this universe, and also in innumerable other universes. This concept is represented by the image of the spoked Dharma wheel, or wheel of life. (Appropriately, a 24-spoked dharma wheel, or 'Ashoka Chakra' is the centrepiece of the Indian flag.)

For the individual, life's real purpose is to seek salvation and release from endless reincarnation and the inescapable suffering that personal existence entails. This can only be achieved, Hindus say, by a superhuman effort, in which one endeavours through countless lifetimes to achieve the self-perfection that will finally liberate one from the selfhood that keeps us chained to this illusory world. Ultimately, that will be achieved when one sloughs off all vestiges of the ego and becomes united with *Brahman*: the ultimate, undifferentiated reality behind all that is.

The Hindu scriptures describe the universe's lifespan as a '*kalpa*', which is a period that varies between 4.1 and 8.2 billion solar years' duration, or 'a day of the god, Brahma'. (Here we need to distinguish between the creator god, 'Brahma', and 'Brahman' the name for the ultimate reality.) Each *kalpa* is made up of four eras called *yugas,* and each *yuga* arrives and passes on like the annual seasons, shifting between periods of creativity and enlightenment and then destruction and ignorance.

Interestingly, these vast Hindu cosmological timescales are of an order similar to those cited by modern astronomers and cosmologists. A *kalpa* is not far from the currently calculated age of the Earth, and is certainly a much more realistic estimate than that of the 17th century Anglican Bishop of Armagh, James Ussher, whose Bible-based, painstaking calculation placed the moment of creation at 4004 B.C.

The '*Puranas*' and other texts describe an infinite number of universes, each inhabited by its own set of gods, worlds and people, with all subject to the same ceaseless cycle of births, deaths, and rebirths.

Buddhism, which branched away from the Hindu faith two-and-a-half millennia ago, teaches that endless rebirth and suffering (a cycle known as *samsara*) is only escaped by being released from the cause-and-effect consequences of one's actions (*karma*). This pathway to salvation is outlined in the Buddha's Noble Eightfold Path.

On this karmic wheel, one is reborn in the form of one of the many sentient forms of life, although one's soul does not transmigrate from one form to another, as it does in Hinduism,

(As a young man I was drawn to the philosophy and practice - but not the religious interpretation - of Buddhism. It all seemed rational and obvious to me, except for the doctrine of the endless cycle of rebirth. Now, with the possibilities opened up by the Multiverse idea, the Dharmic concept of soul-less rebirth might now appear a more acceptable proposition.)

The Buddha was asked several times to comment on metaphysical issues, such as whether or not the universe is eternal, are there gods and what might be their nature, and so forth. On these questions he refused to comment, advising his followers that the task of seeking enlightenment was a big enough task alone without needing the distraction of speculations that hold no promise of any resolution.

Of the other Dharmic religions, Jainism shares the Hindu and Buddhist belief in the endless cycle of birth and rebirth. Sikhism, a monotheistic blend of Hindu and Islamic concepts, also believes in reincarnation and the need to work towards liberation from rebirth.

The Hellenic World
Among the Greeks, and later, the Romans, the idea that the world - and with it, humanity - would be destroyed and then regenerate had wide currency. Largely, this idea drew upon the Chaldean account of 'The Great Year' that measured the phases of the universe's birth, death and rebirth.

Popularised by the Babylonian priest and astronomer, Berossus, in three books written around 290-278 BC and based on much earlier texts, the story of The Great Year spread throughout the Hellenic world and was eventually accepted by both the Romans and the Byzantines. This idea was central to the Stoic school of philosophy that emerged later.

Orphism, a mystical cult that spread throughout Greece from about 600 BC and was based on the hymns of the legendary poet, Orpheus, also held reincarnation as a core doctrine. Reflecting the likely influence of Hinduism, Orphism taught that each soul was fated to endure an eternal cycle of birth and rebirth, with the purging of one's sins and evil inclinations, self-denial and religious observance as the only ways to achieve eventual release and divine enlightenment. This emphasis on battling one's inherently evil nature through relentless asceticism must have helped prepare the ground for the later advent of Christianity.

The concept of the eternal return appears in the writings of many Greek philosophers and is connected particularly with the teachings of Empedocles, Zeno of Citium, and, of course, the Stoics. Pythagoras conceived of the *Metakosmesis* (or 'Great Year') as the complete cosmic cycle that would see all bodies in the heavens finally revert to their original positions. Mentioned by Plato in his *'Timaeus'*, the *Metakosmesis* may have had some similarities with the *kalpa* cosmic cycle in the Hindu cosmology.

The Pythagoreans firmly believed in eternal recurrence, as Eliade observed:

'As to the eternal return – the periodic resumption, by all beings, of their former lives – this is one of the few dogmas of which we know with some certainty that they formed part of early Pythagoreanism.'

In the Roman era, the Epicurean poet Lucretius (c. 99 BC- c.55 BC) had the circularity of existence in mind when commenting on the folly of fearing death, writing in his epic poem *'De Rerum Natura'* that 'everything is always the same' (*edam sunt omnia semper*).

The Abrahamic Religions

In distinct contrast to the Dharmic religions, the Abrahamic religions of Judaism, Christianity and Islam (including their numerous sects, denominations and off-shoots, such as Mormonism) have a linear cosmology: there was once a timeless void within which God, at a definite point, created our universe, which itself in turn, will most likely end at a time of his bidding.

Each unique human being has an immortal soul and after death that soul will continue to exist through all eternity in heaven or hell, according to its owner's conduct on this plane of existence.

Of the three Abrahamic religions (so-called because they each trace their origins to Abraham, with whom God had sealed a covenant), the oldest is Judaism, which is at least 3,000 years old and is one of the first recorded monotheistic religions. Its account of the creation is described in the *'Book of Genesis'*

('*Bereshith*' in Hebrew) that also forms part of the Christian Bible's Old Testament.

Interestingly, in medieval times Judaism's mystical branch of knowledge, the *Kabbalah*, did accommodate a version of reincarnation or transmigration of the soul after death. Termed *Gilgul neshamot* ('cycles of the soul'), this idea was contested by various medieval Jewish philosophers. Nonetheless, reincarnation became embedded as a familiar literary motif in later Jewish writings.

In the Koran, Islam's cosmogony explains that Allah created the heavens and the earth in six days. However, the question is open as to whether or not other, or a multitude of, habitable planets or universes might exist:

'And among His Signs is the creation of the heavens and the earth, and the living creatures that He has scattered through them: and He has power to gather them together when He wills.' (The Noble Koran, 42:29)

Islam's apparent openness to the possibility of other inhabited worlds stands opposed to St. Augustine of Hippo's refutation of the Many Worlds idea of his Neoplatonist contemporaries.

However, in their accounts of the last days (the branch of knowledge known as eschatology) the three religions are in broad agreement. Most Jews, Christians and Muslims foretell a time when God's plan for the world is complete and the resurrected dead will be judged for eternity. Many, but not all, believe that these 'end times' will also be marked by apocalyptic destruction.

Most Christian denominations believe the end times will be heralded by the return of Jesus to earth as the promised Messiah. Likewise, Islam also foretells Jesus, a revered prophet in the Muslim canon, returning at that time to dispel the satanic forces and call the world to Allah.

Thus, all three of these religions, whose adherents are described by Muslims as 'The People of the Book', have consistently promoted a strictly linear vision of the universe.

In the earliest days of Christianity this was a key orthodoxy that had to be vigorously defended against the notions of circularity frequently put forward by pagan philosophers. In his book, *'The City of God'*, St Augustine examined and rejected the common notion that all events followed an eternal cycle:

'...As if, for example, the philosopher Plato, having taught in the school at Athens which is called the Academy, so, numberless ages before, at long but certain intervals, this same Plato and the same school, and the same disciples existed, and so also are to be repeated during the countless cycles that are yet to be, - far be it, I say, from us to believe this. For once Christ died for our sins; and, rising from the dead, He dieth no more.'

For all that, there are echoes still of the earlier belief in time's circularity in Christian and Judaic writings, as we shall read later.

The ancient religion of Zoroastrianism also believes in a judgement day, but with the more appetising prospect that, unlike with the orthodox Abrahamic beliefs, no one is damned for *all* eternity. Sinners are finally admitted to join the elect in heaven after a suitably chastening sojourn in Hell.

Pre-Colombian America

Like peoples on other continents, the pre-Columbian civilisations of the Americas put great store by the circularity of nature. In some cases, it was believed that human cooperation was essential to ensure that this cycle continued with no interruption.

For example, the Aztecs believed that Huitzilopochtli, the god of the sun and of war, could only be sustained in his daily battle with darkness by the copious offering of human blood. Consequently, great sacrifices had to be made to ensure the world did not end at the completion of each cycle of 52 years. According to one 15th century Spanish report up to 80,400 prisoners were despatched during a single such bloody oblation.

The European Alchemists

The Renaissance alchemists were familiar with the concept of the Eternal Return, as is revealed in his *'Religio Medici'* by the writer Thomas Browne:

'And in this sense, I say, the world was before the Creation, and at an end before it had a beginning; and thus was I dead before I was alive, though my grave be England, my dying place was Paradise, and Eve miscarried of me before she conceived of Cain.'

For Browne and his contemporaries, the image of the *Ouroboros*, the snake or dragon devouring its own tail, was a powerfully evocative alchemical symbol of time's eternal circularity.

History as a process of revisiting past events and experiences was a key insight of the Italian sage, Giambattista Vico (1688-1744), regarded as the first proponent of the modern idea of the philosophy of history. Among his views was that human history follows a type of circularity - or, as interpreted by those who reject exact recurrences, a spiralling motion.

Mercea Eliade

Any account of the widespread belief in time's circularity must come back to the Romanian academic and writer, Mircea Eliade, a leading authority on comparative religion whose interpretations were drawn from a vast survey of beliefs past and present, and spanning many cultures. His international reputation was established by the seminal book *'The Myth of the Eternal Return'* (1954), which outlined his theory that the idea of the Eternal Return is what underpins myth and ritual throughout history.

Drawing upon impressive scholarship, he documented how humanity has almost universally (apart from those of the Abrahamic tradition) believed that the world following a cyclical, rather than linear path. The Pre-Columbian Mesoamericans, the Ancient Egyptians, the Hindus and the Chinese and many other cultures, whether sophisticated Greeks or pre-literate tribes, all took their cue from the world they saw around them. The heavenly movements, the unvarying procession of the seasons, the great bird and animal migrations: did they not proclaim life's unending circularity?

Not surprisingly for Eliade, most non-modern and primitive societies have little interest in linear histories, but instead focus on a mythical age with which a people can maintain contact and help keep alive through ritual, taboos and story-telling. A prime example of this tradition can be found in the *Dreamtime* myths of the Australian Aboriginal people.

Eliade believed that modern urban civilisation, by removing us from immediate contact with nature's cycles, has robbed us of an intimate awareness of the rhythms of the world and, consequently, has embedded in our minds the illusion of linearity. Thus, we are not only blind to the tidal nature of reality, but also to the true lessons of, human history.

It is important to note that Eliade's *'Eternal Return'* is distinctly different to the philosophical concept of the Eternal Return. His focus was on belief that regarded all phenomena as being eternally cyclical. As for the 'philosophical' interpretation, the name of its most famous exponent, Nietzsche, is mentioned fleetingly only twice in his book. But it is to his philosophical understanding of The Eternal Return that we now turn.

• THE ILLUMINED PATHWAY

Whether through ancient rites and divination,

closely-read scriptures, philosophical inquiry

or the study of nature itself, humankind

everywhere has always sought to understand

and manipulate the world around itself.

Now that science has applied its own powerful

light to those same mysteries, it is offering

us entirely new insights – while discovering

new perspectives on old insights.

5. The Search for the Ultimate Reality

Across the Ages, Great Thinkers Asked the Same Questions

What exactly underlies reality? Is everything founded ultimately on mind or, if you like, the spiritual? Or alternatively is everything, including even our thoughts and concepts, encompassed within a single, undifferentiated *physical* existence? Or, do both aspects coexist separately in our world?

This ancient debate continues to this day, with most philosophical argument now stimulated by the revelations of quantum physics, rather than theology.

The philosophical idea that a single reality embraces everything, not only the physical world, but mathematical and physical laws, human constructions (such as the notion of beauty) and values (good and wrong, etc.) comes under the name of 'monism'. It stands opposed to the dualistic position that the physical world and the idealistic world are different, but co-existent, realities.

Paralleling this dichotomy is the philosophical idea that creation can be split into *phenomenal* and *noumenal* aspects: that is, the world as we experience and interpret it - and the world as it is, independent of any observer. Immanuel Kant referred to this unobserved reality as *Das Ding an Sich*, 'The Thing in Itself'. He believed that the two realms were separate, while the philosopher Arthur Schopenhauer said that they were simply two sides of the one coin, with the phenomenal merely reflecting how our senses and intellect interpret the noumenal. Consequently, we can assume that Kant was a dualist and Schopenhauer was a monist.

Theologically, monism is most often linked with pantheism, where God is synonymous with, and omnipresent in, all creation - and panentheism, in which all reality is embedded as but one aspect (or, as Plotinus put it, as 'an emanation') of the Godhead.

While some Jewish, Christian and Islamic thinkers subscribed to the monist position, explaining that all reality was ultimately in the hand of God and that God was immanent in all of his creation, the outlook of most orthodox scholars and writers of these faiths was essentially dualistic. They believed that terrestrial and sensory existence was quite different from, and inferior to, what would be found on the spiritual plane that one might encounter in the afterlife: here the Creator stood well apart from the created. By contrast, monism has long been a key feature of the South- and East-Asian religious and philosophical traditions.

Serious ideas about a monist cosmos had emerged in the Western world some seven centuries before Christ. Almost simultaneously across the then-known world, there was a remarkable explosion of reason-driven philosophical ideas challenging the intuitive revelations of myth or religion.

One of the most remarkable epochs in the human story, the period known as 'The Axial Age' spanned five centuries between 700 BC to 200 BC and revolutionised how we thought about ourselves and the world around us. Like a great seismic shock, it spread out across a great swathe of civilisations from the Mediterranean, across the Middle East, through Persia and India and finally to China. Even after an interval of millennia, the profound insights and questions it raised still continue to shape our ideas.

So-named by the German philosopher, Karl Jaspers, The Axial Age produced among the Greeks, Socrates, Plato, Parmenides, Archimedes, Pythagoras and a constellation of other daring and original thinkers and creators. Zarathustra (or Zoroaster) appeared in Persia and the greatest of India's many philosophers and teachers of that period was Siddhartha Gautama, known as the Buddha. Farther east, Lao Tzu's Taoism and the Analects of Confucius (Kung Fu Tse) left a still-enduring imprint upon China and nearby civilisations.

Such a surge of discovery was not to be equalled again until the blossoming of the Renaissance in 14th century Florence. Even here, it could be said that Europe had merely awoken from a thousand-year slumber to discover anew the rich bequest of classical times. The Renaissance led in time to the 18th century Enlightenment, and from there the unabated pulse of enquiry went on to shape our modern era. Some argue that the efflorescence of scientific knowledge over the past three or four centuries actually constitutes a 'Second Axial Age'.

Not surprising then that from this fervid questioning there arose important new speculation about 'the big questions', such as the nature and origins of the universe, time and eternity, the place of sentient creatures within the scheme of things, and other perennial mysteries.

Particularly relevant to the theme of this book are the ideas that relate to the oneness of all creation, as opposed to the dualistic, spiritual-versus-physical view of creation espoused by the monotheistic thinkers, in particular.

The Hellenic Philosophers
Many Greek thinkers described ultimate reality as a single, undifferentiated unity that is the eternal and unchanging crucible of the *phenomenal* world we live in. Referred to by different names, this recurring idea within the Hellenic world would have been well understood by their Hindu and Buddhist contemporaries. Indeed, it is very likely that pre-Socratic Greek philosophy was tinged with several Hindu concepts.

One example of this was the cult around *Hermes Trismegistus* – the 'Thrice Great Hermes'. Derived originally from the veneration of the Egyptian god, Thoth, the cult of Hermes focused on magic rituals and alchemy. However, the cult's forty or so books written over 400 years from around 200 BC also touched on philosophical and cosmological questions. A key precept was that the world is a single, organic, timeless and indivisible whole - and thus each human being is connected to all other entities and, indeed, to the entire Cosmos, in which all creatures are but interdependent components of 'The Great Chain of Creation'.

The roll call of ancient Greek monists is impressive. Among the pre-Socratic monists were Thales, Anaximander, Anaximenes, Heraclitus and Parmenides, and among the post-Socratic monists we have Apollonius of Tyana, Numenius, Plotinus and Porphyry, along with many others.

Anaximander (c. 610 BC–c. 546 BC)
Among the greatest Greek philosophers of the Axial Age, Anaximander was also the first to put his thoughts down in written form, although sadly little of these are left to us beyond a few, tantalising fragments.

One of the Milesian School of philosophers, centred in Ionia, he was a materialist who taught that all phenomena resulted, not from the actions of the gods, but from potentially explicable physical agencies. An inventor who is said to have devised the first sundial and a map of the known world, Anaximander is often credited with being the first scientist.

He described the cosmos as consisting of but one single physical reality, which he described as the *Apeiron,* Greek for 'limitless'. Everything that we see around us, taught Anaximander, is merely an aspect or derived portion of this formless, infinite and eternal unity. The endless procession of ever-changing materials and forms we encounter are all contained within the

Apeiron, and these can neither be added to nor subtracted from it.

This idea of the *Apeiron* profoundly influenced Greek and, later, Roman thought right up to the Neoplatonists and thence until the end of the Classical world and the triumph of Christianity. Besides its obvious resonance with Southern Asian thought systems, the *Apeiron* seems to anticipate concepts familiar in modern physics and philosophy.

Pythagoras (c. 570 BC-c. 495 BC)

As one of Anaximander's pupils, Pythagoras also believed in the *Apeiron* model of the cosmos. The first to describe himself as a philosopher (lover of wisdom), Pythagoras was a great mathematician, scientist and philosopher, and while the little that is known about him was written long after his death, his many recognised achievements include the famous Pythagorean Theorem and a mathematical model he proposed for describing different musical notes.

Since he, apparently, never put his thoughts down in writing, it is hard to disentangle what Pythagoras himself believed and what was later ascribed to him. However, he reportedly thought that ours is probably not the only inhabited world in the universe. He is said to have suggested to Herodotus that the cosmos could host 'infinite worlds both like and unlike this world of ours - with many inhabited by 'living creatures and plants and other things we see in this world'.

Parmenides (515 BC-?)

A giant among the pre-Socratic philosophers, Parmenides was a founder of what became known as the Eleatic School, so-called because it was centred in the Sicilian colony of Elias. A considerable influence upon Zeno and, later, Socrates and Plato, he left us nothing beyond a fragment of a philosophical poem, *'On Nature'*. This 160-line scrap reads more like rather oblique, mystical poetry than a work of heavy logic. It describes a young man's quest to find enlightenment, until, at a temple of an unnamed goddess, he finally finds his answers: one of which is that every existence, and all other things, are eternal.

Indeed, most of what is attributed to him comes second-hand, particularly from Plato's own book, *'Parmenides'*. It is generally reckoned that Plato injected much of himself into what he was writing of others, including in his account of Socrates. Nonetheless, as an avowed admirer and student of Parmenides, Plato is unlikely to have wandered far from the teachings he attributed to a philosopher who was still well known and revered at the time the book was compiled.

Parmenides' insights, it is said, revolve around his argument that underlying all apparent reality is what philosophers came to call the *'Plenum'*, a concept not dissimilar to the *Apeiron* of Anaximander and his followers.

Many of Parmenides' arguments to support his *Plenum* were seen even by his contemporaries as weak - and a philosophy student today could easily overturn several of these 'proofs'. But how exactly Parmenides justified his view does not concern us too much here. More interesting is the fact that his concept of the *Plenum*, from the Latin, meaning (in this context) the fullness or totality of matter, comes so close to describing the vision of the cosmos widely held by today's scientists and philosophers. As an example, consider his idea about a perfect vacuum or nothingness. Parmenides stated that absolute nothingness is impossible; by definition a state of non-existence cannot ever be said to *exist*!

For Parmenides, it necessarily followed that there could be no gaps in reality. The whole universe must be a seamless continuum, rather than an empty vacuum peppered with particles of matter. In this *Plenum*, there are no truly discrete objects and we - and everything - are all elements of the same, single cosmic entity.

'What exists is now, all at once, one and continuous...
Nor is it divisible, since it is all alike;
nor is there any more or less of it in one place
which might prevent it from holding together,
but all is full of what is.'

(Today, the quantum view is that even in the deepest, darkest reaches of intergalactic space, there is no such thing as complete emptiness. For here, where there might be less than one atom per cubic metre, you still have a cauldron of quantum energy, electromagnetic radiation, sub-atomic particles, fields and forces weaving together in ceaseless interplay.)

Also, Parmenides declared, there could never have been a time when the cosmos emerged out of nothing. With this he anticipated the statement centuries later by the Roman poet, Lucretius (ca. 99 BC-ca. 55 BC), *ex nihilo nihil fit* - 'nothing comes from nothing'. Thus, the cosmos and its constituent components (whether in the interchangeable forms of energy or of matter) are eternal, with neither beginning nor end, as the poet Ovid (43 BC-17 AD) was to declare in his epic poem, 'Metamorphoses':

'Nothing in the entire universe ever perishes, believe me, but things vary, and adopt a new form. The phrase "being born" is used for beginning to be something different from what one was before, while "dying" means ceasing to be the same. Though this thing may pass into that, and that into this, yet the sums of things remains unchanged.'

Of course, Parmenides was aware that his view of the universe was at odds with what, at an everyday human level, we seem to experience and observe. He answered this by saying that our awareness of an ever-changing world made up of separate and independent objects and creatures is simply a construct of human consciousness. It is merely the way we interpret what is in reality a static and completely unitary cosmos.

As it happens, Parmenides' insight has gained increasing acceptance since the time of Einstein (whose support for this idea prompted his philosopher friend Karl Popper to jokingly pin on him the nickname of 'Parmenides').

Physicists now generally accept that our concept of a 'now' is entirely subjective - and that from an objective standpoint all the 'nows' that ever were or ever will be are equally real and valid. Our sense of past, present and future is simply how we, as conscious beings, experience our brief passage through the cosmic totality.

'And it is all one to me
Where I am to begin;
for I shall return there again.'

Here Parmenides states his belief that everything that can be conceived in thought must - and does - exist, unchangingly and eternally. To be imagined and to exist are the same thing, providing what was imagined is consistent with logic and the local laws of nature. Thus, some two and a half millennia ago, Parmenides anticipated many aspects of our modern constructs of the Multiverse and Block Time (or Eternalism).

Anaxagoras (c. 500 BC-428 BC)
Another student of Anaximander, Anaxagoras took a scientific, observation-based approach to explaining the world. Balancing the deductive with the inductive approaches, his perceptive insights included the view that the Moon's glow was actually the reflection of solar light.

He taught that the universe and its essential, indivisible constituents were eternal and encompassed within 'The One'. It was Mind (*nous*) itself that created forms and order from this inchoate, primal chaos.

Socrates (c. 469 BC-399 BC)

Beyond that Socrates was probably a monotheist (he is quoted usually as referring to 'God', not 'the gods'), little can be said about his views on the physical world; his teachings and utterances seem very much focused on the human condition and ethical behaviour. In any case, we have to rely largely on his students Xenophon and Plato, and the playwright Aristophanes, for any contemporary accounts. As with Plato's book on *'Parmenides'*, we can never be too sure whether every idea he ascribes to Socrates is authentic - or simply reflects Plato's own view on a subject.

Plato (428/427 BC-348/347 BC)

Along with his teacher, Socrates, and his own student, Aristotle, Plato stands as one of the three pillars of Greek, indeed of Western, philosophy.

The founder of the world's first 'university', the Academy of Athens, he was pre-eminent not only as a philosopher, but also as a mathematician and teacher. Given most classical philosophers' reluctance to write down their thoughts, fortunately he was an accomplished and prolific writer.

In his view of the world, Plato accepted Socrates' belief that reality is ultimately something beyond the grasp of our limited senses, and proposed that there is a more authentic, constant and eternal reality based on non-experiential 'forms' and archetypes. This model dominated Western thought for one and a half millennia, especially in explaining God as a model of absolute perfection.

For example, it inspired the16[th] century astronomer, Johannes Kepler, in his initial attempts to explain the planetary orbits in terms of a set of platonic, perfect forms. However, to his credit, he was willing to abandon this approach when Tycho Brahe's data unobligingly refused to conform to this neat vision.

Zeno of Citium (c.334 BC-c.262 BC)
Zeno of Citium founded Stoicism, a school of philosophy which, developed by later Greek and Roman writers, became a major shaper of thinking and behaviour in the ancient world and influenced Europe through the Christian era and up till modern times. (He is not to be confused with Zeno of Elea, famous for his never-finishing race between the hare and the tortoise.)

The universality of the Stoic prescription for a good life is shown by the fact that in Rome the most widely read Stoic writers were Emperor Marcus Aurelius, Seneca the Younger (a tutor and adviser to Nero) and a Greek slave, Epictetus. The great legal advocate, man of letters and philosopher, Cicero (106 BC-43 BC) also wrote essays with Stoic themes.

The name 'Stoic' referred to Zeno's favoured meeting place in a colonnade of the Athenian agora, called the *stoa poikle*.

Zeno taught a form of pantheism in which the universe was God or a 'World-Soul'. Furthermore, the universe was eternal, although it underwent a continuous cycle of formation, destruction and re-creation. Known as 'The Great Year', each cycle was a phase in a cosmic procession that has neither beginning nor end. Like the Hindu *kalpa,* this is similar to the current idea of the 'pulsating universe' still being debated by some cosmologists.

Zeno also correctly described the sun as a sphere of fire considerably bigger than the earth. Again, like Anaxagoras before him, he believed that the moon shone with reflected solar light.

Epicurus (341 BC-270 BC)

The other great quasi-religious philosophical school to contend with Stoicism for adherents and influence in Rome was Epicureanism. Epicurus taught in his garden in Athens, near where Zeno held his discourses by the Stoa.

Epicurus' approach prefigured the scientific method, inasmuch as he insisted upon a rigorous skepticism that subjected everything to a close observation and logical analysis. His Stoic contemporaries dismissed his teachings as too lax and tolerant, with the result that 'epicurean' still describes a heedless, live-for-today hedonism. This is unfair because it is quite at odds with Epicurus' own advice about a sensible avoidance of pain and for moderation in the enjoyment of life's simple and harmless pleasures. While his balanced and liberal prescriptions for a good life fell short of the Stoics' almost puritanical austerities, Epicurus' was certainly no libertine nor even (in today's sense of the word) an 'epicurean'!

Epicurus subscribed to Democritus' atomism: the idea that matter is fundamentally made up of invisible particles eternally jostling around in space. His view was that these particles moved around in a random fashion: a notion similar to the non-deterministic motion of sub-atomic particles described by quantum physics today. Importantly, because atoms are eternal and they inhabit boundless space, it followed that an infinite number of worlds constantly arise and disappear over eternity.

Roman Thinkers
Plotinus (AD 204/5-270 AD)

Some seven centuries after Parmenides, the founder of Neoplatonism, Plotinus, promoted what he called 'The One': again, a concept not dissimilar to the Apeiron or the Plenum.

(Plotinus may also have been influenced by the earlier Gnostic Christian Valentinius (c. 100-160 AD), whose 'Primal Being' (or Bythos) describes the ultimate unity, or monad, that lies behind the world of differentiated things that we falsely perceive of as 'reality'.) Plotinus said that the ultimate human aspiration should be to find ecstatic union with The One: an experience he himself had achieved on several occasions, according to this chronicler, Porphyry.

An influence upon St Augustine of Hippo, Plotinus was probably born in Lycopolis in Egypt and spent his formative years in Alexandria, finally to settle in Rome after many travels. He attracted numerous followers, including, it was said, the Emperor Gallienus and his wife Salonica.

Once again, no writings of Plotinus survive, but, fortunately, his ideas were faithfully recorded by his amanuensis, Porphyry, and also by others of that era. In the Enneads, Porphyry presents us with his notes and also his edited version of Plotinus' own jottings, which Plotinus was unable to rewrite because of deteriorated eyesight. For Plotinus, *The One* was beyond all categories and description; indeed, it was futile even to attribute to it the states of being or not-being. It could not be divided or multiplied and was neither object nor subject. However, our entire universe, including the chains of events and the lives contained within it, were born of *The One*, without it ever having diminished itself in any way.

Because of its ultimate source within *The One*, all matter shares in its divinity, as do all beings, man included. As recorded in the '*Enneads*', Plotinus declared:

'This universe is a single living being embracing all living beings within it, and possessing a single Soul that permeates all its parts to the degree of their participation in it. Every part of this sensible universe is fully participant in its material aspect, and in respect of soul, in the degree to which it shares in the World Soul.'

And again,

'The One is all things and yet no one of them. It is the source of all things, not itself all things, but their transcendent Principle. . . So that Being may exist, the One is not Being, but the begetter of Being.'

As the highest expression of the known material world, Man's primary task is to seek union with *The One*; a goal and a process very much like the East Asian approach to achieving enlightenment. Indeed, Plotinus is said to have had a great interest in the philosophies of India and Persia, and had once hoped to journey to these lands. One can easily imagine that Plotinus was aware of Indian meditational techniques when we read this quotation:

'Our thought cannot grasp the One as long as any other image remains active in the soul… To this end, you must set free your soul from all outward things and turn wholly within yourself, with no more leaning to what lies outside, and lay your mind bare of ideal forms, as before of the objects of sense, and forget even yourself, and so come within sight of that One.' [6.9.7]

Eustochus, who was at his side in his dying days, wrote that Plotinus' last words of advice were, 'Strive to give back to the Divine in your selves the Divine in the All'.

St Augustine of Hippo (354-430 AD)
As mentioned in Chapter 3, St Augustine's musings about time resonate closely with how modern science understands it. For example, he believed that God, being all-sufficient, boundless and beyond change or modification lived in an eternal 'now' - as distinct from the temporal world we see ourselves occupying in which time is nothing but a crucible of change, of constant becoming and unbecoming.

However, he saw a firm distinction between the creator and the created and was, accordingly, a convinced dualist. What is more, his physical world followed a single, linear path between the moment of creation and its eventual demise. His arguments on this account would ring out across Europe for centuries to come.

Medieval Philosophy

Guided by Church doctrine, medieval philosophers accepted that the universe was created *ex nihilo* by God at a specific instant when linear time itself also came into being - and that the end of the world foretold by scripture would signal the cessation of the material world and of time itself. In this, medieval theologians rejected the speculations of Aristotle and many other pagan philosophers and took their cue, instead, from the arguments of St. Augustine of Hippo.

This was an era when dualism was a central belief among theologians and philosophers everywhere. It was widely thought (but, as we shall see, not entirely) that not only was the earthly world separate from God, but that he had created it neither from nor within himself.

However, that colossus of medieval thought, Thomas Aquinas (1225-1274), argued for a more flexible approach. Even if the material world were eternal, he said, nothing could alter the fact that its existence could only be sustained by divine intention and power. Furthermore, as he neatly explained in his book *'On the Eternity of the World' (De Aeternite de Mundi)*:
'...If we understand "being made" or "being caused" as implying the pre-existence of a passive potentiality, then it should be conceded, according to faith, that something caused cannot

always exist, for it would then follow that a passive potentiality has always existed, and this is heretical.'

Before him, Anselm of Canterbury (1033-1109), thought that, even if mankind was imprisoned in a temporal world, then God himself occupied an eternalist plane of existence and his ability to view all events, past and present made him omniscient, complete and unchanging.

Robert Grosseteste (1175-1253)

The very able Bishop of Lincoln, Grosseteste was also a respected theologian and intellectual whose reputation spanned Christendom, largely as an expert on the recently translated books of Aristotle. For so long lost to most of Europe, Aristotle's scientific books had emphasised an inductive approach, based upon observation and facts as the way to understand nature, and this stimulated a wave of liberated thinking that swept into the Renaissance era.

Grosseteste (the name originally meant 'great head') was also widely regarded as the greatest mathematician of his era, while his enquiries into optical physics shaped that area of study for centuries to come. His writings speculate on the nature of matter at the atomic level, and also on cosmological themes, culminating in his masterwork, *'De Luce'* (1225), which sought to demonstrate that the whole cosmos was subject to a single set of universal physical laws. More than that, he hypothesised that our universe had its beginning in an explosion from a single point, in other words, something similar to what we now describe as the Big Bang.

Of particular relevance is that Grosseteste's reasoning that a Multiverse containing other universes without number and each incorporated its own individual set of physical laws. Well aware that the theological debate in his time about other universes was a hotly contested and dangerous arena, Grosseteste, perhaps wisely, presented his thoughts on the possibility of multiple universes only very obliquely. Nonetheless, today's physicists analysing his works have found tantalising hints that Grosseteste was indeed an early advocate of the Multiverse.

Étienne Tempier (Died 1279)

At a time when French theologians of the day were arguing about the uniqueness of this universe, Bishop Étienne Tempier of Paris examined the question in his famous *'Condemnation of 219 Philosophical & Theological Propositions'* in 1277.

In proposition number 34, 'that the first cause cannot make more than one world', he argued that an omnipotent God could certainly create as many universes as he wished, although scripture pointed to this being the only one. However, this actually re-enlivened debate about other worlds, most famously around the speculations of Nicholas of Cusa, almost a century and a half later. In the meantime, the idea was taken up by such as the renowned French late medieval philosopher, Nicole Oresme (1320 - 82) who had suggested the existence of other inhabited worlds in space.

Nicholas of Cusa (or Kues) (1401-1464)

The German 15th century theologian and humanist, Nicholas of Cusa (like Bruno a century later) proposed that the realm of stars and planets was quite literally unbounded. Anticipating Copernicus, he rejected the Church-endorsed Aristotelian view that the earth was the centre of the universe. If, as he believed, the universe is infinite, then how could it have a centre-point? And would this not inevitably open up the likelihood of other inhabited worlds like ours? In his book, *'De Docta Ignorantia'*, (Learned Ignorance) of 1439-40, he conjectured that extraterrestrials lived on other planets:

'Life, as it exists on Earth in the form of men, animals and plants, is to be found, let us suppose in a high form in the solar and stellar regions. Rather than think that so many stars and parts of the heavens are uninhabited and that this earth of ours alone is peopled - and that with beings perhaps of an inferior type - we will suppose that in every region there are inhabitants, differing in nature by rank and all owing their origin to God, who is the centre and circumference of all stellar regions.

Of the inhabitants then of worlds other than our own we can know still less having no standards by which to appraise them.

It may be conjectured that in the area of the sun there exist solar beings, bright and enlightened denizens, and by nature more spiritual than such as may inhabit the moon - who are possibly lunatics - whilst those on earth are more gross and material.'

This view was in direct opposition to what that revered Church authority, St. Augustine of Hippo, had written almost exactly a thousand years earlier when he dismissed the possibility of other inhabited worlds, believing that it was unthinkable that Christ would have had to endure his blood sacrifice on the cross again and again for each world.

Venturing even further, Nicholas also believed that God was immanent throughout the cosmos, writing: *'God... is the one most simple essence of the entire universe...'*

Not surprisingly, these writings were closely scrutinised by the Church authorities. Of chief concern was that Nicholas of Cusa was promoting the serious heresy of pantheism. Fortunately, he was able to demonstrate convincingly that his views were a form of panentheism, not pantheism. Panentheism (all-within-god) may appear to us to be little different to Pantheism (everything-is-god), but in medieval Europe that two-letter difference was life-and-death critical.

Pantheism is the notion that God is bounded by, and manifest exclusively through, the universe. By contrast, panentheism holds that while God is immanent in every last interstice of the universe, he himself is greater than the infinite universe of his creation. Thus, the universe is, to use the neat phrase employed by medieval theologians, a 'contracted maximum'.

Nicholas satisfactorily demonstrated his sincere belief that God was even greater than his creation. Because Panentheists in the Catholic Church were usually tolerated (admittedly under a watchful eye), Nicholas of Cusa went on to become a cardinal, bishop, papal legate and a renowned thinker of enduring repute.

(It should be noted that the famous 13th century Christian mystic, Meister Eckhart came close to a pantheistic position himself. He believed that everything, ultimately, was contained in an Absolute Unity, and behind all this was the *'Theo Agnosto'*, *θεο αγνωστο*, meaning the 'Unknown or Unknowable God' to which Neoplatonists such as Plotinus had subscribed. Like Parmenides' *Apeiron* or Plotinus' *Plenum*, this ultimate reality was beyond any differentiation and, therefore, beyond all description.)

Avicenna (980-1037)

These debates about the ultimate reality were greatly enriched by deep and sophisticated reflections coming out of the Islamic world. Foremost were the writings of the Persian thinker, *Ibn Sīnā*, whose prodigious intellect carried his renown throughout the Christian world, where he was known as Avicenna.

His protean curiosity led him to write scholarly books upon an improbably wide range of subjects, including astronomy, mathematics, physics, theology, medicine, poetry, and more besides.

Of particular interest here is the argument Avicenna presented for the existence of an eternal cosmos, his version of the *'nihil ex nihilo fit'* (nothing can emerge from nothing) case. He stated that prior to anything existing, the *possibility* of its existence must have been there all along. This prior potentiality would have required some vessel to sustain it: it could not possibly exist in itself or arise spontaneously - and certainly could not exist in an absolute nothingness prior to the creation of the cosmos.

As expected, Christian (and, one imagines, Islamic) theologians counter-argued that a Creator-God was perfectly able to summon forth a cosmos *ex nihilo*, that is, out of nothing, if he so wished.

Nonetheless, we see Avicenna's idea re-emerge later in the form of Thomas Aquinas' speculation about what he called a 'passive potentiality' that must precede something being summoned into existence from nothingness.

Maimonides (1135-1204)

On the question of an eternal cosmos, the other towering non-Christian thinker of that era, Maimonides (Moshe ben Maimon), took a different view to Avicenna. A Sephardic Jewish scholar, astronomer and man of medicine born in Caliphate Spain, Maimonides was an enthusiastic Aristotelian in everything but for one point: rejecting Aristotle's view that the material world was eternal, Maimonides accepted the scriptural description of an *ex nihilo* creation. To his credit, Maimonides stoutly opposed the widely held notion that astrology could interpret how stellar movements shape human destiny.

Renaissance Philosophers

Giordano Bruno (1548-1600)

In 1926 a radio broadcasting licence was granted in Sydney, Australia to a company associated with the local Theosophical Society. It gave their radio station the call sign '2GB' in honour of the 16th century philosopher and secular martyr, Giordano Bruno.

It must be a rare thing that a commercial radio station to this day continues to carry the initials of a long-dead, heretical monk - and equally that astronomers should agree that a 20 km-wide lunar crater would also carry his name. So why these, and so many other, posthumous honours?

Born in Nola, near the slopes of Vesuvius, Giordano Bruno was a Dominican priest who soon earned a reputation for being extremely intelligent, deeply learned - and unsettlingly outspoken and opinionated. For the Church authorities this added up to only one thing - trouble!

Inevitably, Bruno was forced to keep moving across Europe, one step ahead of the long reach of the Papal authorities: first to teach in Paris, next to England's Oxford University and then to Wittenburg in Germany. Wherever he went, Bruno raised eyebrows with his challenging ideas. He wrote, for example, that there was no logical or empirical basis for religious faith, and that the scriptures should not be taken as literally true. Along the way, he dismissed the Genesis story, the Virgin Birth and the Mass, amongst other Catholic verities.

At that time Copernicus' heliocentric model was still far from being accepted by the Church, yet Bruno went well beyond it, proclaiming that the universe was infinite and eternal, and coexistent with God himself. In this pantheistic scheme, the Earth and the Sun were merely elements of a fantastically vast host of heavenly bodies.

In proposing that the Sun, and not the Earth, was at the centre of God's creation, Copernicus' instinct for self-preservation persuaded him to arrange for his heretical book to be published posthumously, but not so Bruno. His repeated affronts to Church orthodoxy, one might even say, ceaseless baiting, could no longer remain unanswered and the former Dominican monk found himself in the Inquisitor's prison where he was held for six years. Given the opportunity to recant and seek forgiveness, Bruno eloquently and obstinately defended his ideas to the last. The Inquisition Cardinals who judged Giordano Bruno included a future saint and one who would, in time, become Pope Paul V.

Sentenced to death, this diminutive heretic was then given eight more days to recant, but he refused to buckle, defiantly holding firm where Galileo himself would, years later, compliantly utter the appropriate exculpatory formula to avoid execution. The impenitent philosopher was then led out to the *Campo de' Fiori* ('Field of Flowers') Square in Rome, bound to the stake and burnt alive, the Church authorities having first taken the precaution of strapping a wooden gag into his mouth lest he pollute the assembled witnesses' ears with his diabolical utterances. The spot where he died is marked today by a statue and monument.

(In the very different fates of the two churchmen - Bruno and Nicholas of Cusa - we see how crucially the Catholic Church differentiated between 'pantheism' and 'panentheism'.)

History presents no greater example of a belief heroically defended, and for this alone, Bruno compels the admiration of anyone who values this struggle. Along with the Neoplatonist philosopher, Hypatia of Alexandria (370-415 AD), who was murdered by a fanatical Christian mob, Bruno is today regarded as science's most famous martyr and a secular saint. Nonetheless, it is what he taught that makes Bruno Giordano of particular interest for this book, for, in the light of what we now know of the universe, and what is being surmised, Bruno's ideas appear startlingly modern and, some might say, prescient.

A Neoplatonist by inclination, Bruno declared that 'all things are one', and that the universe is infinite, with the godhead immanent in its creation, rather than being an external creator figure. In *A Philosophy of the Infinite Universe*, he wrote:

'There are no ends, limits, margins, or walls, that keep back or subtract any parcel of the infinite abundance of things.'

He went on to say that the grandeur of God was not limited to one,

'...but in numberless suns, not in one earth nor in one world, but in ten hundred thousand, of infinite globes.'

Another heretical, but quintessentially modern, insight was Bruno's conviction that our apprehension and understanding of the world is conditioned by our position and circumstances. For him, that there are as many worlds as there are individual observers means no one can confidently postulate an absolute truth valid across all universes, nor put any limit to it. For Bruno, an infinite universe of countless suns and planets, ceaselessly processing from birth to full bloom and then to extinction, all betokened a unity of inexpressible grandeur, beauty and order. Was there any more magnificent testimony to the divine? In *'Cause, Principle, and Unity'*, he wrote:

'This entire globe, this star, not being subject to death, and dissolution and annihilation being impossible anywhere in Nature, from time to time renews itself by changing and altering all its parts. There is no absolute up or down, as Aristotle taught; no absolute position in space; but the position of a body is relative to that of other bodies. Everywhere there is incessant relative change in position throughout the universe, and the observer is always at the centre of things.'

Such a description of the physical world is one that a 21st century cosmologist would own as readily, if not quite so madly bravely, as did that ferocious seeker in the 16th century.

Baruch Spinoza (1632-1677)
Three decades after Bruno's ashes blew across the square of the *Campo de' Fiori*, there was born to a respected family of Dutch immigrant Jews a boy who would reaffirm many of Bruno's ideas - and become one of the titans of modern philosophy. His name was Baruch Spinoza.

In many ways, Spinoza was as defiant of entrenched orthodoxy as was Bruno: he succeeded in having his name placed on the Catholic Index of banned authors and his books were burnt by Dutch Protestants. Then, for good measure, it was said that he had also been excommunicated from Amsterdam's Jewish community: thus achieving the full heretical trifecta!

Luckily for him and for posterity, Spinoza, unlike Bruno, suffered no violence for his confronting views. That is partly because Amsterdam was comparatively more tolerant than the Pope's Rome in Bruno's time, and also that Spinoza kept a judiciously low profile. Turning down honours and teaching positions, he settled for a modestly comfortable living as a grinder of lenses. (It is conjectured that the lung disease that killed him at 44 years was due to inhaling glass dust.)

For Spinoza, mind and matter were all part of the same reality, and so he firmly rejected Descartes' dualistic universe. All that exists is part of the same Nature and follows its unvarying laws (thereby disposing of scriptural miracles). 'God' and 'Nature', said Spinoza were interchangeable names, although there might be aspects and dimensions of God that extend well beyond the physical world we can recognise. Thus, 'God' is identified with the laws and mechanisms of nature, and is certainly not an independent agent able, or willing, to intervene in their deterministic workings.

In Spinoza's view, a fundamental question was: why is there anything whatsoever, as opposed to nothing? Here he was certainly not the first, nor indeed the last, to address this poser, the 20th century philosopher Martin Heidegger included. Spinoza's view was that any notion of absolute and universal nothingness was an absurdity. (As already explained, a state of nothingness cannot *exist,* because that would be illogical and contradictory: merely being in any state must imply a condition of existence, which would straightaway nullify any claim to 'nothingness'!)

On the contrary, Spinoza concluded that if anything exists, then *everything* exists. Thus, Spinoza's cosmos was infinite and eternal: 'eternity cannot be defined by time or have any relation to it'. This might seem to us to be a comfortable way of describing the Multiverse, although Spinoza himself was happy to give the name of 'God' to this impersonal totality. He would have guessed that, as a self-declared theist, this little taxonomical tweak might protect him from the obloquy that went with being a declared 'pantheist'!

Inevitably, though, it was only a matter of time before Spinoza's teachings did identify him as an unabashed pantheist. For all his equivocation, in Spinoza's time and thereafter there were many who labeled him an atheist because the god he described was impersonal: an entity we now recognise as more akin to the Hindu Brahman than the Judeo-Christian Jehovah, with his human-like attributes (anger, partiality, jealousy and pride, need for praise, etc.) and a persistent habit of intervening in human affairs.

Beyond this, our humble lens-grinder's chief focus was ethical and he tried to show that humans living in a deterministic universe could lead good and content lives.

Spinoza was an acknowledged influence on minds as diverse as George Eliot, Johann Wolfgang Goethe, Luis Borges and many others, especially, Albert Einstein. Saying that no other philosopher had done as much to shape his own world-view, Einstein wrote (in a telegram):

'I believe in Spinoza's God who reveals himself in the orderly harmony of what exists, not in a God who concerns himself with the fates and actions of human beings.'

Islamic & Judaic Philosophers

Essentially, Judaism and Islam shared the strong dualistic belief also held by Christianity. However, there were some whose speculations and language edged closer to monism.

For example, it could be said that the Jewish Chasidic scholar, Shneur Zalman of Ladi espoused a weak form of monism when he said that God must continue to be immanent in the physical world he had created because, were this not so, it would instantly revert to its original nothingness. (This reminds us of the Aztecs who feared that, without the regular nourishment of human blood, their god would be unable to continue sustaining the world.)

While the Koran explicitly proclaims the separateness of the Creator and the created, many Sufi mystics looked through monism's glass. For example, the great Persian poet of the 13th century, Rumi, wrote that

'in the shop for Unity; anything that you see there except the One (God) is an idol'.

Hindu & Buddhist Philosophy

The most enthusiastically polytheistic of all main religions, Hinduism paradoxically also comfortably accommodates an ancient tradition of monism, particularly in its Vedanta, Yoga and Shaivist schools. Above the plethora of divinities and transcendent entities, there is an ultimate reality, Brahman, which is formless, undifferentiated and unchanging. Both immanent and transcendent, Brahman contains within itself all that is and ever has been, including gods and mortal creatures. Moreover, Brahman incorporates an infinity of other universes, spiralling through all eternity:

'There are innumerable universes besides this one, and although they are unlimitedly large, they move about like atoms in You. Therefore You are called unlimited.' (Bhagavata Purana 6.16.37)

The Buddhist traditions, in their numerous diverse forms, include many metaphysical speculations and explanations, but the fact is that the Buddha himself chose not to hypothesise about the nature of the universe, eternity or cosmic circularity.

On the other hand, later Buddhist thinkers had much to say about the nature of reality. One insight of lasting importance in Buddhist philosophy was that of Sunyatta, developed by the Indian thinker, Nāgārjuna (c. 150 – 250 AD) who was, after only Siddhartha himself, the greatest single contributor to Buddhist thought. His message was that the only reality was The Void (Sunyatta) which encompasses all things and beings: a concept obviously similar to Greek and Roman descriptions of the ultimate reality. Nāgārjuna went on to say that the illusion that anything has independent existence (our individual selves included) is the source of our unhappiness and feeds a destructive and, ultimately, futile striving. By contrast, enlightenment bestowed the realisation that all beings and phenomena are inseparably contingent and contiguous components, contained exclusively within the Void.

On this subject, the current Dalai Lama wrote in his book, *'The Universe in a Single Atom'*:

'All things and events, whether material, mental or even abstract concepts like time, are devoid of objective, independent existence. To possess such independent, intrinsic existence would imply that things and events are somehow complete unto themselves and are therefore entirely self-contained. This would mean that nothing has the capacity to interact with and exert influence on other phenomena. But we know that there is cause and effect - turn a key in a starter, spark plugs ignite, the engine turns over and petrol and oil are burned. In a universe of self-contained, inherently existing things, these events would never occur.'

The Dalai Lama remarks that the similarities between the world described by quantum mechanics and Nāgārjuna's philosophy of emptiness are apparent to many Buddhists and physicists alike.

Modern Thinkers

Block Universe & Eternalism
Described variously as the Block Universe theory, or 'Eternalism', this philosophical approach describes a reality of four or more

dimensions in which what we choose to describe as 'the past', 'the present' and 'the future' are all coexistent, equally valid aspects of a single block. As mentioned earlier, the Block, or Eternalist cosmos, stands opposed to the idea of 'Presentism', the view that all that exists is the present, which is the handy way with which we intuitively deal with the world. Again, this 'Block' is similar to the concept of timelessness proposed by Dr Julian Barbour.

One obvious characteristic of the Block Universe is that it is fixed, eternal and immutable. This being so, it is hard to imagine how it might contain certain 'fates' and not others; that it selects only some of a limitless range of possible narratives. If this is so, then it is clear that a Block Universe (or Multiverse?) is broadly similar to what the ancients conceived of under such names as 'The Apeiron', 'The One' and 'The Plenum'.

Perhaps one way that we might imagine the Block is that it is like a boundless and eternal, poly-dimensional hologram in which are embedded all possibilities. And, as with a hologram, the reality we draw out of this - and that we experience - depends simply upon our particular vantage point or perspective.

Applying the Razor
A modern argument for the monist position draws upon the Ockham's Razor principle. Quite simply, this states that one should choose the simplest of possible explanations and only proceed to a more complex explanation when it can be seen to offer a better solution.

Widely employed as a general guideline in scientific enquiry, this principle is attributed to one William of Ockham (1285-1349), an English Franciscan friar who made a considerable mark as a theologian and philosopher. It must be said, nonetheless, that the 'razor' maxim, which is Ockham's chief claim to fame in our own era, is not to be found in any of his writings, although he did indicate a general preference for 'economical' explanations.

In their debates with dualists, many philosophers argue that modern physics and cosmology can describe a working universe that no longer has to accommodate both materialist and spiritual planes. Everything, they say, can be or is likely to be accounted for by a materialist or monist explanation.

On the other hand, since there is no independently verifiable evidence for a separate spiritual dimension, the monist account offers the simplest and most comfortable fit with the Ockham's Razor principle. It keeps us within the purview of science.

For all that, we are still left with a monistic cosmos whose fundamental reality may not be of a material nature, but, as some argue, might consist of 'Mind' or 'Idea'. Here they are in the company of the 18th century philosopher George Berkeley and Kant (a self-described 'transcendental idealist'), amongst others. In our own time, Dr Robert Lanza's writings promote a 'biocentrist' interpretation based on quantum theory, saying it is the observer that calls the observed into existence, and not the other way around.

F.H. Bradley (1846-1924)

Bradley was the leading British idealist philosopher of his time and a convinced monist. He said that all reality was one, yet as an equally convinced idealist, he maintained that, despite our perceiving the world as a vast collection of separate entities, true reality is essentially an undifferentiated idea or experience, an Absolute. And within this Absolute, anything that can exist *must* exist in some kind of manifested reality.

Despite his almost mystical embrace of the Absolute, Bradley was a man driven by two intemperate passions: he was an enthusiastic gun-owner and an ardent cat-hater. Often, residents of Oxford University's venerable Merton College would jump from their beds, startled by gunfire during this eminent philosopher's nocturnal expeditions against his feline enemies!

(Some years ago, I visited Merton College, where my son Damien was a student. I am pleased to attest that the eccentric academic is still a protected - indeed, thriving - species in that noble institution.)

6. Thus Spake Nietzsche

The Eternal Return, Superman and the Others

Imagine this scene...

It is a balmy day, and peering out across the dark waters of the Bay of Naples is a thickset individual of mature years, balding and heavy-jowled. His intense eyes proclaim a keen intellect and, in his clothes, deportment and gestures we see the markers of confident, patrician dignity. This is none other than Marcus Tullius Cicero, Rome's most formidable orator and the pre-eminent intellectual of his age; a man whose undiminished reputation reaches to us across more than two millennia.

Standing on a narrow peninsula, he squints under the intense sun at a distant procession of large transport ships heading towards Puteoli, one of Rome's busiest ports and now known as the town of Pozzuli. They bring cargoes of grain from North Africa and the Middle East to sustain Rome's one million inhabitants. Frequently, too, their decks carry caged exotic animals, such as crocodiles and hippopotami from Egypt, all bound for one destination, the Colosseum. In this way, the Emperor is keeping his compact with the ever-volatile Roman citizenry: if they stay quiet, they will be fed and entertained.

Absorbed by this spectacle, Cicero was struck by a thought, which he later recorded for his travelling companion:

'Would you believe that there exist innumerable worlds... and that just as we are at this moment close to Bauli and are looking towards Puteoli, so there are countless persons in exactly similar spots with our names, our honours, our achievements, our minds, our shapes, our ages, discussing the very same subject?'

Cicero, an outstanding lawyer, politician, administrator and consul, was a respected Stoic who left us many writings on his philosophy, including his treatise, *'Academica'* (On Academic Scepticism). It was here that we find the speculative musings you have just read regarding the existence of limitless orbs, and with that, inevitably, the possibility that our own familiar Earth and our very lives might be - must be - recurring elsewhere. Worlds upon worlds of our identical, doppelganger twins!

In fact, the question as to whether there was one universe or, instead a limitless plethora of universes, was a common debating topic among philosophically inclined Greeks and Romans. But on one occasion at least, a pragmatic Roman was willing to leave aside such airy speculation on the plurality of worlds in order to answer a more pressing, earthly concern.

In a letter to a friend, Cicero referred to a lecture by a leading Epicurean philosopher who, as usual, concluded by inviting questions from his audience. An acquaintance of Cicero, one Papirius Paetus, had let it be widely known beforehand that he intended raising the issue of the possible multiplicity of universes. But, instead, his one question was whether his name had been included among the guests invited for the dinner to follow the talk! (Cicero: *'Letters to his Friends'*.)

Nonetheless, the ancients certainly recognised the boundless plurality of worlds as a weighty topic. Peering down the ever-receding corridors of eternity, how could it not be that numberless worlds were arising and disappearing again and again? The Stoics certainly believed and taught this, affirming that all possible phenomena and contingencies would surely be encountered over and over.

The Return of All Things

The ceaseless turning of recurrence must impose itself upon the very rarest of happenings, even upon a conjunction of events that might only pop up once over the accumulated lifetimes of ten or a hundred thousand universes. Earlier, we saw that a dedicated card player might turn up a royal flush (the term for an ace high straight flush) only very occasionally, nonetheless everyone accepts that this lucky hand is likely to occur sooner or later over years of playing. And although the odds, say, of winning a national draw five times in a row would certainly involve numbers inconceivably vaster still, this lucky run would be as inevitable over time.

The fact remains that, across eternity, whatever is remotely possible will inevitably occur: it is just that the periodic intervals between more likely events will be shorter than those between less likely occurrences. However, all incidents will play out an infinite number of times across eternity. For mathematicians, this is accepted as a given.

Recurrence: an Ancient Thought

While the concept of eternal recurrence reaches back to the Ancient Egyptians and beyond, one of the first to address it as a *philosophical* concept was the great Greek philosopher and mathematician, Pythagoras, and this was then taken up by his followers.

The Pythagoreans further developed Anaximander's idea of the *Apeiron* to include the doctrine of the transmigration of souls, together with certain Orphic mystical notions and rituals. As well, they held that, with the right effort and a dedication to philosophy, science and mathematics, an individual could aspire to being reborn at a higher level of existence and, finally, to achieving release from the 'wheel of life': a doctrine instantly familiar to anyone acquainted with Hindu and Buddhist precepts.

The Pythagoreans' belief in eternal recurrence is described here by Eudemus, a disciple of Aristotle:

'Some people accept and some people deny that time repeats itself. Repetition is understood in different senses. One kind of repetition may be in the natural order of things, like repetition of summers and winters... But if we are to believe the Pythagoreans there is another kind of repetition. That means that I shall talk to you and sit exactly like this and I shall have in my hand the same stick, and everything will be the same as it is now and time, as it can be supposed, will be the same. Because, if

movements (of heavenly bodies) and many other things are the same, what occurred before and what will occur afterwards are also the same. This applies also to repetition, which is always the same. Everything is the same and therefore time is the same.' (Eudemus, Frag. 272 in *'The Presocratic Philosophers'* by G.S. Kirk & J.E. Raven - New York: Cambridge University Press, 1957.)

Parmenides claimed that both time and change are illusory simply because past and future already exist and hence the notion of the passing of time is unrealistic. From that he derived that the whole of existence is ultimately a oneness and that nothing can ever be created or destroyed. For his part, Plato believed in reincarnation, with progression to a higher or lower state being determined by one's efforts and virtue in the previous life.

Empedocles (490-430 BC) also accepted the idea of reincarnation, along with an eternally cyclical universe in which all matter reassembles in a primordial form, ready for the next round of gradual diversification and recreation of components and beings. In this ceaseless process, it was inevitable that sentient creatures would, over vast stretches of time, once again relive their earlier lives.

He outlined his thought in written verse, and more of Empedocles' writing survives than does that of any other pre-Socratic philosopher. However, on the question of an eternal corporeal world and the eternal recurrence that this would imply, his view was at odds with the model thought most likely by today's scientists.

Even the Old Testament contains references to the idea of eternal recurrence, as we can read in *Ecclesiastes*, Verses 1:9-11:

'That which has been is that which will be,
And that which has been done is that which will be done.
So there is nothing new under the sun.

Is there any thing of which one might say,
"See this, it is new"?
Already it has existed for ages
Which were before us.

There is no remembrance of earlier things;
And also of the later things which will occur,
There will be for them no remembrance
Among those who will come later still.'

In the third century, the Roman, Plotinus, suggested that all things would come around again in an eternal cycle of Great Years ('Periods') in which each Period would be an exact replay of the one that preceded it.

In the *'Enneads'*, he explained that each of these Periods is:

'...a periodical renovation bounding the boundlessness by the return of a former series . . . The entire soul-period conveys

with it all the requisite Reason-Principles, and so too the same existents appear once more under their action... May we not take it that there may be identical reproduction from one Period to another but not in the same Period?... Thus when the universe has reached its end, there will be a fresh beginning, since the entire Quantity which the Kosmos is to exhibit, every item that is to emerge in its course, all is laid up from the first in the Being that contains the Reason-Principles... As in Soul so in Divine Mind there is this infinitude of recurring generative powers; the Beings there are unfailing.'
Plotinus, *'Enneads'*, trans. S. MacKenna, V.7.1-3.

A century later, Antoninus, a Neoplatonist and contemporary of Hypatia, reinforced this view, saying: *'All things from eternity are of like forms, and come round in a circle.'*

...And Into the Modern Era

Across Europe, medieval debates about the plurality of worlds and the nature of time were greatly refreshed and extended during the Renaissance by the rediscovery, and re-reading, of many hitherto lost classical texts. In short order, this emboldened many thinkers to develop their own original ideas on these topics.

Sir Thomas Browne (1605-1682)

For an unambiguously forthright restatement of the idea of circularity, we need to move forward more than a millennium to 17th century England. Here again we find the remarkable Sir Thomas Browne, a polymath whose curiosity extended across many branches of science and learning. Browne was a prolific author and chief among his works was *'Religio Medicii'* (The Religion of a Physician) a work that was widely circulated across Europe and which, besides affirming a belief in witches, presented his conviction that eternal recurrence was a reality.

As he put it: *'To see our selves againe wee neede not looke for Platoes yeare; every man is not onely himselfe; there have beene many Diogenes, and as many Timons, though but few of that name; men are lived over againe, the world is now as it was in ages past, there was none then, but there hath been some one since that parallels him, and is as it were his revived selfe.'*

It should be explained that 'Platoe's yeare' referred to that Greek philosopher's estimate of the time it might take for all things to complete their full cycle of existence and return to their original state.

Browne went on to say,

'And in this sense, I say, the world was before the Creation, and at an end before it had a beginning; and thus was I dead before I was alive, though my grave be England, my dying place was Paradise, and Eve miscarried of me before she conceived of Cain.'

Gottfried Leibniz (1646-1716)
Browne was not alone in his thinking. To take one impressive example, he was supported by Leibniz, a towering intellect who independently co-invented calculus (Newton also claimed the idea) and had also devised a calculating machine. Leibniz

thought that if humans could only live long enough they would eventually recognise that sequences of events were repeating themselves, including what was said, written and done. (Older readers will recognise this phenomenon when listening to their coevals' anecdotes!) In his work *'Concerning the Horizon of Human Knowledge'* (1693) he comes out clearly on the side of the eternal return as explained by the platonic year's endless cycles and repetitions.

Describing Leibniz's thinking in his magisterial *'History of Western Philosophy'*, Lord Bertrand Russell, said, *'There are an infinite number of possible worlds, all of which God contemplated before creating the actual world. Being good, God decided to create the best of the possible worlds, and He considered that one to be the best which had the greatest excess of good over evil.'*

This was the basis of Leibniz's *'panglossian'* optimism, so named after a character in Voltaire's popular satirical novel, *'Candide'*. The relentless optimism displayed by Professor Pangloss in the face of one setback after another was a waspish tilt at Leibniz's 'best of all possible worlds' proposition.

Going back to the question of recurrence, it must be conceded that in 1701 Leibniz changed his mind, figuring that man would never run out of new and unique things to think, do and experience. Furthermore, he believed that this would be made possible, in part, by humanity's ever-continuing evolution to higher states. Still, long after his death Leibniz's original hypothesis continued to influence eminent thinkers, including Nietzsche.

Bernard Le Bovier de Fontenelle (1657-1757)

The author and essayist Fontenelle interests us because he wrote an immensely popular book in 1686, *'Entretiens sur la Pluralité des Mondes'*, which was translated into several other languages, with the English version undertaken by Elizabeth Gunning and appearing in 1803 as *'Conversations on the Plurality of Worlds'*. While he wrote other works that dwelt on cosmological themes, this was the book that won him lasting fame.

At a time when even sexagenarians were fairly thin on the ground, Fontenelle died just one month short of 100. By all accounts he was mentally and physically lively well into his final decade. Indeed, there is the story that in his late nineties when he encountered a legendary beauty of the time, one Madame Helvétius, he sadly exclaimed, 'Ah, Madame, if only I were eighty again!' (Interestingly, he attributed his vitality to a regular diet of strawberries.)

When not writing in his very accessible way on scientific and other matters - and playing the gallant - Fontenelle was an active member of the French Academy and was Secretary to the Academy of Sciences. Accordingly, Fontenelle, like Bruno, also has a lunar crater named after him: the ultimate accolade.

Always interested in astronomy and cosmology, he was particularly absorbed by the question of extraterrestrial life: a topic of continuing interest to this day, as we know:

'…Surely nothing ought to interest us more than to know how our own world is formed; and whether there be other worlds similar to it, and inhabited in the same way…'

Fontenelle tackled head-on the classic argument laid against a plurality of inhabited or inhabitable worlds: that God could hardly want to be blood-sacrificing his son repeatedly all around his universe. Fontenelle's rebuttal was that there was no need for the Fall and consequent Redemption to occur anywhere else but on Earth, particularly as it was likely that intelligent beings on other worlds might be very different to humans.

Regarding the possibility that only the Earth was created for habitation, Fontenelle wrote in his *'Plurality'*:

'We chuse to believe that every thing in creation is destined to our service; and when we enquire of some philosophers the use of such a prodigious number of fixed stars, of which a smaller proportion would have been sufficient for all the offices they appear to perform; they coolly answer, they were made to gratify our sight. Of this selfish principle it was for a long time supposed that the earth was motionless in the midst of the universe, whilst all the heavenly bodies were created for the sole purpose of journeying round, and distributing their light to her.'

By contrast, he believed in a God who drove a more purposeful creation:

'…and yet we are to suppose that these great planets were formed to remain uninhabited, and that such being the natural

condition of them all, an exception should be made in favour of the earth - yet who will believe it? I cannot.'

Today, we assume that life of any sort is, at best, rare around the Cosmos - and intelligent civilisations even more sparse, if not possibly limited to our own world alone. Fontenelle, however, was convinced that intelligent beings inhabited just about every planet and satellite, including our own Moon. He saw a profusion of life among the heavenly bodies to match the fecundity of our own globe:

'Can you believe that after the earth has been thus made to abound with life, the rest of the planets have not a living creature in them?'

He imagined extra-terrestrials staring skyward in the direction of our own neighbourhood: would they conceive of worlds being so different to ours?

'Were it possible for us to be endowed with reason, and at the same time not of the human species; were we, I say, such beings, and inhabitants of the moon, should we ever imagine that this world contained so fantastical a creature as man? Could we form in our minds the image of a being composed of such extravagant passions, and such wise reflections; an existence so short, and plans so extensive; so much knowledge of trifles, and so much ignorance of the most important things; such ardent love of liberty, yet such proneness to slavery; so strong a desire for happiness, with so little power of being happy?'

These faraway beings might be very different to us, even possessing different senses, he conceded.

Fontenelle believed that manned flight would be attained in time and, even more, that humans would one day find a way to reach the moon.

'The art of flying is but in its infancy; in due time it will be brought to perfection, and some day or other we shall get to the moon. Can we pretend to know every thing; to have made every possible discovery?'

And what would we find there?

He guessed, correctly, that the supply of planets extended well beyond our own solar system (what he called a 'vortex'):

'The fixed stars are all suns: our sun is the centre of a vortex which turns around him; why should not each fixed star be also the centre of a vortex, turning round it? Our sun enlightens planets; why should not every fixed star likewise enlighten planets?...'

Written in 1686, these were remarkably prescient predictions.

Immanuel Kant (1724-1804)
In his *'Universal History'*, Kant describes his awe when contemplating the Milky Way galaxy's cloud of stars, so overwhelmingly vast that our own Solar System 'is hardly seen as a grain of sand':

'Here there is no end, but an abyss of a true infinity, in which all capacity of human thought sinks, even when it is uplifted with the help of mathematics. The wisdom, goodness, and power which has revealed itself is limitless and, to exactly the same extent, fruitful and busy. The plan of its revelation must, therefore be, just like it, without borders and timeless.'

For this reason, he imagined that only a universe that was infinite could be the appropriate creation of a deity of infinite power:

'Where will creation itself cease? We well note that to think of creation in relation to the power of the Infinite Being means it must have no boundaries. We come no nearer to the infinity of the creative power of God if we enclose its revelation in a sphere described with the radius of the Milky Way than if we enclose it in a ball with a diameter an inch long. Everything finite which has its limits and a determined relationship to unity is a long way distant from equalling infinity. Now, it would be absurd to set the Divine into effective action with an infinitely small part of its creative capacity and to imagine its infinite power, the treasure house of a true infinity of natures and worlds, incapacitated and locked into an eternal deficiency in practice. Is it not much more appropriate or, to express the matter better, is it not necessary to present the embodiment of creation as something which cannot be measured by any standard, which is how it must be, in order to bear witness to that power. For this reason the field of the revelation of divine properties is just as infinite as these properties.'

Kant believed that, while the universe had a point of beginning in an act of divine creation, it would continue on into eternity. As he put it:

'Creation is never complete. True, it once began, but it will never cease.'

However, he did not state the obvious corollary, that all temporal events must repeat themselves for ever and ever.

Kant, remarkably, anticipated today's model of cosmogenesis when he argued that the universe began as an inchoate sea of particles which over ages resolved into small clusters and, finally, into galaxies, nebulae, stars and planets. He added that, over millions of years, these would decay back into particles again, and so launch yet another of the cycles of cosmic recreation and death.

Georg Wilhelm Friedrich Hegel (1770-1831)
Hegel's views on infinity and eternity were greatly shaped by the Greek philosopher, Heraclitus, whom he much admired. For Hegel, the universe was an infinite and eternal movement from non-reality into reality. Without this endless 'becoming', both non-reality and reality would evaporate into oblivion. His dialectic - the ceaseless movement from 'thesis' to 'antithesis' and, finally, to 'synthesis' - was to become a foundation stone of Marxist thought.

Hegel held that in nature, things repeat themselves eternally, revisited again and again as a consequence of his dialectical mechanism.

Arthur Schopenhauer (1788-1860)
'Were an Asiatic to ask me for a definition of Europe, I should be forced to answer him: It is that part of the world which is haunted by the incredible delusion that man was created out of nothing, and that his present birth is his first entrance into life.'

Heavily influenced by Hindu and, later, by Buddhist, concepts, Schopenhauer came across the Hindu text of the *'Upanishads'* in a remarkably roundabout way: a Latin translation by the Frenchman Anquetil du Perron from the Persian translation of Prince Dara Shikoh which, one presumes, was from the original Sanskrit or Pali transcription of what had been relayed orally over many centuries earlier.

He later focused his attention on Buddhism and learnt and practised the Buddhist techniques of meditation. He actually called himself a 'Buddhist' and readily acknowledged that its insights informed much of his thinking. To that extent, at least, Schopenhauer would have understood and endorsed the Dharmic view of an endless round of existence and recurrence.

Heinrich Heine (1797-1856)
Heine imagined that, in time, an individual would be born who would have the very same mode of thinking as himself, even in the most minute and individualistic way. What was more, every other person in the world was fated to have their mind cloned in this way.

This was how he put these thoughts on eternal recurrence in his book, *'Journey from Munich to Genova'*:

'...Time is infinite, but the things in time, the concrete bodies, are finite. They may indeed disperse into the smallest particles; but these particles, the atoms, have their determinate numbers, and the numbers of the configurations which, all of themselves, are formed out of them is also determinate. Now, however long a time may pass, according to the eternal laws governing the combinations of this eternal play of repetition, all configurations which have previously existed on this earth must yet meet, attract, repulse, kiss, and corrupt each other again...'

Edgar Allen Poe (1809-1849)
Besides being a prolific and masterful author of gothic stories and poetry, Poe was intensely interested in philosophy and cosmology. He wrote various tracts on these subjects and in one, *'Eureka'*, he speculated on whether there might be an infinite number of universes:

'Have we any right to infer - let us say, rather, to imagine - an interminable succession of the "clusters of clusters," or of "Universes" more or less similar? I reply that the "right," in a case such as this, depends absolutely upon the hardihood of that imagination which ventures to claim the right. Let me declare, only, that, as an individual, I myself feel impelled to the fancy - without daring to call it more - that there does exist a limitless succession of Universes, more or less similar to that of which we have cognizance - to that of which we shall ever have cognizance - at the very least until the return of our own particular Universe into Unity. If such clusters of clusters exist, however - and they do - it is abundantly clear that, having had

no part in our origin, they have no portion in our laws. They neither attract us, nor we them.'

Later, he speculated on the end of our universe, which he imagined as a collapse of all matter back into the primordial singularity from which it sprang; an early anticipation of the 'heat death collapse' model held by some cosmologists in which expansion slows and gravity pulls all matter back again.

'In sinking into Unity, it will sink at once into that Nothingness which, to all Finite Perception, Unity must be - into that Material Nihility from which alone we can conceive it to have been evoked - to have been created by the Volition of God.

I repeat then - Let us endeavor to comprehend that the final globe of globes will instantaneously disappear, and that God will remain all in all.

But are we here to pause? Not so. On the Universal agglomeration and dissolution, we can readily conceive that a new and perhaps totally different series of conditions may ensue - another creation and irradiation, returning into itself - another action and reaction of the Divine Will. Guiding our imaginations by that omniprevalent law of laws, the law of periodicity, are we not, indeed, more than justified in entertaining a belief - let us say, rather, in indulging a hope - that the processes we have here ventured to contemplate will be renewed forever, and forever, and forever; a novel Universe swelling into existence, and then subsiding into nothingness, at every throb of the Heart Divine?'

Arrival of the Superman

We now come to the individual who, of all philosophers, most dramatically defined the idea and implications of the Eternal Return, and whose name is still likely to come first to the mind of anyone who thinks of this concept.

Friedrich Nietzsche (1844-1900)

Both Schopenhauer and Nietzsche are highly regarded for their felicitous literary styles: a rare quality among philosophers in general, and especially remarkable among German philosophers. Unlike Schopenhauer, however, Nietzsche's writing style - very readable, but so often declamatory, allusive and loaded with aphorisms - does little to make all his ideas consistently clear or accessible. Indeed, there are times when I find some of Nietzsche as vague and tantalisingly ambiguous as Nostradamus' quatrains!

Nonetheless, in his very brief but productive life before insanity took him, Nietzsche came up with a number of concepts whose boldness and originality have ensured that he still remains the most-read, and possibly the most misinterpreted, philosopher to this very day.

He is best known for his notion of the *Ubermensch* or Superman. In a complete challenge to the Victorian bourgeois morality and sentimentalism that Nietzsche so despised, his Superman disavowed the Christian ideals of pacifism, forbearance and subjugation of the will.

By contrast, the Superman was someone who accepted life on its own terms, not with world-weariness, passive resignation or a pious hope in priestly promises of better things in an afterlife, but with an iron will and clear-headed courage. For Nietzsche, such a being was the highest development of humankind; one cleansed of resentment or dissatisfaction with the world as it is; neither deluded by notions of the perfectibility of man nor by the urge to devise utopian plans to create a paradise on this earth.

That exuberant *lebenslust*, indomitable to the end, sets aside a hero unfamiliar in these timid and tentative times. It is defined so well in the central character in *'Zorba the Greek'*, the classic novel by Niko Kazanzakis (1946) and played out perfectly in the film version directed by Michael Cacoyannis in 1964, with Anthony Quinn in his career-defining role of Alexis Zorba. Through tragedy and disasters, Zorba remains compassionate, unsentimental, yet irrepressibly buoyant, sustained by the simple joy of being *alive!*

By contrast, the utopians and the believers in world-denying religion are deemed by Nietzsche to be nihilists who reject the only type of existence possible for us. Their efforts fly in the face of the boundless, purposeless energy of a cosmos where ever-changing *being* is all the meaning that can be found. The Superman's ethos balances, and then extends, the qualities of Apollo, representing order, rationality and refined aestheticism - and those of Dionysius, embodying our intuitive and instinctive nature, impelled by action and vitality. It is to wish for nothing but what is, as it is. It is to joyfully embrace *'amor fati'*, the impulse to love one's fate.

Influenced by Schopenhauer's ideas of recurrence and circularity developed from Hindu and Buddhist doctrines, Nietzsche was also particularly impressed by Heinrich Heine's speculations about the Eternal Return. In this possibility he saw the ultimate test for his life-affirming Superman. Thus, in his book, *'The Gay Science'* (1882), he presents this challenge:

'What, if some day or night a demon were to steal after you in your loneliest loneliness and say to you: "This life as you now live it and have lived it, you will have to live once more and innumerable times more; and there will be nothing new in it, but every pain and every joy and every thought and sigh and everything unutterably small or great in your life will have to return to you, all in the same succession and sequence - even this spider and this moonlight between the trees, and even this moment and I myself. The eternal hourglass of existence is turned upside down again and again, and you with it, speck of dust!"

Would you not throw yourself down and gnash your teeth and curse the demon who spoke thus? Or have you once experienced a tremendous moment when you would have answered him: You are a god and never have I heard anything more divine. If this thought gained possession of you, it would change you as you are or perhaps crush you. The question in each and every thing, "Do you desire this once more, and innumerable times more?" would lie upon your actions as the greatest weight. Or how well disposed would you have to become to yourself and to life to crave nothing more fervently than this ultimate eternal confirmation and seal?'

Nietzsche picked up the theme again and made it central to his novel, *'Also Sprach Zarathustra'* (Thus Spake Zarathustra) which was published in 1883-1885. In this, the hero Zarathustra undertakes a long journey that culminates in his finally accepting the full meaning of eternity - and thus finding himself ready at last to achieve 'the supreme will to power'. In this transformation into an *'Übermensch'* or 'Superman' we are invited to witness the ascent into the next stage of human evolution.

(Interestingly, the theme music Stanley Kubrick chose for his film *'2001: A Space Odyssey'* was the Richard Strauss composition *'Also Sprach Zarathustra'* – a tone poem inspired by Nietzsche's book. Not only was it a majestic way to open this epic film, but the theme of the poem resonated very well with the film's storyline which traced our evolution from ape-man to man and finally, to Superman.)

'All beings so far have created something beyond themselves; and do you want to be the ebb of this great flood and even go back to the beasts rather than overcome man? What is the ape to man? A laughingstock or a painful embarrassment. And man shall be just that for the Overman: a laughingstock or a painful embarrassment.'

In the story *'On the Vision and the Riddle'*, Zarathustra, accompanied by his enemy, a dwarf, comes across a gateway:

"Look at this gateway! Dwarf!" I continued, "It has two faces. Two roads come together here: these has no one yet gone to the end of. This long lane backwards: it continues for an

eternity. And that long lane forward - that is another eternity. They are antithetical to one another, these roads; they directly abut on one another - and it is here, at this gateway, that they come together. The name of the gateway is inscribed above: 'This Moment.' But should one follow them further - and ever further and further on, think you, dwarf, that these roads would be eternally antithetical?"'

"Everything straight lies," murmured the dwarf, contemptuously. "All truth is crooked; time itself is a circle."

"You spirit of gravity!" said I wrathfully, "do not take it too lightly! Or I shall let you squat where you squat, Haltfoot, - and I carried you high!"

"Observe," continued I, "This Moment! From the gateway, This Moment, there runs a long eternal lane backwards: behind us lies an eternity. Must not whatever can run its course of all things, have already run along that lane? Must not whatever can happen of all things have already happened, resulted, and gone by? And if everything has already existed, what think you, dwarf, of This Moment? Must not this gateway also have already existed? And are not all things closely bound together in such wise that This Moment draws all coming things after it? Consequently - itself also? For whatever can run its course of all things, also in this long lane outward - must it once more run!

And this slow spider which creeps in the moonlight, and this moonlight itself, and you and I in this gateway whispering together, whispering of eternal things - must we not all have already existed? And must we not return and run in that other lane out before us, that long weird lane - must we not eternally return?"

And, again, in the story, *'The Convalescent'*,

'"O Zarathustra," said then his animals, "to those who think like us, things all dance themselves: they come and hold out the hand and laugh and flee - and return.

Everything goes, everything returns; eternally rolls the wheel of existence. Everything dies, everything blossoms forth again; eternally runs on the year of existence.

Everything breaks, everything is integrated anew; eternally builds itself the same house of existence. All things separate, all things again greet one another; eternally true to itself remains the ring of existence. Every moment begins existence, around every "Here" rolls the ball "There." The middle is everywhere. Crooked is the path of eternity.'

Indeed, for Nietzsche, *the* defining attribute of the Superman was a free willingness to accept the reality of the Eternal Return and unflinchingly face the endless reliving of this life, complete with all its beauty and joy, but also its entire catalogue of pain, horror, ennui, longing, deprivation and disappointment.

The highest honour was due...

'... To the ideal of the most exuberant, most living and most world-affirming man, who has not only learned to get on and

treat with all that was and is but who wants to have it again as it was and is…'. ('Beyond Good and Evil'.)

Christians and other religionists and secular utopians of all types might lay their hopes on a paradisiacal existence, full of joy and free of all sorrow, and for their part Asiatic believers might look for a release from the eternal round of birth, death and rebirth, but the Superman so unequivocally accepted this life, with its many struggles and sorrows and few delights, that he would joyously *embrace* the possibility of retracing it again and again without change for all eternity.

So, far from bowing to the prospect of the eternal return as 'the most abysmal thought', Zarathustra exults instead, *'For I love you, O eternity!'*

Could anyone ever be inspired by the hope for no more and no less than is offered by this life… forever? Yes: for one, we have the Old Norseman whose Valhalla was an afterlife where heroes spend eternity battling and exploring by day and their evenings, (wounds miraculously healed and the slain re-animated), carousing, boastfully recounting their exploits and singing!

Nietzsche himself recognised *'Thus Spoke Zarathustra'* as his greatest work, saying of it in a later work, *'Ecce Homo'*, '…I have given mankind the greatest present that has ever been made to it so far.'

Indeed, as the philosopher Martin Heidegger was to write years later, 'Nietzsche's fundamental metaphysical position is captured in his doctrine of the eternal return of the same.' (*Nietzsche, Volume II: The Eternal Recurrence of the Same.*)

Interestingly, Heidegger and Nietzsche were both adopted by the Nazis as their favourite philosophers. While Heidegger was a convinced Nazi and an early party member, the long-dead Nietzsche would have found much to despise about Hitler. The bald fact is that Nietzsche, who had always espoused a rigorous individualism, would have abhorred the Nazis' brutal collectivism and certainly their ideas and methods were completely antithetical to his own stated views, particularly in their persecution of the Jewish people, whom he held in high regard. Nietzsche's undeserved role as an inspirer of national socialism had much to do with Reich Minister of Propaganda Joseph Goebbels' very selective reading of his thoughts - and the promotional efforts of Elizabeth, Nietzsche's sister, herself an ardent anti-semite and Nazi supporter who, as curator of his works, put their prestige entirely at Hitler's disposal.

I have two comments to make about Nietzsche's Eternal Return. First, we cannot consider the Eternal Return of the Same without also taking into full account the Eternal Return of *All* Possibilities. The essential corollary of Nietzsche's Eternal Return is that while over eternity an individual existence must be endlessly recycled in every exact detail, it will also be re-enacted with every possible variation of condition and experience. What is more, these variations on one's present life will necessarily occur much more frequently.

Nietzsche, who employed the familiar analogy of an eternal game of dice in which every possible combination would appear again and again, recognised that recurrence meant that the identical, similar and dissimilar phenomena would recur, as we read in his *'The Will to Power'*:

'If the world may be thought of as a certain definite quantity of force and as a certain definite number of centers of force - and every other representation remains indefinite and therefore useless - it follows that, in the great dice game of existence, it must pass through a calculable number of combinations. In infinite time, every possible combination would at some time or another be realized; more: it would be realized an infinite number of times. And since between every combination and its next recurrence all other possible combinations would have to take place, and each of these combinations conditions the entire sequence of combinations in the same series, a circular movement of absolutely identical series is thus demonstrated: the world as a circular movement that has already repeated itself infinitely often and plays its dice game in infinitum.'
'Friedrich Nietzsche, The Will to Power', trans. W. Kaufmann & R. J. Hollingdale (New York: Random House, 1968).

I suspect that, while it may take the promethean fortitude of a Nietzschean Superman to elect to go through *this exact life* again and again, the prospect of being able to try all sorts of alternative lives in between times might make it all a little more palatable for the rest of us.

The second comment I would make when considering Nietzsche's Eternal Return is this: if we accept Nietzsche's own definition of the Superman Question, that one would eagerly endure all the dolours of this existence recycled endlessly, would one not experience each identical round of life as if for the first time? In other words, would not the dreamless state described by esoteric philosophers as *interbiosis* intervene between each of one's lives, so that we embark upon each new cycle completely unaware of being about to follow a path already well-trodden, our memory a total *tabula rasa* or blank slate?

On the other hand, if there were a continuing thread of consciousness linking each run of these countlessly repeated lives, I would agree that such a choice would be heroic, if not unendurable. Think about it: would it not be a Hell worse than the fiery torments described with chop-smacking relish by medieval pardoners?

But we must remember that if the Eternal Return is a reality, then we have *already* lived this life - both exactly the same and also with all those myriad variations - an infinite number of times. Happily or otherwise, none of us seem to have any recollection of a past life, and we remain quite unoppressed by any 'here we go yet again!' ennui. Nor are we burdened by the anticipation of all-too-familiar, ever-recurring ills and setbacks, even though what we most dread is usually worse in the anticipation than in its realisation. Thus we would be immune to both *déjà vu* and its opposite, *jamais vu* ('never seen', i.e., the sense that one has never witnessed what one knows to have been previously encountered).

In short, as we journey through eternity, in each life we are as unaware of the experiences of our other lives as we might be of the phantoms of a long-forgotten dream. We are as oblivious to the pain and trauma of our other lives as is one who, waking up from dreamless coma, knows nothing of what has transpired around them during their long sleep. So, we know nothing of our other lives; and we should be glad that this is so. As I said, very few of us, I fancy, have the mettle to be a true Superman!

Eternal Return: Reverberating into the 20th Century
Johannes Gustav Vogt (1843-1920)
While no thinker has done more then or since to firmly impress the notion of the Eternal Return upon our minds than Nietzsche, it had been anticipated earlier by Heinrich Heine (1797-1856), Fyodor Dostoevsky (1821-1881), and by many other near or actual contemporaries of his. Nietzsche makes little mention of these. Even Auguste Blanqui, who had already articulated the idea in a work of great originality and imagination, *'Eternity by the Stars'*, is hardly referred to, although we shall return to this sad and strange individual later.

The one we know who did impress Nietzsche most was the German natural philosopher, Johannes Gustav Vogt, who conceived of the Eternal Return, not as a sequence of endless cycles, but as a static and ageless block of space and time (what he called 'The Force') in which all possibilities are coexistent and, within each version itself, unchanging. His monist and mechanistic view was outlined in his book, *'Force: A Realistic and Monistic Worldview'* (Die Kraft. Eine Real-Monistische Weltanschauung) (1878), which we know was highly regarded by Nietzsche himself.

Closer to our own time, the prominent French philosopher, Gilles Deleuze seems to have endorsed Vogt's static model. As he said in an article on the Eternal Return in 2000:

'We misinterpret the expression 'eternal return' if we understand it as "return of the same". Above all, we must avoid believing that it refers to a cycle, to a return of the Same...'

Ludwig Boltzmann (1844-1906)
Born in the same year as Nietzsche, Boltzmann was an Austrian physicist, mathematician and philosopher of great brilliance and originality who was already a full professor at 25.

One of the questions that had most intrigued Boltzmann was how it was that the universe appeared so remarkably orderly when the law of thermodynamics would have suggested much greater disorder, or entropy. The answer, which he presented in 1897, was that such an anomaly could only be explained by space-time being infinite. Since within such a vastness, particles would necessarily be found that display every possible position and momentum, eventually we must find a pocket - our own universe, for example - where, against all odds, there would exist an oasis of comparative order. Thus, over countless eons, a universe would eventually find itself back in its original state of order, just as our endlessly re-shuffled pack of cards is statistically fated to reappear in the original order in which it appeared when the deck was first broken open.

Suffering, it is likely, from an undiagnosed bipolar disorder, Boltzmann had frequent bouts of profound depression, probably worsened by the many attacks on his strongly-argued and correct belief in atoms and molecules. Sadly, during one such attack, he hanged himself.

Henri Poincaré (1854-1912)

One of the greatest mathematicians of all time, Poincaré published a proof in 1890 showing that in certain closed and finite systems, such as a universe, every state will eventually return to something very near to its original condition. Known as the Poincaré Recurrence Theorem, it states that it may take an enormous time for this to appear within any complex system, possibly far longer than the likely lifetime of a universe. The interval between an event or state and its recurrence is known as the 'Poincaré recurrence time'. (Thus, while Boltzmann saw recurrence as an inevitable consequence of infinity, Poincaré argued that eternity would achieve the same outcome.)

Arthur Oncken Lovejoy (1873-1962)

One of the leading 20th century philosophers, Lovejoy devised the term 'The Principle of Plenitude' to describe a cosmos that, being both infinite and eternal, would necessarily see that all that was potentially possible would actually and necessarily exist. In his book, 'The Great Chain of Being', he also stated that these linked possibilities constituted an unbroken connectedness.

Here he was restating the notion of a natural hierarchy that goes back all the way to Plato's ideas in *'Timaeus'*.

As Lovejoy put it:

'The existing species exhibit a hierarchy of status and so compose a great chain, or ladder, of being, extending from the lowliest condition of the merest existence up to God Himself. In this chain man occupies the middle position between the animal kinds and the angels, or purely spiritual beings.'

Pyotr Demianovich Ouspensky (1878-1947)

A Russian esoteric philosopher and mystic, Ouspensky was greatly attached to the idea of higher dimensions and, particularly, was convinced of the reality of eternal recurrence. He believed that time and the spatial dimensions were actually linked in a complete four-dimensional form: his *'New Model'*. Thus, all the moments of a man's life, for instance, were a complete and deathless reality, not simply, as we imagine, a series of discrete moments linked by our memory of them. He saw this as a four-dimensional form which was curved, with the end meeting the beginning again. While we can only ever be aware of the life we are living and can have no knowledge of anything before our birth or after our death, that life is nonetheless endlessly recycled. In each circuit of life, we encounter the same chances and decisions anew and, being exactly the same person, cannot but elect to choose the same fate every time, exactly.

Albert Einstein (1879-1955)

Within a reality, in which whatever could be, must be, Einstein similarly believed that there was a seamless continuum ('the chain of being', as he described it) that connected all existences from God down to the merest creature and beyond to the most basic building block of inanimate matter. Here he restated the notion of a natural hierarchy that also goes back, like Lovejoy's idea, to Plato's 'Timaeus'.

Martin Heidegger (1889–1976)

Heidegger was one of the 20th century's giants of philosophy, largely because of the impact of his book, 'Being and Time', which had a considerable impact on the existentialist thinkers and writers of his era. An enthusiastic interpreter and proponent of Nietzsche's 'eternal return of the same', Heidegger explained its logic very simply. If events are finite and time is infinite, then events must be repeated endlessly over eternity.

A committed National Socialist, publicly unrepentant even after the defeat of Hitler's Germany, Heidegger's instinct was that bold action was a virtue in itself ('The possible ranks higher than the actual.'), and this comes through in his statement, 'Only by way of nihilism and the moment is the eternal recurrence of the same to be thought'.

Heidegger, whose second volume on Nietzsche, 'Nietzsche, Vol. II: The Eternal Recurrence of the Same' (1954) described Nietzsche as 'the last Western metaphysician', whose 'fundamental metaphysical position' ('the infinitely reiterated circulation of all things') was an idea powerful enough to displace the visions of Plato and Christianity.

With his message that mankind needs to rediscover its pre-Platonic, pre-Christian 'openness to being', Heidegger saw the ultimate affirmation of this ideal in the Nietzschean Superman's embrace of the eternal return of the same.

David Kellogg Lewis (1941-2001)

A leading analytic philosopher of the later 20th century, Lewis was the creator and great champion of the 'modal realism' theory. This stated that every *possible* world must exist, and while each of these worlds is completely separated from, and inaccessible to, the others, they all have the same concrete existence as our own. Some of these worlds may be similar or even identical to our own, but many more may be quite different.

Echoing some of the thoughts of the German philosopher Leibniz about possible worlds, Lewis, an American, presented his construction on the basis of philosophical argument alone, saying that one of its chief attractions was that it neatly disposed of a number of persistent philosophical questions. Nonetheless, his papers and books (including *'Counterfactuals'*, published in 1973, and *'On the Plurality of Worlds'* (1986), certainly did not enjoy a ringing endorsement from his academic peers at the time: many dismissed his idea as utterly implausible.

Yet before he died in his 60th year, Lewis might have found some satisfaction, certainly interest, in the ideas voiced ever more confidently by respected physicists, such as the Many Worlds hypothesis, M-Theory and the Multiverse. Like the physicist Everett (who appears in the next chapter), Lewis was lucky enough to see his counter-intuitive and disregarded ideas eventually become respectable. It would be interesting to know if the two had ever talked.

It is worth noting that Kellogg Lewis' other main insight was that events we describe as 'past', 'present' and 'future' are all contemporaneously real - and exist, if not in our own temporal sphere, then in another 'timescape'. In this, he could be said to have taken an eternalist stance.

And the Debate Continues
This chapter has shown that philosophers well understood the idea of an infinite universe many long centuries before modern scientists talked about a 'Steady State Universe', a 'Pulsating Universe' or a 'Multiverse'. Thus, the boundless plenitude of worlds is a proposition that many, then and now, have thought more than capable of standing on its philosophical legs alone.

Nonetheless, physicists, astronomers and cosmologists focused on this area are informing the debate with plausible models that seem to fit current theoretical frameworks, observational data and mathematical bench testing.

So, it is now time for us to move from philosophical and metaphysical enquiry to the, possibly, firmer ground of physics and cosmology. Accordingly, this is the focus of the next chapter.

7. The Quantum Leap

Science Uncovers a New Reality

In 1957 a small, chirping silver ball circled the world, proclaiming to an astonished world the message that mankind had at last truly broken 'the surly bonds of earth'.

Russia's lofting of the Sputnik satellite into space was certainly an astounding achievement, and surprising, too, considering that just a year earlier Britain's Astronomer Royal had dismissed talk of space travel as 'utter bilge'.

Yet very few people then, even in the world of science, could have guessed that this year would also launch us into another realm with a novel idea that many now consider the equal of that pioneering space flight. For this was also the year that saw the publication of an unknown student's paper proposing an astonishing solution to some of the most perplexing problems in quantum physics.

In his thesis, Princeton student Hugh Everett considered the event-collapse thought to happen whenever an observer looked at, or measured, paired sub-atomic particles. The famous Schrödinger's Cat thought-experiment, for example, had examined how the act of observation might determine whether the cat lived - or died.

In physics, quantum states are described as 'wave functions' and these embody all the possible configurations (including both the dead and living cat options) prior to when they are observed, at which point they then collapse into only one of the previously co-existing superposition possibilities. It was believed in those days that with this, the unrealised options were then banished from existence.

Everett's bold solution was that, in fact, upon observation *all* the alternative possibilities - on both the micro and macro scales - are also played out, albeit only one in any single universe. For that to happen, there must be other universes, and indeed, as many universes as it takes to enable every single possible state in a quantum system to become reality. He called this phenomenon the 'Universal Wave Function', expressed by the Greek letter 'Ψ' (psi) - and it was his firm belief that it described all reality.

Compared to the impact when Copernicus upturned the earth-centred Ptolemaic model of the universe, or when Darwin challenged the literal interpretation of Genesis, it has to be admitted that the Many Worlds idea crept onto the stage in a very low-key and tentative fashion.

Certainly, his outlandish proposition drew very little attention at the time it came out. Indeed, when Everett travelled to Copenhagen to present his conclusions to the famous theoretical physicist, Niels Bohr, 'The Father of Quantum Mechanics', he was politely shown the door. Bohr, it turned out, was quite unimpressed with Everett and his Many Worlds idea.

Apart from the fact that such a startling idea had come from a relatively obscure individual, Everett's paper was burdened with a less than electrifying title, *'Relative State Formulation of Quantum Mechanics'*.

After such a discouraging reception to his paper (his first and last) Everett decided upon gaining his Ph. D. to work for the Pentagon in the necessarily anonymous field of weapons research. (By way of comparison, imagine if the young Albert Einstein had published his paper on General Relativity and then elected to spend the rest of his life in the obscurity of the Bern Patents Office!) However, it must be added that Everett did make quite a successful career, and a few million dollars as well, in his new field.

The insights and possibilities Everett's paper raised would only be unearthed a decade later, starting with an article that appeared in *'Physics Today'*. By the time his ideas were written up in the *'Analog'* science fiction magazine, Hugh Everett was already becoming something of a cult figure among younger physicists and students. He was regularly invited to address interested groups and there had even been talk of his heading up a research institute. Unfortunately, Everett, a chain-smoker and heavy drinker, died of a heart attack at the young age of 51.

Since then, Everett's startling idea has been considered seriously by ever more theoretical physicists, astronomers and scientific philosophers. Even as far back as 1995, a survey of 72 leading physicists by the researcher David Raub showed that almost 60% believed in the Many Worlds interpretation. Today, that figure is likely to be considerably higher.

The term 'Multiverse' came into being in 1960 when the vice-chairman of the Scottish branch of the British Interplanetary Society, one Andy Nimmo, coined it as a handy label for Everett's Many Worlds. If the Latin 'uni-' ('one') was the prefix for a single universe, then it made sense to describe many ('multi-') universes as belonging to a 'Multiverse'.

The roll call of those who take 'multiversalism' seriously is impressive and includes not only Stephen Hawking, but also the august figure of Martin Rees whose many titles include Professor of Cosmology and Astrophysics and Master of Trinity College Cambridge, British Astronomer Royal and former President of the Royal Society. For good measure, he also sits as Baron Rees of Ludlow in the House of Lords after having received a life peerage.

With the endorsement of Rees and others, the 'Many Worlds' or Multiverse approach has, in its various versions, won over a considerable number of theoretical physicists and provoked much debate. Among those taking such ideas seriously is Frank Wilczek, the distinguished American physicist, mathematician and Nobel laureate, who has written a number of papers about the various ways in which the existence of a Multiverse might be revealed.

Years ago, a leading theoretical physicist, the Russian-born Andrei Linde, addressed a number of anomalies and paradoxes in quantum physics with his hypothesis that outside the universe we know is a higher domain called the Multiverse wherein exist in a state of potentiality every possible universe and every possible event.

Among the most enthusiastic advocates is Oxford University's David Deutsch, a prominent theoretical physicist who promoted the view that the Multiverse's existence is verifiable. More than that, he maintained, this proof would arise from his idea for an unimaginably powerful quantum computer. (With this device now moving towards practical reality, he is now known as the 'Father of the Quantum Computer'.) Regarding the Multiverse, Professor Deutsch declared:

'...I issue this challenge to those who still cling to a single-universe worldview: if the universe we see around us is all there is, where are quantum computations performed? I have yet to receive a plausible reply.'

Whether or not such a device is accepted as proof of the Multiverse, the fact is that the quantum computer itself is already well beyond a proof-of-concept reality. Promising to vault over the brick wall presented by the silicon chip's physical limits, working quantum computers are now being developed around the world. While daunting obstacles remain, mainly relating to the extreme fragility and volatility of the data being generated and processed, progress has exceeded expectations and, given its astonishing potential, a fully-fledged quantum computer will certainly arrive very soon. In the meantime, quantum technology is already embedded in a considerable array of everyday devices, including cell phones and laptop computers.

One interesting area of study is gravitational waves. Now that these have actually been detected, emanating from the collision of two massive black holes, physicists may look for the other gravitational waves that may still be pulsing around our universe from the time of its cataclysmic birth. Their discovery, they say, could provide evidence for the Multiverse.

Different Models of the Multiverse

An awkward problem with the Multiverse proposition is that it offers not just one plausible model, but a basketful of candidate explanations - and not all of these may be mutually exclusive. It is almost as if we may already have the correct answer, but are simply waiting to decide upon the right explanatory hypothesis and its verification!

Since just one Multiverse must necessarily encompass an infinite number of worlds, the possibility of several such realms would seem to be redundancy on a heroic scale: and here we might recall Bernard Fontenelle's dismissal centuries ago of a universe uselessly replete with lifeless planets. After all, as has been said, infinity multiplied by infinity - or just by four - is still infinity, no more and no less.

Generally speaking, while most physicists accept the possibility of one or another of the Multiverse models, quite a few do not subscribe to Everett's Many Worlds hypothesis. Others, however, see the two as quite compatible descriptions which really only describe the same reality from different angles of attack. There is no single theory of the Multiverse in physics: the concept is based on a range of conclusions based upon other theories, some of which are quite speculative and others grounded on demonstrable science.

To examine the tally of possible Multiverse models, we might start first with Max Tegmark, an internationally renowned, Swedish-born cosmologist and physicist who is a Professor at the Massachusetts Institute of Technology. (Preternaturally intelligent, he and a classmate had designed a commercially successful word processor while still teenagers.)

According to a paper he presented in 2003,Tegmark described these four classes of possible parallel universes:

Level 1: Regions Beyond the Cosmic Horizon
The easiest model to explain and grasp, this supposes that our universe extends infinitely beyond our observational horizon of some 46 billion light years distant. Assuming that matter is distributed outside this more or less uniformly, and encompasses a wide, but still limited, number of configurations, then it is only logical to assume that we will somewhere encounter an exact copy of our galaxy, our solar system, our world and finally, ourselves. (It has been calculated that your twin self would probably be found within some 10 to the 10^{28} meters from where you are now!)

Level 2: Other Post-Inflation Bubbles
According to what is known as inflation theory, other island-universes could pop into being as bubbles of ever-expanding

space-time. While some of these universes may be similar to ours, others, possibly most, might incorporate radically different physical laws that preclude any type of life.

Level 3: The Many Worlds of Quantum Physics
This picks up on an interpretation of quantum physics which says that every single event must simultaneously manifest itself in every single possible way, but since only one way is allowed for each universe, all those other outcomes have to be allocated across countless other universes. (We could call this the Everettian 'Many Worlds' model.)

Level 4: Other Mathematical Structures
The most difficult model to grasp, Tegmark's idea is of a 'mathematical' Multiverse which houses every conceivable mathematical structure, not just those that appear as physically real in this universe. Furthermore, those other universes would be governed by mathematical equations quite different to what drive our own physical world. For example, in some universes our mathematical constant π might not correctly represent the ratio of a circle's circumference to its diameter - or Einstein's famous equation, $E = mc^2$ might not accurately describe how the speed of light affects energy and mass.

Thus far we have looked at Tegmark's models of parallel universes. Although four models might seem enough to be getting on with, Tegmark's list is a parsimonious offering compared with the array presented by the well-known physicist and string theorist, Professor Brian Greene of Columbia

University. In his 2011 book, *'Hidden Reality'*, he proposes no fewer than nine classes of parallel universes.

Type 1. Quilted Multiverse
As with Tegmark's Level 1 version, if space extends infinitely, we will eventually find an exact twin copy of our own world and its region: in fact, countless such replicates.

Type 2. Inflationary Multiverse
Again, this is the endless sea of 'bubble universes' of every possible type, as predicted by Inflationary theory.

Type 3. Brane Multiverse
When string theory was modified to incorporate 11 dimensions, it opened up the concept of the 'brane'. Branes are conceived of as membrane-like physical entities adrift in space-time and, driven by quantum mechanics. These countless branes may contain entities with variously-configured dimensions, our own type of universe being but one example.

Type 4. Cyclic Multiverse
This presents the possibility that branes (which have mass) are drifting around in hyperspace and occasionally collide gently with one another. The result would be that the point of contact would set off a Big Bang - and so bring yet another universe into being. Carried out over eternity, this process would have delivered an infinite number of universes.

In their book, *'Endless Universe'*, theoretical physicists Paul J. Steinhardt and Neil Turok, suggested that in this way time did not begin at the moment of the Big Bang, but that this universe's genesis event was simply one of endlessly repeating cycles of universe-creation, each involving the generation of new matter and, over a long duration, the formation of galaxies, stars, and planets.

They stated:

'...What we think of as the moment of creation was simply part of an infinite cycle of titanic collisions between our universe and a parallel world'.

It should be mentioned that in earlier years, 'genesis' suggestions included a 'Pulsating Universe' in which our universe exploded into being with the Big Bang, slowed down and contracted into a 'Big Crunch' and then exploded once again in an eternal oscillation between creation and destruction.

Once considered in the 1930s by Einstein himself, this model, also known as the 'Oscillating Universe', was apparently a closed system and quite independent of the existence of any other universes. In any case, since it continued through all eternity, the implications regarding eternal recurrence would be similar to those of a full Multiverse as we think of it today. Certainly, the intervals between recurrences might be vastly wider with this physically circumscribed model, but remember that we are still dealing with *eternity* here!

Type 5. Landscape Multiverse. Here we have a cocktail made up of the various fundamental properties which, according to

String Theory, are inherent in a universe, and the effects of an inflationary Multiverse which work together to produce an endless stream of bubble universes operating to variously-configured physical laws.

Type 6. Quantum Multiverse. This is the still-argued 'Many Worlds Interpretation' originally proposed by Everett and which posits that whatever can occur, must occur in some universe somewhere, including with all possible variations and outcomes.

Type 7. Holographic Universe. A hologram is a three-dimensional image that has been captured on a two-dimensional plate and, when illuminated by a laser beam, for instance, can be seen as if viewed from different angles. The other interesting property of a hologram is that the plate can be cut or broken into smaller pieces which each contain the original image, albeit with reduced resolution. A hologram can store an immense amount of information, with each item of information diffused equally right across its surface. Likewise, a Holographic Universe employs these principles to suggest a Multiverse in which are mirrored exactly all possible versions of various universes.

First proposed in 1990, the idea that our universe is actually encoded in a two-dimensional structure was strengthened in 2017 by an announcement from astrophysicists at the University of Southampton in the UK, working with Canadian and Italian colleagues. Their studies of the cosmic microwave background revealed, they believed, significant evidence to support the idea of a holographic universe. Along the way, the team reported, this might also offer a way to resolve modern physics'most challenging dilemma: how to unify general relativity (which describes reality at its biggest, cosmic level) and quantum theory (which explains reality at its very smallest level).

Type 8. Simulated Multiverse
This suggests that our universe - and countless others - might simply be constructs of a vastly powerful computer engineered by some super-intelligent beings who, presumably, might themselves occupy some other cosmic plane. Thus, unsuspectingly, we inhabit one of countless artificially created virtual universes! Considering the recent advances in immersive virtual reality engineering, this option today seems a little less implausible than only a few years ago.

Type 9. Ultimate Multiverse
Even more speculatively, this model for parallel universes tables the idea that all possible theories are actually manifested in one form or another somewhere in the infinite Multiverse. Thus, all suggested mechanisms to support the idea of the Multiverse are at work. This model seems to me to echo Plato's theory of the timeless universality of his idealised, quintessential Forms.

Which Model of Universe?
Does the proven existence of one of these models negate the existence of the others? Not necessarily we are told, and we do well to remember that there was a time when no less than five seemingly incompatible, yet plausible, models of string theory were being vigorously debated. Then someone suggested increasing the number of proposed dimensions from ten to eleven, thereby creating what is known as M-Theory in which

strings were replaced by membranes. Now, *mirabile dictu!*, all five string theories clicked together very neatly: it turned out that, as different aspects of the same wider reality, each of the string theories was right after all. Rarely in physics are so many fiercely contested positions all reconciled so amicably, but it may yet turn out that several of the proposed Multiverse models are also found to coexist quite happily, too.

Nonetheless, when considering this bewildering choice of Multiverse models, it should be added that some physicists think that this Sorcerer's Apprentice type of proliferation may be subject to some limitation after all. While generally admitting that the Multiverse could contain all possible universes in their *potential* state, they say the only universes that are summoned into existence are those containing sentient life. Why? Because it is precisely that only conscious observation can summon them into their differentiated existence. By this reasoning, there are only as many physically-manifested universes as there are universes that have observers.

Indeed, along these lines Stephen Hawking suggests that, instead of numberless universes, what are contained within the string theory landscape are actually all possible *histories*. Here, every single possible version of a universe exists in a state of quantum superposition, and every time a measurement or observation is made, a subset of histories pops up. In this way, you encounter a history of the universe that *you* have chosen at a self-serve Cosmic Buffet!

How are we to imagine being surrounded by a swarm of parallel universes, all equally authentic and each following its own path? One useful analogy is supplied by Nobel laureate Steven Weinberg who suggests that we think of our consciousness as being like a radio receiver which at all times is simultaneously bathed in the countless transmissions of radio stations from all over the globe. However, while a radio set is capable of receiving any one of these numerous different broadcasts, it can only receive one at a time: the single transmission from the station to which it is tuned at a particular moment. In like fashion, we can only experience the one universe to which our consciousness is tuned. And lucky for that!

Looking at Everett's Many Worlds Interpretation (where every single event causes a universe to split into parallel universes) and the Multiverse model (based on endless inflation, for example), the two ideas together seem to represent a rather uneconomic approach to diversity, especially given that each suggests its own, infinite suite of universes. It is hardly surprising, then, that some physicists are asking whether the two models are, in fact, simply aspects, or different explanations, of the one reality. Obviously, a successful attempt to marry the two will necessarily also have reconciled the apparent differences operating at the quantum and the cosmological levels. And that is probably the biggest challenge facing physics today.

To both the layperson and the professional physicist, some of these propositions may seem unacceptably fanciful, or at least untethered speculation. But the fact remains that the idea of the Multiverse, however it may be explained, is deeply attractive to science. It has been mathematically 'road-tested' extensively and has passed, thus far, with flying colours. More than that, the Multiverse works in very neatly with all sorts of known phenomena at both cosmological and quantum levels.

Apart from making explicable a number of bothersome questions in physics, the Multiverse idea neatly disposes of some philosophical issues, as well. These we shall look at in due course.

Multiverse vs. Anthropic Universe

How diverse is our natural world, where life thrives in the sea, on the land and in the air, leaving no possible niche unoccupied! Yet this lavish fecundity must seem even more miraculous when one considers how fragile and tenuous life really is. In truth, the emergence of even the lowest organism anywhere in our cosmos must hinge upon an astonishing array of coincidental factors, most exquisitely fine-tuned.

Take just this one, close-to-hand, example. Gases chilled to a liquid become much denser and, as they are frozen into a solid state, denser still. Almost uniquely, water frozen into ice actually becomes less dense than liquid water and this is evident from 4 degrees C and below. Only a half a dozen other substances share this exceptional quality: silicon, gallium, germanium, antimony, bismuth and plutonium. In every other case, the solid form of a material is heavier than the liquid form.

Now why is this property so important? Quite simply, if water did not lose density as it approached its frozen state, life could not exist on Earth. Ice would rapidly form at the bottom of our oceans and, unexposed to sunlight, would soon build up until it reached the surface. With most solar heat reflected back into space by the massive build-up of white surface ice, the world would turn into a ghostly, giant ice-ball. Apart from those few simple and adaptive life forms that cling tenuously to deep-sea volcanic vents, our once-verdant globe would be a sterile wasteland.

Again, if the strong nuclear force were a mere 2% stronger than it is, the very physics that shape the stars would change utterly, making life on smaller bodies impossible. In all, Martin Rees nominates no less than six 'dimensionless physical constants' as being necessary for life, such as the strength of the force that binds nucleons into nuclei being 0.007. If that were only 0.006, only hydrogen could exist and nothing else - including the carbon that makes up and sustains living organisms. On the other hand, if that number were adjusted to 0.008, hydrogen, the most abundant element in the universe and the primary fuel of our Sun, could no longer exist since it would have fused into other elements almost immediately after the formation of our universe.

As mentioned, the complexity of matter in the universe is made possible by the ability of stars to break down their hydrogen and helium and, in the process, release energy and forge new elements. This conversion process, sustained over hundreds of millions or billions of years, takes place in the fusion engine at the heart of each star, our own Sun included. Carbon is produced precisely because an alpha particle, a helium nucleus, and a nucleus of beryllium-8 are able to cohere to form carbon-12 - and that depends on a very precise level of excited energy. If this level were only slightly different, a stellar furnace would stop at that point and so would be unable to produce carbon or any heavier elements. This, as the astronomer Fred Hoyle once declared, would leave us with a stillborn, lifeless universe.

Among many other examples: if the power of gravity in our universe were only a little weaker or a little stronger, the stars and galaxies strung across our night sky would simply not exist. Here we should note that observable matter seems to account for only 15% of the total matter necessary to provide the gravitational pull required for the galaxies to form and then continue to hold together. The hunt is on to prove the existence of the invisible, but probably very heavy, particles that account for the rest of our universe: the 85% that is called 'Dark Matter'.

At the other end of the cosmological scale, let us look at the ratio of the mass of the neutron to that of the proton, which is approximately 1.001. As it happens, this is precisely the ratio that makes nucleosynthesis possible - and with it, the generation of new atomic nuclei in the boiling core of each star, such as our own Sun. Again, without this exact balance, no life... and no us.

Remember, this is just a small selection of the unlikely 'coincidences' that make possible our life-friendly universe. Yet even so, scientists keep uncovering yet more critically-balanced factors essential to sustaining life.

Can you now begin to imagine how inconceivably, bizarrely improbable it is that such a universe as ours could have ever occurred? Meticulously balanced upon an ever-ascending pyramid of critical factors, everything is delicately assembled with the precision of a skilled watchmaker, it is all so implausible as to stretch both credulity and imagination to the outer limit.

But before we dismiss this as an impossibly rare chance made real, let us consider another incredible lottery: the vanishingly small likelihood that *you* exist, in this here and now. Of all the possible beings that ever appeared over uncounted ages, human and non-human, you alone occupy this selfhood of yours, this instant, this flash of existence between the two eternities!

And of all their countless possible encounters, what are the chances that your parents would ever have met, bonded and created this individual baby that became you? During one very special act of love, around 100 million sperm, each with its own set of genetic characteristics, were set off in the race against all the others for the single prize of fertilising your mother's egg, thus helping create an embryo with its own unique make-up and carrying into life its own point-of-experience... yours.

How could you possibly measure the odds against such a lucky win? Some have tried. By one estimate, the probability of any one individual existing is one in more than 100 million - and another estimate puts the odds at one in 12 billion! I find it hard to see how one might compute such a number with any precision, but these odds still seem unrealistically short given even some of the variables. It may be that there are as many potential 'points-of-experience' in the universe as there are points of singularity: a number virtually limitless.

Yet, for you and me, this lucky win *did* happen, and we are the living proof of the fact. Against such unimaginable odds, suddenly the extraordinary confluence of factors required to create our life-infused universe now seems just a little more believable.

The need for so many razor-thin coincidences, each one essential for a life-accommodating universe, suggests to many people that a deliberate and intentional design was needed for us to be. In short, this they say is evidence of a designer's hand - and that, in turn, points to a God. Not unexpectedly, many physicists have challenged this assumption, referred to as the 'Fine-Tuning' Argument, on various grounds. One of these is that, rather than physical laws having been tailored for life, an organism in some form or other will organise itself to thrive in all sorts of physically different universes, much as life on this planet thrives in the very different environments of the sea, the land and air and in extremes like solid ice and steaming volcanic gas vents, acid pools, depths with immense underwater pressure, and so on.

Without necessarily acknowledging that an Intelligent Designer's hand is at work, cosmologists and astrophysicists recognise various lines of argument here, but principally for answer they look to either the Strong Anthropic Principle or the Weak Anthropic Principle. The Strong Anthropic Principle takes into account some unknown force or influence that somehow selects or favours universes that can eventually host life, particularly sentient life - and so, *voilà,* here we are! The Weak Anthropic Principle, by contrast, suggests that no universe can ever be observed if it is not of the anthropic sort to begin with: all others are fated never to be encountered. Neither one of these alternatives, by the way, is incompatible with the idea of the Multiverse.

The Anthropic Argument, that the universe was fine-tuned for us, has been around for a long time and still carries much weight for many people, particularly religionists. Most scientists struggled to present a clear and convincing counter-argument until the arrival of the Multiverse model. This could explain with irrefutable logic that whatever is possible, including those inexpressibly rare universes whose physical laws are precisely arranged for life, must exist in infinite number in an infinitely large Multiverse. Inevitably, and happily as it has turned out for us, among the estimated 10^{500} types of physically different possible universes even thinking life must be abundant. To put that vast number into perspective, remember that a piddling mere 10^{25} grains of sand suffice to make up the entire Sahara desert!

So, while the likely odds would not remotely compare with your far better chances in an office draw, they are still encouraging.

Miraculously, we can deal with such stupendous numbers mathematically, but how could we ever intuitively grasp the chilling immensity of such scales, when we deal with numbers far, far beyond any human analogy or point of reference?

The nearest I can come to any comparison is that within the observable universe with a radius of some 46 billion light years there are anything up to 300 sextillion stars spread across 500 billion galaxies – and still all their atoms added up come to only 10^{78}, or 10^{82} at most - far, far short of the 10^{500} estimated types of universes.

To summarise, there must be countless corners of the Multiverse where thinking creatures, as Fontenelle guessed centuries ago, are looking up at the night sky and wondering how they came to be.

Again, remember that, within eternity and infinity, what is possible must happen - and that what can happen once must recur an infinite number of times. The fact that we have the good fortune to live in a 'fine-tuned', life-friendly universe can be explained by the fact that if any of the physical constants required to sustain any form of life were absent there might not be anyone around to experience or observe such a state. We are here because this, or some similar universe, is the only place where we *could* be.

As a note of caution, no model of a Multiverse suggests any form of cosmic evolution in which universes appear and die, leaving some beneficial and cumulative bequest to the next tranche of creation. In other words, we are not moving, step-by-step, towards a glorious end destiny, such as one where universes are ever better adapted to sustain conscious life. And even if that were possible, would we not have arrived at that happy point a whole eternity ago? Quite simply, every possible variant is ready to appear, whether 'good' or 'bad', life supportive or not, an infinite number of times. It does so with a periodicity that reflects only the rarity or likelihood of its particular configuration of physical laws being pulled out of the hat. In any case, how can we entertain the idea that the Multiverse is guided by an overall teleological purpose when there is no evidence of any such direction apparent at the level of our own existence, particularly in biological evolution itself (despite widespread assumptions to the contrary)?

Proving that the Multiverse Exists
Can we - *could we* - actually prove the existence of the Multiverse? Even if this proposition appears to offer a neat solution to many questions puzzling physicists, and has passed every mathematical challenge, the passageway from speculative metaphysics into hard physics must remain closed until acceptable proof beckons us inside.

An immediate challenge is that, apparently, each universe is a locked-off system; but it is as well for us that this is so. Just consider the indescribable chaos if all the information from one area of the Multiverse could flow freely to another and everywhere in-between! If we were even capable of seeing it, every single possible variation of every phenomenon and every event would be piled up simultaneously, one atop the other. Luckily, our realities are firewalled from one another, and this mechanism, according to David Deutsch, ensures that information almost always is exchanged only *within* small pieces of quantum calculation, and not *between* these pieces, which he says, are actually separate universes.

We go back to the suggested proof of other universes offered by Deutsch: that the only plausible explanation for the massive power of a quantum computer is that it disperses its sub-atomic level calculations across other universes besides our own.

Then, at the macro end of the scale, there is other intriguing cosmological evidence that could point to a Multiverse, an infinite universe or at least, the presence of another universe next to ours.

Unseen 'Tugging Force'
Astronomers have observed that certain far-away groups of galaxies are being tugged away towards the edge of the known, i.e., observable, universe. This phenomenon is also supported by anomalies in the temperatures of our universe's cosmic background radiation, which was the after-effect of the Big Bang and has been recorded by NASA's Wilkinson Microwave Anistropy Probe.

Analysing the data, a team from the Goddard Space Flight Centre found that, instead of expanding at a uniform rate, certain groups or clusters of galaxies were moving in a particular direction and at a faster rate than normal. This has been called the 'dark flow' phenomenon. Located some three billion light years away, these galaxies appear to be pulled off their normal path by some unimaginably dense force outside our own universe.

Unknown Fingerprints
The fingerprints of another universe that was once near ours are believed to appear on the Cosmic Microwave Background

map of our early universe taken by the Planck satellite. What is shown on the map is remarkably uniform… except for several anomalous ring patterns. Thought to be the signatures of bumps from other universes in the remote past, these 'bruises' are exactly the same as what was created by computer-modelled collisions between universes. This evidence of an ancient cosmic 'fender-bender' could be our best clue yet to the reality of the Multiverse.

Inconsistent Densities

On top of this, there is yet another anomaly which could point in this direction. At any specific area in space, one can see immense variations in the density of astronomical bodies. However, it has been regarded as axiomatic that, as one zoomed out to take in an ever more extensive field of space, one would see an ever greater uniformity in the distribution and density of galaxies and galaxy clusters. The amount of observable matter would tend to average out over enormous areas, making the universe appear pretty homogenous on a macro scale: an assumption so fundamental that it was dubbed 'the cosmological principle'. However, more and more observations are highlighting anomalies that seem to challenge this by revealing vast areas, up to two billion light years across, of unaccountably high densities, and also low densities, of matter.

It is a riddle, along with the 'CMB cold spot', that requires some explaining. One suggestion being examined is that another universe - a 'brane' - is overlapping our own and is distorting our measurements in that area, giving the impression of anomalously high and low densities. Work is being done to put this idea to the test and, if it is confirmed, we could have the firm proof that our universe is not unique.

Black Hole Portal
Again, it is possible that a black hole could provide us with a portal to another universe, thereby proving that our own universe is not unique. This suggestion by the redoubtable Stephen Hawking, is in a paper published in '*Physical Review Letters*', co-authored by Professor Andrew Strominger of Harvard University, and Professor Malcolm Perry of Cambridge University. Their argument is that an object falling into a black hole leaves its store of information at the black hole's event horizon or boundary and this may enable that object to pop out again somewhere else in this universe - or in another universe.

Cosmic Triangulation: 'Flat, Eternal Infinite' Universe
A pointer to the universe being 'flat, eternal and infinite' came in 2014 when scientists at the University of California, Berkeley, announced that they had just mapped the universe more accurately than ever before, using a high-powered telescope at the Apache Point Observatory in New Mexico.

They began by looking for clusters of galaxies called Baryon acoustic oscillations (or baryons) which were formed by pressure ripples from when the universe was formed about 13.4 billion years ago, with the radius of each cluster always being the same. Using these as 'yardsticks' of 500 million light-years' length, the scientists were able to build up this data into the most-accurate yet 3D map of the universe. Thus equipped, they began their triangulation measurements across truly vast cosmic distances, and what they consistently found was startling: viewed on this enormous scale, the universe was everywhere found to be uniformly 'flat'.

To put this simply, if you carefully measure out a triangle on a completely flat surface, all the angles of this triangulation will add up precisely to 180 degrees. However, draw a triangle on a globe, for example, and the sum of the angles will add up to more than 180 degrees. That number will be greater as the degree of curvature is greater.

'One of the reasons we care is that a flat universe has implications for whether the universe is infinite,' explained team leader David Schlegel in their announcement. 'That means - while we can't say with certainty that it will never come to an end - it's likely the universe extends forever in space and will go on forever in time. Our results are consistent with an infinite universe.'

Bruising 'Bubble' Encounters
In 2017 came news of yet another promising strategy already underway to prove the existence of a Multiverse by detecting the signatures of other universes.

Most current theories suggest that each universe in the Multiverse, ours included, is contained within a bubble. It is thought likely that individual 'bubble' universes may gently collide from time to time, and so the search is on for the ring-like 'bruises' left by such encounters, as evident on the cosmic microwave background (CMB) radiation map that charts the heat radiation still evident from the Big Bang. The challenge until now is that it is very difficult to search for this evidence across such a vast area. Then there is the difficulty in determining whether one has found such a telltale ring - or simply an anomalous or random pattern.

In two papers, a team of cosmologists at University College London (UCL), Imperial College London and the Perimeter Institute for Theoretical Physics describe how they designed a powerful computer algorithm that greatly refines this search for authentic markers of such 'bubble' collisions. While the first evidence does not conclusively point to there being a Multiverse, they expect new data coming from the European Space Agency's Planck satellite to bring them closer to an answer.

The Falsifiability Test
Despite all these promising avenues of enquiry, for many scientists the Multiverse will remain only a hypothesis unless convincing evidence is provided that it is real. Particularly, they say, such evidence should be *falsifiable.* As proposed by the philosopher of science, Karl Popper, falsifiability is the necessary test for any scientific proposition – and this requires a description of what demonstrable evidence, calculation or observation would be required to disprove that claim. To illustrate this, although Einstein's Theory of Relativity of 1915 explained a number of astronomical observations, it was not finally proved empirically and convincingly until extremely precise variations in gravitational fields were measured almost six decades later. Regarding his theories of time dilation linked

to a body's relative speed, a convincing test involved comparing an amazingly accurate caesium atomic clock on the ground with its exactly synchronised twin which had circled the globe several times in a jet: the tiny time difference was exactly as predicted all those years earlier.

Every scientist accepts that Karl Popper's falsifiability doctrine is a very reliable test of what is or is not science: it is a handy tool for separating the phenomenal (what can be experienced, observed and measured) from the noumenal (what cannot be known in this way). It is, understandably, the first yardstick against which any significantly new proposition is measured. Nonetheless, it should not be taken as an entirely non-negotiable, *religious* truth, particularly in an area like theoretical physics where the gap between an insight and its demonstrable proof can be years long and tortuous, as Einstein was to discover. On this score, the cosmologist Sean Carroll has warned that we should be wary of ignoring an as-yet unproven possibility in this speculative field, 'on the grounds of some *a priori* principle'. We do well to remember that at one time the existence of such things as black holes, extra-solar planets, etc., was entirely a matter of theoretical conjecture - and now we are finding them all over the cosmos! And many are confident that we are closing in on the hypothesised dark matter, whose spoor is being found in more and more places.

So, again we confront another of science's axiomatic benchmarks: the Ockham's Razor test. One of the most common objections to the Multiverse concept is that postulating an infinite number of unobserved universes to explain why we live in this life-friendly universe is superfluity of 'astronomical' proportions, and is certainly a massive violation of Ockham's tried-and-tested principle.

Not so, according to physicist Max Tegmark. In his view, the Multiverse theory, considered in whichever of the main versions, represents the simplest and most elegant answer to a whole host of cosmological and quantum quandaries. Otherwise, science would have to construct theoretical scaffolding of much greater complexity: all based on unproven hypotheses and conjecture. On this count, he believes, the Multiverse model answers Ockham's preference for a 'parsimonious' explanation much more efficiently than the idea of a single universe.

This view has the support of Russell K. Standish, a computational scientist and adjunct professor at the School of Mathematics and Statistics at Australia's The University of New South Wales. In his book, *'Theory of Nothing'*, he wrote:

'...The burden of proof is actually with the singular view of reality. For there to be a single reality with but a unique strand of history is actually less plausible than for all possible histories to exist side-by-side...'

By now, though, we can appreciate the difficulties of proving the existence of the Multiverse when we are locked within the inescapable temporospatial boundaries of this universe, with no known way of directly observing anything outside it.

To illustrate the dilemma, I suggest this analogy. Imagine that you are one of a number of goldfish in a large fishbowl. The bowl is illuminated by a single light source, adequate but sufficient only to reveal what is inside the bowl, and no more.

Unknown to you, your bowl - the only world you are aware of - is on a stand in a large, unlit room. Around you are other identical fishbowls, each with an internal dim light source, so weak that it is invisible to any fish in the adjacent bowls. So, looking out through the glass of its own bowl, each fish in every bowl sees only an inky blackness surrounding it.

Since it is impossible to escape your own bowl or to see anything outside it, how can you ever ascertain whether or not other fishbowls - and other fish - exist? Is your bowl everything, and the only thing, that exists?

Being a particularly intelligent goldfish, you look for ways to put the question to the test. For example, you repeatedly flick your tail on the surface of the water, creating a loud, splashing sound that travels around the inky darkness beyond your bowl. With the help of your fellow goldfish you precisely measure the almost imperceptible echoes bouncing back to your bowl, in the same way that sonar devices can detect hidden submarines or bats hunt insects at night.

Repeatedly scanning from different angles, you detect slight variations and anomalies, which can build up into a crude soundscape map. These may be interpreted as indicating, the presence of other objects similar to your own bowl, each of which returns a similar echo signature. While short of positive proof that other bowls exist around you, this be taken as inferential evidence.

Alternatively, as a remarkably resourceful goldfish, you could construct a super-sensitive light meter and scan through the bowl's glass walls. While invisible to your eyes, the thin flow of photons from the other bowls' dim lights may be captured by your meter, which in turn suggests the possible existence of nearby fishbowls.

In a way, this metaphor indicates roughly where physicists and cosmologists are now in their various investigations into the existence of the Multiverse. We may never actually observe other universes directly, but we might just build up a case by accumulating enough circumstantial evidence.

Here we can consider the 'bruise mark' on the Cosmic Microwave Background Map, the total flatness (suggesting it is boundless) of the universe as measured in triangulation experiments, the neat way the Multiverse proposition answers a range of cosmological questions (such as the weakness of gravity), Deutsch's quantum computer challenge and various quantum effects, all taken together incline towards a Multiverse. And on top of these and other arguments, the Multiverse has been subjected to many, and extensive, mathematical crash-tests and has come up unchallenged each time.

True, all this only suggests the *possibility* of a Multiverse; it only allows us to infer that an infinite number of universes might exist. But if that seems a little frustrating, we should remember that we have been in this position before. Remember, several of Einstein's chalkboard calculations had to wait years before we were able to see them verified: his 1919 idea that light was bent by gravity was not conclusively and accurately proven until 1959 - and his 1905 paper on Special Relativity had to wait until 1971 for the synchronised caesium-beam atomic clocks test. Closer to our own time, the theoretical prediction in 1964 of the Higgs Boson needed the construction of the Large Hadron Collider at a cost of $13.25 billion to prove its existence in 2011-2013.

The Multiverse & 'Platonia'

Finally, how does the concept of the Multiverse sit with our current understanding and speculation about the nature of time, some of which we looked at earlier in this book? It appears possible that the two approaches might actually reinforce one another.

Several years ago, the quantum mechanics expert and a leading exponent of the Multiverse theory, Dr David Deutsch, met with fellow-physicist Dr Julian Barbour, a world-recognised thinker on the nature of time. Approaching the question from their respective standpoints, they concluded that there was no incompatibility between the two theories and that they could be simply looking at the same reality from different viewing angles. They agreed that each instant of time could be regarded as a self-sufficient universe in itself - and that quantum mechanics, long thought of as only able to make sense in the world of the very small, could actually describe the universe on the vastest scale conceivable. So, from their own informed perspectives at least, the Multiverse and 'Platonia' or Block Time might just be one and the same thing. Interesting…

8. The Ocean of All Possibilities

A Transforming Vision of the Cosmos... and of Ourselves

A full half century ago, just graduated in film editing from the BBC Film & Television School, I was working in the cutting rooms at Ealing Studios. Located in suburban London, this was where many of the best-loved British comedy classics had been produced in the post-war years.

One day, after returning some reels from the viewing theatre to the film storage vault, I glimpsed up from my paperwork and idly scanned the tall racks of film canisters, reflecting on how many thousands of hours of drama, documentaries and feature films were stacked on those shelves. In my reverie I imagined the countless scenes, faces and moving images, each frozen on celluloid and with their words, music and sounds mutely embedded in magnetic or optical sound tracks; and all equally free from time's linearity. Here, every single frame of celluloid shared the same frozen potentiality and validity as all the other frames in its reel.

Furthermore, I mused, each one of those many reels preserved its own constructed world, its unique story, completely self-contained and autonomous - and quite unconnected to all the other reels close by, yet again with each still sharing an equal and parallel existence. Before long, I began to see in all this archived celluloid a handy metaphor for reality itself. Remember, had not the 18th century Scottish philosopher David Hume speculated that time itself consisted of a vast collection of contingent, interlinked, but static, instants - just like the single frames in each of these reels of film?

Considered in this way, our consciousness might simply be processing those innumerable instants of our lives in the way that a film projector's shutter mechanism jerks its way through a strip of film, transforming a rapid succession of still images into the illusion of seamless continuity, just as I described earlier in Chapter 3. Similarly, might our real-life experience of action and motion (flowing time) be as illusory as what we see on a screen; with all the becoming, being and dying of our lives no more than a phantom narrative created by our own consciousness?

These ruminations left a lingering impact on me from that time, but I could not guess that one day they would supply a powerful analogy to help me handle some of the ideas implicit in Block Time and what came to be known as the Multiverse. Pictured as a cosmic film vault containing all narratives, here was *the* Reality that houses every subsidiary reality!

Few in higher-level physics think of time only in the way that nearly everyone else intuitively experiences and understands it. Their usual position is that what are called 'past', 'present' and 'future' are, in fact, equally valid, co-existent entities. Many, but not all by any means, look to the concept of Block Time as a way to describe this insight. Likewise, not all astronomers, cosmologists and theoretical physicists, or philosophers for that matter, accept the Multiverse as a possible or likely model, although more and more are becoming converts and most are open to the idea.

At this time, of course, it remains unproven science; very interesting speculation only. However, should one or both of these propositions turn out to be true, then we must brace ourselves to adjust to some astonishing, even bizarre, but nonetheless logical, realities.

Block Time

Think of Block Time as the vessel that contains the iteration of every possible universe, every phenomenon, every event and every being, and all their multitudinous fates. Everything exists in the form of unique, frozen slices of information, each of which can link to countless alternative pathways alongside them. Along these open networks, countless destinies and narratives will tack and weave from moment to moment, with each pathway made actual by one sentient being's errant consciousness.

Now we may ask, as some have, what if the Multiverse itself should exist in Block Time? What if these concepts simply turn out to be two versions of the same reality? Straightaway, we could do away with the need for the constant *physical* bifurcation of worlds into their possible component versions, triggered by each event-collapse of the most trivial events, as described by Everett's Many Worlds scenario. Likewise, we would need only a limited, although still indescribably vast, portfolio of universe-templates to account for the universes popping in and out of existence in other Multiverse models.

In a Block Multiverse all variants already exist in a state of timelessness. Of course, if one version of every variation and alternative were sufficient, we would eliminate the redundancy of absolutely identical versions being created again and again to clutter up the, admittedly boundless, Multiverse. Clearly, then, looking at the Multiverse as an aspect of Block Time does open up certain benefits and, indeed, some physicists seem to accept this, going so far as to actually refer to the Multiverse itself as 'The Block'.

Now, were all versions of reality to coexist eternally in this way, might it be that what is new is not a freshly-minted universe, but instead the individual journey that a conscious entity experiences for itself as it makes its way through innumerable pathways and options that already exist at some level. To revert once more to the ever-handy movie film analogy, our life is simply a re-spooling and viewing of a long pre-existing reel of film: there is no need to send our camera crew out on location with a dog-eared old script to re-shoot the same footage for every repeat viewing of the same story!

Since there would be no need to re-forge every world and its histories anew with each telling, we now have the simplest and certainly most economical way of containing all the possibilities that could be. At this level, we would surely be hosting the stillness and totality of *Apeiron* or Plotinus' *The One* - and it would be vast beyond any description.

We read that if you set out across an infinite or sufficiently large universe, you will eventually encounter your own world, and yourself, once again. The countless elements that shape the world as you experience it, consisting of the memories, experiences, psychological and neurological profiles, in fact every single element that makes your own unique *Umwelt* or personal reality, will be faithfully curated and replicated in every detail. That unimaginably vast distance to your other self has been computed, in one instance, at a googolplex of metres - or as one widely accepted cosmological model suggests, you have a twin self on a planet some $10^{10^{28}}$ metres from where you are right now. To be sure, this is a distance incomprehensibly enormous - even for cosmologists to whom 'billions' and 'trillions' are everyday metrics.

But even within such a universe, vast but not infinite, the same set of physical laws may prevail from one side to the other. By analogy, the sea girdling our planet is boundless, having neither beginning nor end, but it is certainly finite, as the sailors under Ferdinand Magellan and his successor, Juan Sebastián Elcano, discovered when they eventually ended up back in Spain after circumnavigating the world.

Here is another thought.

As mentioned before, in his *'Our Mathematical Universe: My Quest for the Ultimate Nature of Reality'* physicist Max Tegmark proposed that mathematics is the fundamental underlay for all that is; that our physical world is the creation of mathematical structures. Taking up that idea, could we then imagine Block Time as simply a gigantic algorithm that spits out the appropriate 'reality' when prompted by the actions and choices of a conscious being? Think of a 3-D printer that, within it, contains no defined objects, but can produce a vast range of items on demand, providing it is fed the right software instructions and raw material.

In any case, like other scientists, theoretical physicists are attracted to the simplest plausible explanation and are naturally averse to unnecessary complexity and redundancy - especially when it comes to expending energy - and this is the type of economy that could be offered by the Multiverse-Block Time option.

I imagine William of Ockham would be pleased with such an option.

Pushed from Centre-Stage!

For five centuries, science has steadily rolled back the boundaries of the known universe, so that we now peer far, far deeper into the cosmos than was conceivable even a lifetime ago. But, we know there is a price to pay for this most magnificent privilege. As our field of vision widens, so also does our significance continue to shrink apace; by ever more humbling degrees, we are relegated yet farther from the centre of creation.

This demotion began when Ptolemy's Earth-centred cosmos was displaced by Copernicus' solar system, relegating our Earth to one of the dutiful retinue circling Mighty Sol. Then, in turn, our Sun itself was revealed to be no more than a minor star quietly minding its own business, just one among billions in the outer fringe of the Milky Way.

Then on January 1, 1925, came yet another Copernican moment. Astronomer Edwin Hubble discovered that the far-distant smudges on his telescope's long-exposure photographic plates were not gas-and-dust nebulae after all, but other galaxies just like our own. Originally thought to number at least 150 billion, this was recently recalculated at some *two trillion* galaxies stretching over an observational bowl of more than 90 billion light years from rim to rim.

Now, when it seemed that we hardly needed yet another humbling dismissal to the wings of the celestial stage, eminent astronomers, cosmologists and physicists now seriously propose that our universe, for all its numbing vastness, is itself only one of a suite of countless other universes.

Not many have yet absorbed the philosophical or religious implications of this emerging perspective, but just as before, the stage may come when most of us will accept it as the new reality. Only this time, we are looking at much more than today's astronomical scales infinitely expanded: we may have to confront the inescapable logic of eternal recurrence. Whether we are dealing with a ceaseless linear sequence of universes (the pulsating universe option) or an endless supply of co-existent universes with a limited life, or both, then the outcome must still be the same eternal return.

You, You... and You!

That there are other versions of you all across infinity is not fantasy, but a mathematical inevitability once it is assumed that space or time are limitless. Hard to comprehend, true, but because we are applying straightforward probability calculations to *infinity*, this is a pretty solid conclusion. Furthermore, there is not simply one mirror-you out there, but rank upon rank of your *doppelganger* twins who are all living real lives, confronting every sort of possibility.

As Parmenides put it some two-and-half millennia ago,

"There is not a Being which existed only during some past time, or will exist only in some future time, because at the present all Being is in being, together with itself, in one single continuum.'

Just imagine: somewhere a version of you is now reading this very book - and wondering about you wondering about *them.* Somewhere, you have just completed a project that you are, in this here-now, struggling to start. There is a 'you' that has to face an unheralded crisis or tragedy that in your present life you were just lucky enough to have avoided, had you only known it.

A version of you is lying in bed surrounded by your grieving family who watch as, with a gentle sigh, you let go of your last breath. And elsewhere, countless universes away, you kick and thresh as you struggle to gulp your very first lungful of air and, with a triumphant cry, proclaim the first day of your newly independent life.

This vision of a mirror-maze in which there is no one 'reality', but instead an infinite range of equally-true narratives is suggested by the opening line in the Qing Dynasty novel by Cao Xueqin, written in the mid-18th century, *'Dream of the Red Chamber'*:

'Truth becomes fiction when the fiction's true;
Real becomes not-real where the unreal's real.'
(trans. David Hawkes)

In this way, the author introduced his semi-autobiographical account, involving long-dead or half-forgotten acquaintances and lovers, reminding us that the line between the false or imagined world and what appears as the real world is forever opaque. In a sense, the unreal has its own reality.

Lives Outside Time

The logic of an infinite Multiverse means that all the moments and experiences of your life, and each one of your possible lives, coexist as real events and are endlessly playing out *right now*, somewhere within its unbounded matrix.

The reason for this simultaneity is that these infinitely replicated versions of you dwell in universes that have their own independent space-time continuums. Each of those timelines is self-contained and unconnected to the past-present-future timeline that we experience in our own universe. Relative to our world, what happens to your mirror-twins in other island universes cannot be described as happening in *our* future or past: that would be meaningless. Their 'now' cannot be linked to what we perceive as 'now' here, and so it must follow that, viewed from outside our universe, all moments of this life are equally real and coexistent within the Multiverse. To each other version of you, our timeline here would appear like a single compendium of moments, just as if looking at an entire reel of a film in its individual canister. Or, if you prefer, an enormous table covered by a large spread of many photographs spanning all your life till now - and beyond.

If this notion of time seems utterly bizarre, it would be well to remember that most physicists believe that time as we know it in our daily lives is, essentially, a human construct. Like the notion of independent will, it may well be just another illusion, albeit a *necessary* illusion.

Can we even begin to conceive of this 'Self', whose every trivial encounter prompts endlessly bifurcation, one life into another life and on and on, extending over limitlessly varying existences; an explosion of dendritic branching out that explores every possibility? Who better to help us here than the man who first conceived the idea for the Many Worlds Interpretation, Dr Hugh Everett? In the first draft of his doctoral thesis, he wrote:

'As an analogy one can imagine an intelligent amoeba with a good memory. As time progresses the amoeba is constantly splitting, each time the resulting amoebas having the same memories as the parent.

Our amoeba hence does not have a life line, but a life tree.

The question of identity or non-identity of two amoebas at a later time must be rephrased. At any time we can consider two of them, and they will have common memories up to a point (common parent) after which they will diverge according to their separate lives after this point. It becomes simply a matter of terminology as to whether they should be thought of as the same amoeba or not, or whether the phrase "the amoeba" should be reserved for the whole ensemble.

We can get a closer analogy if we were to take one of these intelligent amoebas, erase his past memories, and render him unconscious while he underwent fission, placing the two resulting amoebas in separate tanks, and repeating this process for all succeeding generations, so that none of the amoebas would be aware of their splitting. After awhile we would have a large number of individuals, sharing some memories with one another, differing in others, each of which is completely unaware of his "other selves" and under the impression that he is a unique individual. It would be difficult indeed to convince such an amoeba of the true situation short of confronting him with his "other selves".

The same is true of [sic] one accepts the hypothesis of the universal wave function. Each time an individual splits he is unaware of it, and any single individual is at all times unaware of his "other selves" with which he has no interaction from the time of splitting.

We have indicated that it is possible to have a complete, causal theory of quantum mechanics, which simultaneously displays probabilistic aspects on a subjective level, and that this theory does not involve any new postulates but in fact results simply by taking seriously wave mechanics and assuming its general validity. The physical "reality" is assumed to be the wave function of the whole universe itself. By properly interpreting the internal correlations in this wave function it is possible to explain the appearance of the world to us (classical physics etc.), as well as the apparent probabilistic aspects.

With this imaginative analogy, Everett certainly left his many baffled human 'amoebas' with a useful insight into how his elusive idea might affect them within the Plurality of Worlds!

Creators of Universes?
Let us now turn to the implications of the Multiverse, Block Time and the Eternal Return for *us*.

Newtonian physics, rational, mechanistic and essentially materialistic, gave impetus to the Enlightenment - and Einstein's theories certainly had their impact on wider society a century ago. On the other hand, while the quantum has long been embedded in our technology (some 40% of domestic gadgets use quantum effects in their electronics), it is only now shaping the thinking of wider contemporary society, even if many experts cannot yet fully guess where this will take us.

However, there is one aspect of quantum theory that may yet make the biggest impact upon us. While unable to restore us to a central position within an anthropocentric cosmos, quantum theory does secure an essential place for the *observer* in the scheme of things - and that is unequivocally demonstrable. Indeed, there is even debate as to whether the physical world is not after all simply a summoned-up creation of the one, true reality: *Mind!* Back we go again to Bishop George Berkeley and his theory of immaterialism, commonly referred to as 'subjective idealism'.

(The late John Wheeler (1911-2008), one of America's most eminent theoretical physicists and one-time colleague of Albert Einstein and Niels Bohr, came up with what he called 'genesis by observership'. He suggested that, by the very act of observation, we contribute to the creation of physical reality. No mere witnesses of the cosmos, we play an important role in shaping a 'participatory universe'.)

As a conscious being, you live in a world that you create in your head. Here you assemble all the available sensory inputs in real-time, and processing them in a fraction of a second, create a version of reality that makes sense to you, as a human being. Furthermore, how you then interpret this 'reality' depends upon many sorts of in-built psychological, social, cultural and experiential factors. Since no two people are exactly the same, neither will they construct, experience and interpret the world around them in exactly the same way: a fact noted by philosophers many centuries ago. The point here is that, in a sense, each one of us shapes - and inhabits - our own unique 'universe'.

So, maybe we humans, as conscious and sentient beings, *do* count for something, after all. We create universes.

Does thinking of your inescapable fates overwhelm you - or does it liberate you to know that any dream that is possible is inevitable? While striving to secure a tolerable life in this timeline, with all its inevitable pain and setbacks, can you find here the consolation of knowing that elsewhere, elsetime, it is all very different? Count upon it, compared with what you contend with here, things are certainly a good deal worse for some of your alter egos; but, yes, just as surely you are also enjoying other lives where you are much, much better off.

The Ocean of All Possibilities

How are we to picture one's passage along a 'lifeline' in Block Time? This is my favourite image…

When swimming underwater, one is moving in a medium of four-dimensions (length, height, depth and time) and can turn at will in any spatial direction and follow any one of innumerable invisible and ever-branching potential pathways, each of which offers its own unique set of possible encounters and experiences. Think of this ocean as encompassing all that is or could be, presented as a vast medium comprising countless frozen 'nows'. Next, imagine the swimmer as your consciousness gliding through the sequences of static moments, all the while stringing these together into a continuous narrative, a self-created continuity which takes you through what are deemed to be a past, present and future.

As a conscious observer, you encounter one of these possibilities with every passing instant, leaving the other alternative realities to other versions of your self or other selves. And let us not forget that you, in this life, are just an unrealised possibility for countless other 'you's' in another universes.

The idea of the Multiverse as being embedded within Block Time forms what I describe as *'The Ocean of All Possibilities'*. I call it such because I imagine reality as a boundless medium containing every possibility and every moment. Within it are to be found, not just all your own lives, actions, thoughts and emotions, but also the countless lives of everyone you have ever known. Here too in in their own, real world are being played out the ever-vital narratives of your dead friends and relatives, your ancestors and even those of your descendants, for these, too, are as real as you suppose your present living self to be.

No one in the this-here world has, or could have, any direct awareness of their multiple existences elsewhere in the Multiverse. Luckily for our need to focus on this life, and for our very sanity, an impenetrable curtain separates us from our innumerable other versions: the dreamless state between existences I have described earlier as *interbiosis*.

A Share of Immortality

Considered from the viewpoints of both secular philosophy and of theology, eschatology is what describes the debate about the 'end times', that is, the final fate of the universe and, particularly, the final destiny of humanity.

This is a scenario that preoccupies nearly everyone, whatever their creed or philosophy. Many religionists, understandably, see the end of the world as the final battle between the forces of good and evil and the time when everyone is judged on their mortal lives. Quite a few non-believers, unaccountably, are themselves anxious that our Sun will one day consume the last of its hydrogen fuel, expand and swallow our Earth, and then in the far, far distant future our universe will either slow down and implode inwards or, more likely it currently seems, will expand forever into a chilly, black and lifeless entropy. Yet these events are billions of years away, countless generations ahead, should humanity survive that long in any form that would be recognisable to us now.

While one or another of these final scenarios for this universe seems inescapable in the utterly distant future, a Multiverse seeded with numberless other versions of our universe, forever spinning around in their separate domains, will always host sentient creatures who will be there to worry about the fate of *their* universe.

And some of them will be you... or versions of you, at least.

As I said, the most astonishing implication is that we are eternally embedded in this vast realm. In all sorts of guises, our mirror-selves are forever coming and going in different universes, confronting every fate. And interspersed between these, often starkly-different, life narratives, what of the fragile and evanescent phantom-images, voices and experiences that one recalls upon waking from a fast-evaporating dream - or were glimpsed in a reverie? Will they, too, finally have their chance to become real and accessible in far corners of the Great Ocean?

Against the scale of the universe we know, each of us, and our lives, are inexpressibly insignificant in scale and consequence, to be sure - but we know that. And, if of little account in one universe, how much the less might we be we within a Multiverse?

But think of this: yours is not one solitary life that lights up and is then extinguished forever. The Multiverse and Block Time both promise that there has never been a time when you did not exist and nor will there ever be such a time. Everything about you, and everything you have seen and known, are all of them immortal, to be lived and encountered forever. Your every experience and every possibility are frozen, not for eternity, but are frozen *in eternity*!

With this, every instant of your life, of your every life, is deep-etched on the crystalline surface of the infinite and is fated to be encountered, again and again. And so, in this endlessly recursive realm where there is no beginning and no end, you are, in a sense, deathless.

Amor Fati
A Stoic concept, which we recall was a favourite of Nietzsche, is *'amor fati'*, Latin for 'love of one's fate' and it describes an attitude of joyous acceptance of all that life offers, including both its inescapable vicissitudes, as well as its pleasures. Clutching no specious hope in eternally-sustained good fortune

or happiness, this is the instinctive embrace, not of what life may endow, but of *living itself.*

Of course, the idea of repeated existence will surely be received differently from one individual to another. Already weary of living, some may gaze upon any form of deathlessness with horror. Then there will be those who argue that it is the very fact of mortality that impels us to achieve and strive so our fleeting moments are as rich as possible.

Look at the diametrically different attitudes to the prospect of eternal life held by the world's two great religious families: the Abrahamic tradition comprising Judaism, Christianity and Islam (described collectively by Muslims as 'The People of the Book') - and the Dharmic faiths, principally the Hindu and Buddhist religions. While the one group holds out the promise of eternal life to believers, the other consoles its faithful with the possibility of final escape from the endless wheel of birth and rebirth. On the assumption that there is no easy pleasing of everyone, perhaps the likelihood of endless parallel, but unconnected, existences for each of us might represent an acceptable, third-option compromise!

Perhaps also there is that rare individual, an exemplar of Nietzsche's Superman, who would lunge at the prospect of endless cycles of life, fully mindful of all the ennui and turbulence that must season every existence.

Here, I suggest, we should think of Ludwig van Beethoven, the tempestuous genius who composed many of the greatest works of music ever heard. A famously talented pianist, he played all over Europe and was well rewarded with acclaim and financial success. Then, to his horror, he began to lose his hearing and was forced to exchange his secure career as a virtuoso performer for the struggles and uncertain rewards of a composer. Feverishly, he tried to outpace his advancing deafness with a prodigious output of works, but all the while struggling to hear the instruments. Finally, when composing his majestic 9th *Choral Symphony*, Beethoven was driven to resting his head on the piano, hammering the keys with his fist in the hope that their vibrations would resonate as notes in his skull. After the first performance of his *Ninth*, he was not even aware of the rapturous applause it evoked, and had to be turned around to see, but sadly not to hear, the astonished audience's response to his superhuman masterpiece.

What cruel irony, that this creative titan should forfeit his most important faculty in his early forties, at the very height of his powers, and be forced to retreat from the company of others into a world of perennial and bitter silence. Thwarted in love, his was a life of solitude, poor health and worries, with no consolation but the music that played silently in his leonine head. Such a Promethean struggle might have driven Beethoven to suicide. Instead he passionately embraced life, even on the terms dictated by this cruellest of destinies. Writing to his childhood friend, the physician Franz Gerhard Wegeler, he declared:

'Free me of only half this affliction and I shall be a complete, mature man. You must think of me as being as happy as it is

possible to be on this earth - not unhappy. No! I cannot endure it. I will seize Fate by the throat. It will not wholly conquer me! Oh, how beautiful it is to live - and live a thousand times over!'

On his deathbed, the genius was slipping in and out of consciousness when those keeping solemn vigil beside him were startled by a violent thunderclap. Beethoven suddenly opened his eyes and, raising an arm, defiantly shook his clenched fist at the heavens - and then sank back into his pillow, dead at only 56. Despite his struggles he had never flinched from Zarathustra's challenge nor faltered in his faithful embrace of *amor fati*. Now he was at peace - and his name safely entrusted to the ages.

9. The Intuitive Grasp

Where the Mystic and the Metaphysician Meet

Assuming an intellectual grasp of at least some of the scientific and philosophical arguments for the Ocean of All Possibilities, we are still left with the question: how to *intuitively grasp* this ultimate reality? And is this even remotely possible?

In truth, we draw upon two types of knowledge and understanding: the objective and the subjective. The first is based upon hard data, logic and rational examination. This process is the essential tool we employ to make sense of the outer world - and to manipulate it. It is why 'left-hemisphere dominant' engineers are the designers and dispatchers of spacecraft to the outer planets, rather than poets and artists. And it is why engineers are rarely called upon to design public sculpture, although they are often asked to put it together.

The other way of understanding is intuitional, relational and experiential and, drawing upon subconscious powers, is often incomplete and fuzzy, but it is also what is actually *lived and felt*. This is the so-called 'right-hemisphere dominant' approach to apprehending the world around us.

Of course, no single mind is exclusively given over to one type of thinking only. At such extremes one would become either an unemotional robot or, alternatively, a completely instinctual animal. This explains why, to temper the stereotypes just quoted, we are able to read some astronauts' moving and surprisingly poetic descriptions of their experiences - and why Leonardo da Vinci, the painter of the *Mona Lisa* and *The Last Supper*, was also an engineer and scientific polymath driven by an insatiable curiosity about the physical world.

The Intuitive Brain

So, to deal effectively with our existence, we must draw upon both of these complementary mental instruments: the intuitive and rational 'brains'.

If this is true for the individual, it is also true for a well-functioning society. In ancient Greece, Sparta was notorious for having expunged all artistic expression, humanity and luxury from its society lest anything impede the creation of a military super-state. Athens, by contrast, cultivated not only its military might but also endowed the ages with a glorious bequest spanning art, literature, architecture, mathematics, science and philosophy. As a result, the Spartans of Lacedaemon left little to posterity but impressive military victories and the adjective, 'laconic', which describes their grimly terse, unemotional demeanour.

Closer to our own era, a healthy society's need for balance between these two aspects of the mind was proclaimed by the British intellectual C. P. Snow. He wrote and spoke of the lamentable and, he thought, widening gap between science and the humanities. A successful scientist who was also a novelist, literary critic and commentator, he was well placed to pronounce on this concern and his book, *'The Two Cultures and the Scientific Revolution',* caused wide debate when it was published in 1959. Snow warned that this decline in the dialogue between what we now term the left and right brains was becoming culturally, socially and educationally institutionalised, and thus was diminishing society in important ways.

That there are two complementary modes of thinking is something well understood by cybernetic scientists working on a human-like artificial intelligence. Currently, computers possess remarkable powers when it comes to left-brain typical, algorithmic processing, which is one reason why they can beat even the greatest chess masters and are well ahead of humans in many areas. However, when dealing with 'fuzzy logic' and incomplete templates which only intuition, creativity and imagination can make work, today's best computers are still little better than dullards, although impressive progress is being made in this area.

It takes vastly more computing power and an enormous repository of experience-templates to achieve what computer designers refer to as 'heuristic' reasoning, the ability to deal with ambiguities, analogies, paradoxes, incomplete information and, especially, the ability to play a hunch. Software with self-tutoring feedback offers a great step forward here.

(Interestingly, for the cinema's most famous self-aware computer, and the central figure in the epic *'2001: A Space*

Odyssey', the name of 'HAL' served as an acronym for 'Heuristic-Algorithmic': which acknowledged the mind's dual aspects. Another explanation circulated that it was *'IBM'* with the letters alphabetically and - anticipating possible copyright infringement - prudently moved back one space!)

While we have always seen much art and creativity in science and technology, and rationality and logic employed in art, the general convention is to regard science as the special domain of the left-brain exemplar and art as the preserve of the typically right-brain dominant, creative person. (We may remember that the ancients apotheosised these archetypes in the form of Apollo, the god of cool and temperate reason - and Dionysius, who embodied instinctual and unrestrained self-expression.)

Holding for the moment to this simplification, let us illustrate the two approaches this way. Being asked to describe a sunset to one blind from birth, our caricature of a left-brain, scientist might put it thus:

'Streams of photons emitted from the sun are reflected by illuminated objects at different wavelengths and pass through the lens of each eye to activate the optic nerves in the retina. Employing the principles of triangulation, the brain utilises the different angles in the images presented by each eye to create a stereoscopic image that provides a sense of three-dimensional depth. Compensating for the fact that this combined image is received upside down, the visual centre in the occipital lobe at the back of the brain then creates a 'corrected' right-way-up analogue picture. Because the setting sun's rays are refracted

at an increasingly oblique angle through the atmosphere, we see an interesting spectral spread that changes rapidly as the sun sinks below the horizon. Different wavelengths of light are processed by the brain to create analogous equivalents that are then interpreted by the mind as "colours"...'

Something along these inflexibly reductionist lines might give an informative and accurate insight into the mechanics of viewing a sunset, but your sightless listener would still have not the least idea of the actual *experience* of seeing a sunset.

The right-brain approach might do a little better by drawing upon the closest analogies available to a sightless person. Here we might talk about a pleasant image evoking an effect on one's sight similar to what the blind person experiences with their other senses when gently tracing a finger over velvet or a flower petal, when smelling fresh pine needles - or listening to a soothing melody.

But could we ever hope to impart to a congenitally blind person any real sense of what it is to *see* a sunset? No. And so there are some things that will forever remain out of our reach. With these we must remain experientially ignorant: just as a mollusc, marooned in the eternal dark of the deepest ocean trench, can never witness the *Aurora borealis*!

Each day takes us through a flurry of fragmentary instants - fleeting, lightly-limned and impressionistic - whose impact is often unique to the individual. Philosophers and psychologists use the term *'qualia'* (sing. *quale*) for feelings, sensations or impressions that may not be easily described (if at all, even to oneself), but are only properly grasped as a direct, personal experience. Such a moment can be linked to a deeply embedded emotion, as when lavender's perfume evokes a warm childhood memory of a grandmother's dressing table.

This explains why the most elevated experiences can often only be communicated in an allusive way, through poetry, for example. A sense of the numinous, like a brush with the enlightened state that Zen practitioners call *satori* (often revealed in an *'augenblick'* - the blink of an eye, a fleeting second) is almost impossible to convey to those who have not experienced it, or something close to it.

So, our minds operate at two levels: the rational-objective and the intuitive-subjective. Of course, some mental processes are exceptional in that they overwhelmingly draw upon one of these levels only. For example, we do not need to tap into our intuition or experience to understand why *pi* can describe the relationship between a circle's radius and its circumference: logic alone suffices. And neither do we need to look to logic to deconstruct the heart-warming appeal of our toddler's laughter. Finally, should we accidentally touch a hot kitchen plate, an instinctual and reflexive response alone is called for: we need neither the reasoning nor the emotional 'minds' to tell us to quickly move our hand away!

However, it is different when we look for an over-arching philosophy or intellectual framework to help explain not only where we fit into the scheme of things, but how we might also be *inspired* by it. Our question is: how to achieve an intuitive grasp of the ultimate reality that complements what is illumined by science and philosophy?

Metaphysicians and Mystics

We now turn from the cosmologists and physicists to those who also share their intense interest in the most fundamental questions of existence: the metaphysicians and, in many instances, mystics. What can they tell us of their own more abstract and intuitive explorations? While the average reader is likely to struggle with their accounts, particularly when concepts and insights are described in language so often paradoxical, allusive *and elusive* – and strewn with negatives. Typically, Hinduism conveys the ineffability of the ultimate reality, Brahman, with the Sanskrit term, *neti, neti*, 'not this, not that…'. Again, taking their cue from the insights of Plotinus and other pagan Neoplatonists, Christians of the Apophatic theological tradition employed a similar device: the *via negativa* in which God, and the experience of God as the Ultimate Good, could only be described through negatives or, at best, paradoxical or allegorical language.

There is a straightforward answer to explain this apparent slipperiness. A mystical insight is an intuitive encounter that is beyond all previous personal experiences and is therefore, by definition, also beyond mere shared words or common intellectualising; it is a glimpse into an undifferentiated realm in which familiar tags such as self, time and place, names and descriptions have little meaning. By employing commonplace words or images to directly describe this experience, one inevitably reduces it to our limited, earth-bound understanding or experience. To go back to our earlier example, it would be like sharing a sunset's beauty with one blind since birth.

Such a mystical experience, when it occurs, carries many names, including 'enlightenment', 'cosmic consciousness', and 'metagnosis': all of which mean the knowledge of, or insight into, a level of reality that is beyond what is normally apparent or explicable.

Those individuals displaying signs of 'cosmic consciousness' are drawn from every philosophical and religious tradition, practices, idioms, historical eras and locations. Some are agnostics or atheists, scientists even. That they employ surprisingly similar images and analogies to describe their encounters, suggests essentially similar experiences. I cannot imagine that anyone convinced of the Multiverse or Eternalist model, and reflecting on its astonishing implications, will not be driven to reshape utterly their own intuitive sense of place in the ultimate scheme of things.

The Timeless Void

This is where we must begin. Whatever other terms are used to describe this super-reality, 'The Void' is the essential concept we must confront. Speaking of this central focus of their philosophy and practice, Buddhists refer to an emptiness that is replete with all that ever can be. That is very much how many others describe The Void, whether they refer to it as *The One*, *The Plenum*, the *Apeiron*, the *Summum*, the Gnostic *Absolute*, Buddhism's *Shunyata*, *The Tao*... or also, I suggest, *The Ocean of All Possibilities*.

In each case there is a unifying vision of The Void as the ultimate reality: a static oneness that is formless, featureless, all-encompassing, and without boundaries or place in space or time. This may seem conveniently evasive, but consider how could one possibly describe what is, quite literally, ineffable and offering no differentiated quality or experience.

Thus The Ocean of All Possibilities is the vessel of all that is or ever was or could be. Remember, when we describe any single feature or object we can only do so by isolating certain characteristics (colour, weight, size, shape, position, etc.) and signaling or implying the absence of others. But here we are talking about the simultaneous and equal presence of all qualities, including their opposites. And so, where every single negation is encompassed we can, therefore, only be left with a complete, featureless and indescribable *Void*. And, by the same reasoning, if what we are talking about could be described in any way that relates to a physical characteristic or to our own direct experience of the world, then it is by definition not this Void of which we speak.

Consider this analogy. Commonly, we regard something that is pristine white, a sheet of paper, for example, as being blank and having no colour. Yet, as Newton discovered, when pure white light is projected through a glass prism it breaks up into the constituent visible colour wavelengths of red, orange, yellow, green, blue, indigo and violet. Put this spectral rainbow through another glass and it can be made to recombine back into white again. In this way, high school students can see for themselves that white light is actually the combination of *all* visible colours - and not simply an absence of colour. Likewise, what makes the Void indescribable is the very fact that it contains *all* descriptions.

Towards the Infinite

When ascending a mountain, climbers may (theoretically) set out from any one of hundreds of different starting positions. However, as they gain height the distance that separates them becomes ever smaller until, at last they may find themselves standing at the very same spot at the summit.

Thus it is for those working towards an intuitive vision of the unity of all things and, as I said, why mystical adepts use a language that is almost interchangeable, whatever their widely disparate traditions, or religious or non-religious points of origin. Some of this concurrence can be seen from these brief samples from different traditions:

Hinduism

In the Hindu religion, Brahman (or *Parabrahm*) names the reality lying behind the apparent and illusory world that we think of as 'objective reality'.

The classic text, '*The Bhagavad Gita*', talks of Brahman as having no beginning and that it:

'*...Can be called neither being nor nonbeing... It is both near and far, both within and without every creature; it moves and is unmoving. In its subtlety it is beyond comprehension. It is indivisible, yet appears divided in separate creatures. Know it* *to be the creator, the preserver, and the destroyer. Dwelling in every heart, it is beyond darkness. It is called the light of lights, the object and goal of knowledge, and knowledge itself.'*

Brahman is undifferentiated, encompasses every phenomenon, including all contradictions, and lies outside the realm of space and time, and therefore, of cause and effect. It is, for this reason, ultimately inexpressible and unknowable.

For the Hindu, the path to salvation lies in escaping from the endless round of existence and reincarnation, thereby to achieve eternal unity with Brahman.

Greece & Rome
Clearly inspired by Indian traditions, the cult of Orphism was enormously influential throughout the ancient Greek world. Like Hinduism, it taught that each individual soul is trapped in an endless cycle of reincarnation and that only by purging itself of sin over a succession of lifetimes could the soul become united with the eternal reality.

Sometimes, a prepared mind was spontaneously vouchsafed a view of this greater reality. The Neoplatonist Plotinus, who was at least as much a mystic as a philosopher, related to his aide Porphyry that he had experienced a mystical ecstasy at least four times. As he put it:

'Often I have woken to myself out of the body, become detached from all else and entered into myself; and I have seen beauty of surpassing greatness, and have felt assured that then especially

I belonged to the higher reality, engaged in the noblest life and identified with the Divine.' ['Enneads', iv.8]

Judaism
The Kabbalah teachings importantly express Jewish mysticism. Their primary focus is on what is called *Ein Soph* (or *Ayn Sof)*, the infinite, unchanging nothingness that God inhabits and which lies outside the created and ever-changing world that we inhabit.

Again, the *Ein Soph*, which is outside all differentiation or conceptualising, can only appear to us as nothingness and therefore cannot be comprehended or described by the human intellect.

The German-born Israeli philosopher, Gershom Scholem (1897-1982) described it as:

'...the absolute perfection in which there are no distinctions and no differentiations, and according to some even no volition. It does not reveal itself in a way that makes knowledge of its nature possible, and it is not accessible even to the innermost thought... of the contemplative.'

He added:

'Essentially, this nothingness is the barrier confronting the human intellectual faculty when it reaches the limits of its capacity. In other words, it is a subjective statement affirming that there is a realm which no created being can intellectually

comprehend, and which, therefore, can only be defined as "nothingness."'

Christianity
In contrast to the other two Abrahamic religions, Christianity comes closest to personifying God, chiefly by identifying Jesus Christ as one of the divine trinity and by using his life, teachings and sacrifice as the object of reverence.

Despite Christian worshippers' intense meditative focus on this anthropomorphic aspect of their deity, there has been a long tradition of speculation on the ultimate nature of the Godhead, and once more we hear familiar ideas and language, such as those expressed by the German 15th century theologian, Nicholas of Cusa (Kues):

'God is not something... God is beyond nothing and beyond something... God cannot be called "this" rather than "that"...'

Again, we can turn to the German Dominican theologian Meister Eckhart (born Johannes Eckhardt, around 1260) who is still revered as one of the foremost of Christian mystics:

'God is nameless, for no man can either say or understand aught about Him. If I say, God is good, it is not true; nay more; I am good, God is not good. I may even say, I am better than God; for whatever is good, may become better, and whatever may become better, may become best. Now God is not good, for He cannot become better. And if He cannot become better, He cannot become best, for these three things, good, better,

and best, are far from God, since He is above all. If I also say, God is wise, it is not true; I am wiser than He. If I also say, God is a Being, it is not true; He is transcendent Being and superessential Nothingness. Concerning this St Augustine says: the best thing that man can say about God is to be able to be silent about Him, from the wisdom of his inner judgement. Therefore be silent and prate not about God, for whenever thou dost prate about God, thou liest, and committest sin. If thou wilt be without sin, prate not about God. Thou canst understand nought about God, for He is above all understanding. A master saith: If I had a God whom I could understand, I would never hold Him to be God.'

An indispensable handbook for many Christian mystics was, and still is, *'The Cloud of Unknowing'*. Written by an anonymous English cleric in the second half of the 14th century, this spiritual guide emphasised that the Godhead was a pure and essential entity whose true nature was beyond human comprehension.

'God is neither soul nor angel ... nor can He be described or understood ... He neither stands still nor moves ... He is none of the things that have no being, none of the things that have being... Nor is there any way by which we can reach Him through reason or understanding...'

Therefore, the unknown writer counselled, meditative prayer should focus, not on what might be deemed about God or deduced from his actions, but upon an emptying of one's mind of all conjecture: a high spiritual state of *'unknowing'*.

Islam

Central to Islamic teaching is that God is unknowable and, therefore, indescribable. Accordingly, any attempt to portray God in art is deemed blasphemous because, in making Him accessible to mere humans, it must inevitably diminish Him.

The great Persian Sufi mystical poet, Jalal ad-Din Muhammad Rumi (1207-1273), emphasised this when he wrote:

'God created suffering and heartache so that joyful-heartedness might appear through its opposite. Hence hidden things become manifest through opposites. But since God has no opposite, He remains hidden... God's light has no opposite within existence, that through its opposite it might be made manifest.'

Closer to our own time, 'Abd al-Kader (1807-1883), wrote in his book of spiritual meditations, *'Kitab al-Mawaqif'*:

'The absolutely Non-Manifested cannot be designated by any expression which could limit It, separate It, or include It. In spite of this, every allusion alludes only to Him, every designation designates Him, and He is at the same time the Non-Manifested and the Manifested.'

The Sufi branch of Islam sees everything as a reflection of God, whose essence is universal love. The Sufis strive to see the beauty in all phenomena merely as manifestations of God's single unity, including both what is deemed good and evil, beautiful and ugly. Since it contains all that is, including opposites, this divine unity or reality (*'Tawhid'*) is devoid of every form and quality, and so is indescribable.

214

To try to experience this divine unity, the Sufi must flee from every idea of duality, especially that between the self and the rest of creation.

Buddhism

The inexpressibility of a formless reality and, with it, the ephemerality of differentiated existence, is central to the Buddhist account of things, whether it is interpreted as a religion or as a philosophy only. 'The Void' (*Sunyatta*) and 'Emptiness' (*Shunyata*) are at the very heart of the teachings of Siddhārtha Gautama Shakyamuni, known to us simply as 'The Buddha'.

As was mentioned before in Chapter Five, this concept was extended and refined by the Indian Buddhist philosopher, Nāgārjuna some twenty-two centuries ago. He regarded all things, humans included, as fundamentally empty of any independent being, with their existence totally contingent on conditions and causes.

Further, Nāgārjuna argued, it is our erroneous belief in intrinsic existence that sustains the self-perpetuating dysfunction in the way we deal with the world, its creatures and with one another. Under this illusion we ascribe their own false reality to various qualities deemed attractive or repulsive; we react to certain objects and events with deluded attachment or aversion. Nāgārjuna tells us that grasping at the independent existence of things, being delusional, leads to dissatisfaction and disappointment, which in turn, prompts a chain of destructive actions, reactions and suffering. Accordingly, Nāgārjuna believed, this notion of emptiness goes well beyond being merely a philosophical insight into reality: it also presents us with profound psychological and ethical implications.

This is the description from the patriarch Bodhidharma who brought Zen Buddhism from India to China in the fifth century AD:

'The ultimate Truth is beyond words. Doctrines are words. They're not the Way. The Way is wordless. Words are illusions...'

He added:

'... this Mind, through endless kalpas without beginning, has never varied. It has never lived or died, appeared or disappeared, increased or decreased. It's not pure or impure, good or evil, past or future. It's not true or false. It's not male or female. It doesn't appear as a monk or a layman, an elder or a novice, a sage or a fool, a buddha or a mortal. It strives for no realisation and suffers no karma. It has no strength or form. It's like space. You can't possess it and you can't lose it.'

The influence of Hui Neng (638-713 AD), the Sixth and last Patriarch of the Chinese Chan (Zen) school of Buddhism, continues to this day on account of his instructive *'Platform Sutra'*. In it he talks of the Void in this way:

'The illimitable Void of the universe is capable of holding myriads of things of various shape and form, such as the sun, the moon, stars, mountains, rivers, men, Dharmas pertaining

to goodness or badness, deva planes, hells, great oceans, and all the mountains of the Mahameru.'

Again, Yung-chia Ta-shih, the revered Chinese Buddhist sage who also died in 713, explained this elusive concept in verse:

'When the absolute Reality is known, it is seen to be without any individual selves, and devoid of any objective forms;
All past actions which lead to hell are instantly wiped away.
After the Awakening, there is only vast Emptiness; this vast universe of forms ceases to exist.
Here, one sees neither sin nor bliss, neither loss nor gain.
In the midst of the eternal Serenity, no questions arise;
The dust of ignorance which has accumulated on the unpolished mirror for ages,
Is now, and forever, cleared away in the vision of Truth.'

Taoism
The *Tao* in Taoism simply means 'The Way' (or 'The Path') and it tells of a formless, nameless Totality, outside of which there is, and can be, nothing. This is the crucible within which all the phenomena that we are or observe are generated and, in time, must revert into non-being in an endless cycle. We individuals, as components of this whole, are charged with living lives that are in balanced accord with nature.

Here we should turn to Lao Tzu, the founder of this belief system, for his own description of the Tao in his book, *'Tao Te Ching'*:

Look, it cannot be seen - it is beyond form.
Listen, it cannot be heard - it is beyond sound.
Grasp, it cannot be held - it is intangible.
These three are indefinable;
Therefore they are joined in one.

Nahua Meso-American Religion
The Nahua native American people of Mexico and Central America, whose population once included the Aztecs, founders of one of the major pre-Columbian civilisations, describe an ultimate reality which, in many ways, seems remarkably similar to what was understood by distant cultures in other hemispheres, even though they had no contact with them.

To this day the Nahua talk of *teotl*, an eternal, still and all-encompassing reality within which resides all that ever is, ever was or ever will be. Nothing exists which is not part of *teotl,* or is outside it. It is both a small pebble and also the stars and the entire cosmos, seen and unseen.

Like other accounts of the ultimate reality in other traditions, philosophies and belief systems, *teotl* transcends any description or differentiation; within it are all forms and all contradictions; it contains all change, but is itself outside change.

And What of... God?
On this I am unsure of my footing. Before I can even start working on an answer, I need to know what one means by 'God'. Is it the amorphous Providence of the Stoics and the Enlightenment's deists, or the personal deity of the Abrahamic

traditions? Is it the pantheistic God, immanent in all things, that was espoused by Spinoza and others? Even within Christianity, it seems that the God implied in *Leviticus* is quite different from the God of St Francis, that of the Unitarian Newton, of Calvin, and so on.

Besides those many versions of a Supreme Being (or Beings!), I suspect that every believer's notion of an ultimate reality is a highly individual and internal construct that reflects their own personality, way of thinking, culture and experience, just as much as it does the explicit revelations of their religion. Thus, even if I share your interpretation of fundamental truths, I may still perceive of our 'God' differently.

If we are talking about a personal god in the form of the Jehovah of the Old Testament, then I have nothing much to say in his favour. It seems impossible to me that a deity responsible for managing the endless immensity and diversity of the Multiverse should see mankind as the jewel of all this creation and, indeed, would in any way recognise in us his own mirror image. Besides, a jealous and vengeful god, inordinately partial to his believers and given to annihilating those who vex him, seems seriously out of keeping with modern sensibilities!

That great Rationalist philosopher, Spinoza, conceived of God (or 'Nature') as an impersonal and ultimately unknowable power that had little direct involvement or interest in human affairs and was concerned only with ensuring the orderly running of the celestial clockwork. This pantheistic reality accounts for all creation, is self-sufficient and is the impulse behind all events and phenomena. It seems that Einstein was attracted to this idea.

Spinoza wrote: *'Whatsoever is, is in God, and without God nothing can be, or be conceived.'* And, again: *'God is the indwelling and not the transient cause of all things.'*

It is interesting that any 'Name Your God' challenge would pose less difficulty for a Hindu. In that marvellously accommodating religion, an orthodox believer can bed down with polytheism, monotheism or even, as some say, atheism. At one level we have a diverse pantheon of gods, each with their own attributes and myths, including Devi, Krishna, Ganesh, Hanuman and Lakshmi. But above them all is the over-arching entity, the ineffable and impersonal Brahman, which transcends and yet includes all that ever is, was or will be. Thus, we and all other beings and even the very gods themselves are simply manifestations of different aspects of Brahman. To me there are obvious parallels between Hinduism's *Brahman*, Anaximander's *Apeiron*, Plotinus' *The One*, Spinoza's *Nature*, and so on with the Multiverse and Block Time or, as I would call it, the Ocean of All Possibilities.

In the end, the choices we make on this matter reflect, as much as any rational argument, one's cultural conditioning, psychological make-up and emotional needs. It could get down to an aesthetic, as much as an intellectual, preference. Perhaps, in this regard, the Buddha had it right. Replying to a question as to the nature of deities, he would not answer but said that even if a god or gods did exist, they too would be subject to the eternal laws of causality. The Buddha must have understood the futility of trying to definitively disprove the existence of such persistent entities.

Looking at the Multiverse proposition, if this offers a way to answer the Anthropic argument, it still says nothing about whether or not there is a God. Believers are free to see it as interposing simply another remove between creation and a creative agency, who or whatever that may be. We must remember that this has happened a number of times in the past (the issue of evolution, for example) without seriously weakening the faith of many believers, nor need it do so in the future.

Insight

I firmly believe that, however one comes upon it, the intuitive experience of the oneness of all existence and the deathlessness of all forms and events is a real and attainable prospect. It is an insight that can be the reward of a life-long, patient quest - or it can come quite suddenly in an instant of unbidden recognition. However it arrives, this intuitive experience of the Absolute is deeply and permanently transformative and is not to be unlearnt. The lives and thoughts of many seekers over many ages proves that so.

• <u>EVERY DESTINY IS YOURS!</u>

Limitless in extent, and bounded

by neither beginning

nor end, the Multiverse insists

we dramatically reshape

our understanding of reality. And it also opens up

a radically new way of interpreting human destiny.

You are told that your unique, linear existence,

bounded eternally by a single

birth and a single death,

instead opens into a vast spectrum of

lives, some similar, many different, but

together promising immortality.

What are you to make of this?

10. Why Me?

This Improbable 'Point-of-Experience'

'Why am I me?'...

I think I was about six or seven years old when, without any warning, I posed this question to my mother. I am not sure what reply she came up with, but I do recall she was busy in the kitchen preparing the family's evening meal. I imagine her response was somewhat awkward, along the lines that I was here because she and my father had wanted me.

If this question sometimes taxes the minds of youngsters (and their parents), it also perplexes many of the most distinguished intellects, philosophers included. Needless to say, it has certainly baffled me to this very day, which is precisely why I remember when I first addressed this puzzling mystery.

I must make it clear that I am not talking about the race of life in which the odds against securing a physical existence are so astronomically high. The issue here is about the incalculably remote likelihood of ever occupying *this* selfhood, *this* viewing position looking out onto creation; *this* very seat of consciousness so unique and utterly separate from all those other possible conscious entities, whether close or far distant, in our own time, in the past or as yet unborn.

Perhaps guessing that only eternity might finally grant corporeality to every possible or imagined being, the Victorian essayist and life-long bachelor, Charles Lamb, expressed the sheer improbability of existence beautifully in his essay, *'Dream Children: A Reverie'* (1822). He describes a dream in which his two fantasy children visit him, and then depart forever, whispering:

'We are nothing; less than nothing, and dreams. We are only what might have been, and must wait upon the tedious shores of Lethe millions of ages before we have existence, and a name.'

As these longed-for children fade from his view, he wakes up and:

'I found myself quietly seated in my bachelor armchair, where I had fallen asleep.'

(*'Lethe'*, one the five rivers of Hades in the Greek underworld, here means 'oblivion' or 'forgetfulness'.)

In his acclaimed Gifford Lectures delivered at the University of Glasgow between 1935 and 1937 (later published as the best-selling *'The Human Situation'*), Professor W. Macneile Dixon posed the question thus:

'In each family a few, a very few, out of legions of possible human beings came into existence. They are, shall we say, among the favoured few? Why were they, like ourselves, so singled out? And at what moment did this self of ours, so

precious to us, this 'I', this individual person attach itself to the chromosomes from which our bodies have sprung? And are there somewhere souls awaiting their opportunity to be born? "I stand terrified and amazed", wrote Pascal, "to see myself here rather than elsewhere, for there is not the slightest reason for the here rather than for the elsewhere, or for the now rather than for some other time." And we may add, '"for any time at all", no reason why your "I" or mine should ever have entered into the world or life.'

Indeed, why *am* I me? We may evade Martin Heidegger's challenge in *'Being and Time'*, 'Why are there beings at all instead of nothing? That is the question', but we are still left with the solipsistic riddle: why is it that *I* am anchored to *this* consciousness – and why am I, if I were to be anything at all, not simply one of the other 'not-me' conscious entities that surround me – even one that is otherwise identical in every detail to my own self?

Your Unique 'Point-of-Experience'

Let us look more closely at the one aspect of each sentient existence that is truly unique, remains fixed from childhood and is unaffected by any changes in the development of personality. It is what definitively sets us apart from each and every other sentient being in this universe, even from an identical twin, and does so much more emphatically than any differences in particular mixes of personality traits or experiences.

What makes each of us absolutely individual is what I call our unique 'point-of-experience' or ('point of view'), Let me explain:

you are the only person who is seeing the world through *your* eyes, constructing and interpreting impressions in *your* mind, experiencing *your* life. And, in turn, that implies that the universe you inhabit, that you construct in your mind, is ultimately unique to you. For the simple reason is that while others may infer much about you and your personal world, no one else can directly inhabit or experience it - nor you theirs

Others may try to look into your window, but only you can look *out* through it. Furthermore, this point-of-experience is the one thing about ourselves we can all really be certain of. In this sense, we might see it as simply another way of interpreting Descartes' famous *Cogito* proposition. Thus, 'from my unique vantage-point, I experience, therefore I am this self'.

The actual incidence of sentient life in our vast universe is likely to be vanishingly small, and, as mentioned, for all we know at this time it may be limited to our little world alone. Yet no one wonders that there should be other self-aware, thinking people around us on this planet. Neither, is it very hard to grasp that there should be room in it for a comparatively unremarkable individual such as oneself.

As I said, the real conundrum relates to why I, rather than any one of the vast repertoire of *other* potential identical selves, should be occupying *this* point-of-experience, being uniquely involved in this one-off sense of self.

This 'point-of-experience' is your unique attribute that belongs, in its own form, just as validly to every single individual, whether old or young, stupid or intelligent. But several observations have to be taken into account. First of all, if such a 'point-of-experience' is an essential component of self-aware consciousness, it is dependently linked to memory, otherwise nothing beyond a reflexive response can be prompted by external stimuli. Secondly, while this point-of-experience implies a continuing sense of how we perceive the world, it is not changeless. The brain is continually remodelling itself to adjust to acquired experiences and learning over the years, to hormonal changes. As well, it can be interrupted by deep and dreamless anaesthesia or induced coma, injury, disease, age and so on.

In 2017, I had arranged to meet up with an old friend from my BBC days in London, to start editing the TV pilot documentary we had just finished filming. With another project already being scripted, we certainly were working to tight deadline pressures.

That morning I felt strangely breathless and fatigued. I remember pausing to rest on a park bench opposite Wynyard Station in the centre of Sydney and then... nothing. After an indeterminate interval, I then became aware of repeated and violent hammering on my chest. I opened my eyes to see a ring of people anxiously staring down at me as a tall, solidly-built young man rhythmically thumped my sternum. I smiled weakly and he made way for the two doctors and several nurses who had sprinted out of the medical centre, just metres away. I whispered thanks to everyone and was loaded onto the ambulance that had just drawn up.

I learnt from the paramedics that before being resuscitated, I showed no vital signs: my skin was chalk-white, eyes rolled back, pulse flatlined and I had not drawn breath for at least four very long minutes.

I came to with no sense of time lapsed, no dreams or visions, nothing – and certainly completely unaware of the drama that had ruffled several dozen commuters. But I was still connected to the same 'point-of-experience' that I had just before my brief excursion to the 'other side. (It was very similar to my experiences in coming out of deep anaesthesia after major surgery.)

Nursing cracked ribs and soon to receive a new atrial heart valve, my consolation was that I now had convincing proof that, while the process of dying might be uncomfortable, the actual exit itself need not be feared.

There is, though, the question that, if my body and mind were to be somehow deconstructed and then reconstructed exactly, atom for atom, would there be any continuity of my self, in my point-of-experience? Or would I be a new, 'other' person, in the way that an otherwise identical twin still has a different consciousness to that of their otherwise extremely similar, monozygotic sibling?

This takes us to the 'Beam me up Scotty....' conundrum so often debated by some fans of the long-running 'Star Trek' science fiction TV series. While that precise request was, apparently, never actually made, it became a popular catch-phrase reference to Captain Kirk's frequent order to be 'beamed' from some planet back to the orbiting *Starship Enterprise*. The unresolved question for many 'Trekkies' is whether the 'beamed up' Captain Kirk is really the same person or consciousness as the one who had been standing on a planet's surface just seconds earlier, or is he now simply an utterly convincing simulacrum?

Several years ago, scientists succeeded in teleporting information from one atom to another across a three-metre space in a laboratory. More recently, the University of Science and Technology of China employed this 'quantum entanglement' mechanism to teleport information from a photon on Earth to its paired twin in a space station orbiting 500 kms away. A very small-scale beginning to be sure, but there is no telling whether that the 'beam me up' issue may not one day need some serious examination.

In Eternity, Why Me... Now?

That I should ever have been granted existence at any time is mystery enough, but with it comes an equally perplexing question. Why am I alive and conscious here and now – and not at any place in the eternal past or the eternal future? How can it be that in a timeline of billions of years (never mind the spans of all those other possible universes!) I should exist in this hairline present, this precise intersect between the two eternities? Surely the actual occurrence of my truly unique 'point-of-experience' is so unlikely as to be virtually impossible?

The odds of a life of, say 85 years' duration, being lived now and not at sometime in the infinite past or infinite future can be roughly calculated at the odds of:

$$\frac{1 \quad \text{in } \underline{\text{infinite time}}}{85 \text{ years}}$$

Which, of course, is.... one in infinity!

So, we must now take a different approach to the conundrum. If there can be no such thing as a completely unique event or entity within eternity, then it is axiomatic that whatever conjunction of conditions that gave rise to any single phenomenon must be reassembled again and again through all time (or 'times'). Logically, there is no argument why that should exclude even something as special as one's own consciousness or point-of-experience. That being the case, then your life will be, and must be, recreated again and again, both with and without variation from your present existence.

Now we may be dealing with something a little more manageable. The Eternal Return, as Nietzsche proposed it, guarantees that a version of each life can be expected to appear periodically, in what we perceive as the future as well as in the past. We are no longer grappling with a unique event fated to be lost in the unplumbable depths of eternity. Granted, it may take the duration of quite a few universes (or *kalpas*, as Hindu cosmology describes these cosmic cycles) for an individual life to be rerun, but that still means that there will be intervals of time between our lives that must be infinitely shorter than eternity. To find myself living at some here-and-now point, in whatever universe, becomes not only possible, but also, inevitable.

Finally, the Ocean of All Possibilities, this limitless repository of every possible entity, phenomenon, event and instant, is also the home for every conceivable self – and version of a self. These range across 'editions' differing by only the slightest permutation all the way to those with ever-wider divergences and then on beyond until we might no longer recognise ourselves at all. All these numberless versions of selves can be imagined as fusing into a single continuum of being in which time past and present are all time present; in which all conditions, events, experiences, features and characteristics are encountered. This ultimate reality behind our illusory world of differentiated forms and flux has now become a seamless continuum, or if you like, the *Apeiron* that Parmenides spoke of. In truth, I believe, it is where we really live.

Jorge Luis Borges put it this way:

'There is a concept which corrupts and upsets all others. I refer not to Evil, whose limited realm is that of ethics; I refer to the infinite.'

'This felicitous supposition declared that there is only one Individual, and that this indivisible Individual is every one of the separate beings in the universe, and that these beings are the instruments and masks of divinity itself.'

'This web of time – the strands of which approach one another, bifurcate, intersect or ignore each other through the centuries – embrace every possibility.'

It should be mentioned that, apart from sharing the same aquatic metaphor, the Ocean of All Possibilities differs from the *'Ocean of Souls'* imagined by the mathematician-philosopher, Gottlieb Wilhelm Liebniz. As I conceive of it, our 'Ocean' is an ultimately completely fluid and undifferentiated, single reality, just as with the Greek *Apeiron*. By comparison, the Liebnizian reality is a 'God-as-Ocean' fundamentally composed of immutable and differentiated basic physical and spiritual units he called *monads*, which he deemed to be the smallest possible perceivable particles, even more minute than atoms.

Mind & the Universe

More than ever before, much debate centres on what place the mind, or consciousness, has in the cosmic scheme.

Is self-awareness, with its ability to observe, simply a useful survival mechanism evolved over many millions of years to enable our vulnerable species to carve out a niche in a hard-scrabble natural world? Is a sentient mind of no greater consequence within nature than, say, the spring-like quality of a cheetah's spine that enables it to run faster than any other land animal or the chromatophores in the squid's skin that endow it with rapid, colour-changing camouflage? Or, on the other hand, does mind have a central and essential place in the greater creation, as some suspect?

Eighteen-year-old Sheryl is lost in her world. Lied to by her mother about who her absent father was and why he left them when she was thirteen, Sheryl turns to alcohol and sex to escape her frustration, her lack of self-knowledge, and her nagging mother.

Sheryl has never lacked for casual lovers, but only when she starts having feelings for Isaiah, a guy she sleeps with regularly, does she begin to figure out who she really is. As she finds herself falling quickly and deeply in love, she and Isaiah keep their relationship a secret. Sheryl is determined to escape her past, but will that help her learn the truth about herself? As an unexpected bump in her plan shifts her outlook on life, the past she's running from catches up with her in a way that may threaten her life and the lives of those she loves.

In this contemporary novel, a young woman struggles with knowing herself and with allowing true love into her life.

ISBN 978-1-5049-0872-6

 authorHOUSE®

51995
9 781504 908726

I would start by asking what it is that proves to us that any thing whatsoever in our universe can be said to exist. One might answer that, to exist, a discrete entity must possess describable characteristics. If that is so, then straight away we need someone to describe, or cause to be measured, those features. In other words, a *conscious observer* is required.

This is no mere philosophical wordplay: it has a demonstrable basis in science. We know from the earliest experiments in quantum mechanics that the presence of an observer actually has a physical effect. To take one example, in what is called Young's Experiment, particles behave either as waves or as particles depending on whether or not they are being observed. Performed in the first year of the 19th century and in ordinary classrooms to this day, the 'double-slit' experiment has scientists still struggling to find a definitive explanation for the phenomenon it demonstrates.

But its chief implication remains very clear. As Heisenberg once explained, 'A path comes into existence only when you observe it.' Without a conscious observer, time and motion as we intuit them, do not exist in terms of their being objective realities. Together, they are a construct (some would say an illusion) created within our own minds.

It could be argued that by demonstrating how an observer, or 'mind', can impact upon the physical world, we are led back again to some version of the immaterialism proposed by that 18th century Irish philosopher, Bishop George Berkeley.

Many Minds – Many Universes

Trying to imagine an observer-less universe, we confront a great mystery. Without an onlooker, there is no differentiation between what is deemed to be large or small, close or far, relatively still or moving, past or present, and so on. Especially, at a sub-atomic level, the very sub-atomic particles that make up matter itself are lost in the unresolved and ghostly haze of quantum superposition where, being unobserved, they are neither here nor there, but are simultaneously both. And, finally, without the presence of a conscious observer, human concepts like beauty become utterly meaningless. Here we are in the realm of what the philosopher Kant called the noumenal world, whatever physical reality is when it is stripped of the connotations and descriptions attributed by sentient observers. This objective, unfiltered reality he labelled *Das Ding an Sich*, 'the thing in itself' – and, so defined, it is essentially unknowable to us.

By contrast, we live in the world of the phenomenal; that is, the realm of appearances, qualities, measurable and, especially, *describable* features and attributed values and connotations. But it is important to understand that it is only summoned up and made possible by the workings of a thinking mind that recognises or ascribes characteristics, relying upon our senses, memory, logic, recognition of context, and so on.

Remember, according to our individual make-up, we each see the world around us in our own fashion and in this way construct a completely original version of the universe. If my hearing is impaired or you suffer from partial colour-blindness, it is not only that we have an impaired sense of a single reality around us; the 'universes' we each perceive and know will be that much less similar. Beyond that are the different ways in which we interpret things: what I find commonplace you may see as awe-inspiring, threatening, comforting, intelligible, mysterious and so forth.

As well, there is the fact that we usually never see things from the very same physical position – and always differences in distance, perspective and context can make a significant difference.

Finally, we must accept that what we see is not the world 'out there', but an analogous world that we construct inside our own brain from external stimuli. Photons excite nerves in our eyes that, in turn, prompt the brain to assemble a picture in the brain – and ascribe to it what we think of as colours. Likewise, sound waves trigger special hairs in the ear that generate nerve impulses, which are translated into what we experience as 'sound'. Equivalent mechanisms give us our sense of touch, balance, taste, etc.

So, in a real sense, we already do create a version of the universe that is uniquely our own. It is not the complete picture of reality: we will not know how it might appear if we were equipped with the super-hearing of a bat, the extraordinary olfactory powers of a beagle, or a shark's sensitivity to electrical fields. Two and a half millennia ago, Plato recognised this limitation and illustrated it with what came to be known as the 'Plato's Cave' analogy. Imagine, he suggested, that a group of chained-up individuals had been confined in a cave all their lives and had never seen the world directly, but could only infer it from the sounds and the lights and shadows thrown onto the cave wall by the passing events and people from the unseen, outside world. Likewise, he said, our limited human faculties allow us only a very partial sense of reality.

Of course, no thinking being could ever apprehend the complete reality of the world: it will always be filtered and incomplete. As I said, *Das Ding an Sich* is ultimately unknowable to our experience. Yet still the only way for the universe to be known at any level at all is through an observer, no matter how limited their capabilities and understanding - and the unique 'point-of-experience' that makes this possible is a truly astonishing feature of our cosmos.

The 'Self-Selected' Universe

While the 'reality' we each inhabit is something we craft in our own brains, this question remains: how is it we are so fortunate as to be in one of the, presumably, very rare and lucky universes that can sustain life?

Going back to what was mentioned in Chapter 7, one answer may be that all theoretically possible universes exist in a latent state, and only become actualised or 'real' when perceived by a sentient observer. In a way, this is simply extending to a cosmological level the central feature of quantum mechanics at the micro-level where information about a sub-atomic particle (spin, position, etc.) is only settled by an act of observation or measurement. Until then, the particle can exist in multiple, mutually contradictory and equally valid states all at the same time.

Recall that the physicist Everett's key insight was that quantum mechanics might be applied right across the entire cosmos, and not be limited only to the ultra-small realm of the quantum. This idea that there is, after all, no division between the worlds of quantum and classical physics has been taken up by a number of physicists, but the experimental challenge is in determining at what scale quantum effects are masked in everyday life. This brings us back again to the idea that the only possible 'actualised' universes are those that can sustain observers, human or otherwise. What remain of the 10^{500} universes predicted by string theory must hang in a ghostly, unresolved state. And with that, the anthropic universe in its however many viable iterations just might be the only game in town!

Another thought: what if the observer effect of humans and other sentient beings could have the retroactive effect of making their universe happen before they appear on the scene? While retroactive effects have been observed whereby future actions shaped past events at a sub-atomic level, I shall sensibly leave that conjecture to others.

The 'Solipsistic' Argument
Our examination of the 'point-of-experience' mystery also suggests to me something important about reality at the very grandest scale. Indeed, I see here another supporting argument for the very Multiverse itself.

Let us go back to the proposition that this 'I' (or point-of-experience) could not exist as a single or unique phenomenon occupying only this particular here and now, yet within an eternal and infinite cosmos. Logically, we would always be irretrievably lost in either the eternal past or the eternal future: the 'now' which we occupy could only ever be a theoretical and never-encountered intersect between the infinitely receding past or horizonless future. And here we must also recall the axiom that there can be no once-only events in eternity: whatever happens once, must recur again and again, endlessly.

As well, it might also be argued that my encounter with this distinct point-of-experience calls for such an improbable convergence of innumerable chance factors that its occurrence is well beyond the odds available within a single-universe cosmos restricted to a time-line of limited duration.

This logical impasse seems to mandate some form of Multiverse. Only the Eternal Return with its endless succession of universes can comfortably accommodate the longest odds imaginable.

I would not expect these 'solipsistic' arguments to gain traction with many theoretical physicists or cosmologists. However, I do think that this might offer more fertile ground for philosophers and metaphysicians.

11. All Other Histories

Alternative Histories and Counterfactuals

It was September 28, 1918, just weeks before the armistice brought a weary end to the four-year slaughterhouse that was the First World War. The German lines were buckling, but along the Western Front bitter fighting still raged on, and it was here, near the French village of Marcoing, that a battle-hardened British soldier saw a grey-uniformed figure lurch into view.

Henry Tandey, a private in the 5th Duke of Wellington Regiment, raised his rifle and took aim. As he focused he noticed that, while still armed, the German was clearly wounded and, although aware that he had been spotted, he appeared too weak to raise his weapon in self-defense.

As he related later, Tandey could not bring himself to shoot someone so incapacitated and so he slowly lowered his rifle. Gazing at him for several seconds, the German slowly nodded his head in gratitude and then painfully made his way back to the comparative safety of his own lines…

Twice wounded, Private Tandey emerged from the blood and mud of 'the war to end all wars' as Britain's most decorated private, with the prized Victoria Cross among his awards for bravery. The lucky German corporal, himself the winner of two Iron Crosses, went on to become the Führer of Nazi Germany.

Although some disputed the story, Hitler himself recognised Tandey from a painting based on a photograph of the much-decorated hero that appeared after the war. He actually mentioned the incident to Prime Minister Neville Chamberlain at the time of the Munich Crisis meeting and asked that he convey his best wishes to Tandey.

Knowing so well what horrors were to unfold only two decades later, we need hardly ask how different things might have been had Private Tandey acted, as many Allied infantrymen would have done, and shot the armed enemy combatant on sight, wounded or not? Could anyone be certain that the Second World War, with its toll of 60 million dead, would still have happened? Of course, other calamities might have emerged in its stead, but surely only Hitler's uniquely inhuman fanaticism and indomitable will could have authored a murderous disaster on such a scale?

(It is worth noting that Tandey himself came to regret reprieving Hitler, especially after he lost his home during the Coventry Blitz in 1940.)

The Multiverse: Sum of All Possible Histories
With every remotely plausible turn of events embraced within a Multiverse, it follows that in countless worlds Private Tandey raises his Lee-Enfield rifle, squeezes the trigger and a German corporal with a strangely clipped moustache slumps, mortally-wounded, into the mud.

In such scenarios, a devastated family in the Austrian town of Linz is reading and re-reading a telegram announcing the death of their young Adolf, shot on the Western Front just before the Armistice. Neither they, nor Corporal Tandey nor anyone else could know that with their heartbreaking loss, history's greatest catastrophe had just been averted.

Unfolding in other universes, countless variations of this narrative are real events, and that is why a Multiverse is able to endow any plausibly conjectured history with a life of its own.

Counter-factual Narratives

Whenever hit by unexpected misfortune or having ducked a lucky near miss, our natural reflex is to ponder on what might have been. This explains why we are fascinated by news reports of individuals whose late connection caused them to miss a doomed flight - or of the improbably unlucky soul felled by a falling meteorite. Even on a far wider stage, powerful destinies can still pivot tantalisingly on one or two chance factors that could propel millions of lives either way towards very different fates. Speculating on the arbitrariness of historical events and how they might have so easily unfolded otherwise inspires what is known as 'counter-factual' or alternative history.

A quick flip though a history book shows that many, if not most, epochal events could very easily have gone one way or another. A small, arbitrary decision or a mere happenstance event might have diverted fate along an entirely different trajectory, setting off unimagined chains of causality that, in turn, could have taken us to who knows where.

As Chaos Theory tells us, in a 'deterministic non-linear system', an initially insignificant factor can have a compounding effect over successive phases so that it ends up greatly affecting the final outcome. Thus most of us are familiar with the example of the Amazonian butterfly's wing-beat that hypothetically triggers a disastrous hurricane.

Accordingly, the counterfactual historian can draw upon an inexhaustible lode of great and well-known crossroads moments when one of vastly different and far-reaching histories had a chance to 'collapse' into actuality.

Not surprisingly, the richest of such sources are decisive military engagements where 'knock-on' effects can pile up and extend particularly rapidly and dramatically. Speculative or counterfactual military narratives give historians, war-gamers and military strategists ready-made exercises to demonstrate how specific decisions and tactics can deliver radically different outcomes. Here, valuable lessons are offered about accumulating consequences, contingency planning, being able to respond rapidly and opportunistically to fast-evolving circumstances amid 'the fog of war', etc.

A good example of this genre is *'What If?'* edited by Robert Cowley, which brings together conjectural essays by military historians that analyse crucial military conflicts over two and a half millennia. Starting with how the plague thwarted the Assyrian siege of Jerusalem in 701 BC, the book ends by examining how easily things could have gone awry during the Berlin Wall confrontation, when Soviet and American tanks squared off at Checkpoint Charlie – and missile silos were readied to unleash a nuclear apocalypse.

Often, the weather is a powerful shaper of destiny. What if, in 1588 Phillip II of Spain's massive invasion fleet had not been blown into catastrophic disarray by a violent storm in the North Sea? A largely defenceless England might have become a reluctant vassal under the suzerainty of His Most Catholic Majesty - and not a mercantilist super-power fated to build its own vaster global empire. Today's world language, English, might instead now be just another West Germanic language, largely confined to several European islands.

Centuries earlier, fortuitous storms in 1274 and 1281 rescued another island-nation when a massive Mongol invasion fleet was blown into chaos by what the Japanese reverentially call *Kamikaze* - 'the Divine Wind'. How different things might have been, even up to our present times, had proudly militaristic Japan been reduced to a compliant tributary state under the Golden Horde of Kublai Khan?

One of the most studied and passionately argued 'what-if' scenarios relates to the Battle of Waterloo, the decisive battle that finally ended Napoleon's plan to dominate Europe.

On the morning of this titanic clash between France and Britain (supported by its allies), the battlefield was still sodden from heavy overnight rain, thus putting the French infantry, cavalry and gunners at a disadvantage. Napoleon accordingly had postponed his attack until the afternoon to allow the ground to dry off.

After long and savage fighting, Wellington's army was wilting under the relentless French pressure and Napoleon saw a real prospect of victory. But the last-minute arrival of Field-Marshall von Blücher's Prussian army tilted the battle against the French. In Wellington's own words, the battle was 'the nearest-run thing you ever saw in your life'.

Without the previous night's torrential downpour, the battle and the war could very easily have been decided long before the Prussians arrived. And what if the iron-willed von Blücher had listened to his weary troops' pleas to rest awhile, instead of maintaining the forced march that brought them to the field at the most critical moment?

In the event, the Allies did win and, historians tell us, the peace settlement of the Congress of Vienna profoundly reshaped the continent. British dominance was assured, the path was created for a unified Germany under Prussia and a century of relative orderliness was only finally broken by the needless outbreak of the First World War. According to an alternative account, under Napoleon's unchallenged tyranny, Europe's history would have been incalculably different. His victory at Waterloo would have curtailed Britain's and Germany's power and, possibly, a united Europe might have been a reality a century earlier than actually happened. Along the way, there would have been wars, but it is unlikely we might have seen anything like the two world wars of the last century.

Influenced by G.M. Trevelyan's 1907 essay which imagined a Europe shaped by a Napoleonic victory at Waterloo, J.C. Squires wrote a best-selling anthology, *'If It Had Happened Otherwise'* (1931) which explored a number of such counterfactual historical episodes.

Chaos Theory in Action

Sometimes, seemingly insignificant factors can be decisive. In 1914 Archduke Franz Ferdinand of Austria and his wife Sophie were on a state visit to the restive Serbian town of Sarajevo. Unknown to him, would-be assassins had been foiled in their plan to kill him. Then, his chauffeur became lost and went down a side street - and right past one of the plotters, the Serbian nationalist assassin Gavril Princip. The Archduke and Duchess were shot dead and this in turn, precipitated a conflagration that was played out in two acts: the First World War and what some regard as its inescapable consequence, the Second World War.

Professional historians are often sharply divided about counterfactual historical hypotheses. Some do not regard this as a legitimate branch of serious academic historical study, believing it trivialises and clouds a rigorous academic discipline with a kind of post-modern relativism. One can certainly sympathise with historians wanting to keep things as unspeculative as possible. Already, they have a difficult enough task unravelling hard facts from overlays of myth, contradictory accounts and bias.

On the other hand, there is the argument that counterfactual exercises, by examining what might have happened, can help us better evaluate the impact and consequences of actual outcomes. Realistically, this tally should also factor in the opportunity cost when things have turned out badly - or quantify the potential benefit of narrowly avoiding an adverse event. We must also remember that prior to major events, the main actors often anticipated quite different outcomes: Napoleon engaged at Waterloo confident of victory, while Wellington was fearful of defeat. Thus, among several competing and entirely possible outcomes, all but one became counterfactuals in this world only *after* fate had made its call.

Especially, counterfactuals highlight how easily destiny turns upon trivial and arbitrary factors, and thus they serve as a useful corrective against post-hoc assumptions of inevitability favoured by historical determinists. As so frequently in science and history, we must be ever vigilant against teleology's temptations.

Counterfactual or alternative histories typically require only a slight tweaking of real-event narratives to deliver a plausible account of how things might have gone from there, based firmly on what is known of the protagonists and the circumstances.

On the other hand, writers of counterfactual novels take this one step further to create a whole fictional structure that simply starts with certain reimagined possibilities. An example is the collection, *'The Best Alternate History Stories of the 20th Century'*, edited by Harry Turtledove. This contains fourteen of the most acclaimed works of counterfactual fiction by well-regarded writers of science and fantasy fiction.

Many such counterfactual novels have gone on to become best-sellers, including *'Fatherland'* by Robert Harris and Len Deighton's *'SS-GB'* which look at how the world might have appeared had the Nazis prevailed: possibly the most popular topic for counterfactual writers.

However, some speculative fiction that launches off from actual historical events might better be described as science fiction or fantasy writing – and so will fall more properly within the purview of the next chapter.

Sum of All Counterfactual Histories

Of course, what should make these alternative histories even more readable is that, where they deal with what might *possibly* have happened, one can be sure that they are actually playing out in some other corners of the Multiverse.

Apart from counterfactual histories, much general fiction also has its chance of being enacted in a real world, so long as the stories are logically consistent with a plausible reality. Conversely, we should remind ourselves, the real-life historical events and narratives we have lived through in our world may be no more than imagined tales and fantasy in countless *other* worlds.

Just consider this celebrated instance where life replicated art with uncanny accuracy.

In 1898, the struggling American short story author Morgan Robertson published his novella *'The Wreck of the Titan: Or*

Futility', about the world's biggest liner and its doomed voyage. Written a full 14 years before the disastrous maiden voyage of the *'Titanic'* - and well before even the idea of building such a vessel, his book almost exactly mirrors the tragic narrative of the *'RMS Titanic'* so familiar to us today.

The author's descriptions of the dimensions, tonnage and overall features of his *'Titan'* very closely matched those of its close namesake of 1912. Each described as 'unsinkable', both were triple-screw vessels travelling at similar speeds, and met disaster exactly 740 kms from Terranova in Newfoundland. Robertson even foresaw the precise cause of this tragic loss of life: a collision with an iceberg in the North Atlantic and a completely inadequate supply of lifeboats.

This set of remarkable coincidences should make it easier for us to accept that across a limitless Multiverse, every storyline or scenario will have its chance of being played out, providing it is based on events that hypothetically *could* happen, somewhere and sometime.

So, not just the plots and characters in many novels, but also those in films, stage plays and scenarios or narratives you could have encountered, are sure to be flesh-and-blood reality - somewhere.

And it may well be that, far, far out there in the Multiverse, a very real, handsomely saturnine Mr Darcy has just entered a room and fixed his penetrating gaze on a young Miss Elizabeth Bennet...

12. The Continuing Journey

Finding Ourselves in the Great Cosmic Scheme

Slipping in and out of delirium, Europe's most famous observational astronomer was fast approaching his end.

In a way, it was an absurd exit for the prominent Danish nobleman, Tycho Brahe. Only days earlier at an important banquet, he had sat through one long speech after another and, although desperate to empty his bladder, he had stoically stayed at table lest he be thought in breach of etiquette. The sad consequence was a rapidly worsening bladder blockage, infection, and now his present, final agony.

Tycho Brahe had certainly lived a picaresque life. A notorious carouser, he wore a brass prosthetic nose (having forfeited the original in a duel) and he had kept a full-grown pet elk, until it killed itself by drunkenly falling down the stairs of his palace! He usually dined with a supposedly clairvoyant court jester, the dwarf named Jepp.

Yet, for all his dissolute ways, Brahe was also a serious and respected scientist who, amongst other significant achievements, had compiled a vast collection of precise data on the movements of the planets and stars. From this he was able to challenge the belief, held since the time of Aristotle, that the celestial arena was immobile. But he knew that his meticulous sidereal logbooks still contained many more secrets yet to be uncovered.

The problem was that there was only one man in all of Europe who had both the astronomical and mathematical skills, not to mention the tireless perseverance, needed to tease out from this inchoate data the answers to questions that had puzzled generations of astronomers. His name was Johannes Kepler (1571-1630), a German who was in almost every way different to Brahe. While Kepler's reputation as an astronomer was, if anything, greater than that of the aristocratic Dane, his character and his life were otherwise the complete opposite. He was insecure and anxious, beset by constant financial problems, unhappy in his domestic life and, to cap it all, his own mother was an incautious spell-peddler who several times came close to being burned as a witch, only to be rescued at the last moment by her already over-burdened son.

Despite their mismatched temperaments, Brahe engaged Kepler. But, jealous of his precious data, Brahe only grudgingly fed out enough observational notes to keep his employee occupied, but little more. Again and again, he fobbed off Kepler's anxious pleas to see the body of his observational logbooks. But now, on his deathbed, this resistance changed: he accepted at last that he had to relent and hand over his data to the one individual who could realise its true worth. Only by so doing had he any hope of saving his lifework from being forfeited as a cartload of incomprehensible jottings.

As the sombre Kepler contemplated the pain-wracked noble who, for years, had been both his benefactor and tormentor, the ever-patient mathematician was finally granted full access to all the precious data. With that, the door swung open to astronomical discoveries that would resonate across ensuing ages. Fervently, the Danish noble implored Kepler to devote all his energies to releasing the secrets they both knew were buried in those notations, compiled so laboriously by Brahe and his assistants over many years.

These were his sad and desperate words: *'Let me not seem to have lived in vain!'*

The Eternal Yearning

Tycho Brahe's touching plea often comes to my mind whenever I ponder the perennial human longing to scratch one's name on Eternity's heavy iron door.

Our universe is a cold and lonely place for a mere mortal. It is incomprehensibly vaster than anyone could have imagined only a few decades ago and, as well, we now know that every single star and every single planet is on its own path to eventual extinction. Despite its enormity, our entire universe's inescapable fate is death: either in a fiery implosion or, more likely, in a long dying in the cold and dark night of eternity. Nothing escapes mortality, as the Buddhist scripture, *'The Diamond Sutra'*, reminds us:

'Thus shall ye think of all this fleeting world:
A star at dawn, a bubble in a stream,

A flash of lightning in a summer cloud,
A flickering lamp, a phantom, and a dream.

To be born, to live, to die... then to disappear, leaving nothing to remembrance and with the wheels of passing ages grinding on as if you had never been: who would not recoil from this prospect? Of course, some are sufficiently consoled by religion's promise of an afterlife, but for many others the best hope is that their life's achievements might outlive them just a little.

This is the yearning described by Schopenhauer thus:

'In the furthest depth of our being we are secretly conscious of our share in the inexhaustible spring of eternity, so that we can always hope to find life in it again.'

But is it possible, we may ask, to look for another way to avoid being swallowed up forever in complete oblivion? How are we to find an answer to this most profound question? And where are we to start looking?

The Cosmic Signpost
Over the centuries, sages and seers wanting to understand the world almost always started by looking to the heavens. The essential backdrop to every creation story, it was here, if anywhere, that we could hope to find our place and our compass points in the great cosmic scheme. From their long and close observations, our forebears built a cosmological platform and upon this they erected a full scaffolding of religion, laws, behaviours, rituals and sciences. Above all, they could

see in this celestial immensity a direct vision of the eternity transcending our brief lives and the most likely haven where one's soul might one day find deathless repose.

So deeply embedded was this habit that most Greek philosophers were impelled to anchor their schools of thought and prescriptions for living to a proprietary cosmology. Nearly always, this started by defining a simple building block as the basis of all matter. This approach, described as 'ontological reductionism', usually cited one of the four basic elements (fire, water, earth, air) as *the* primary substance upon which the material universe was constructed. Thus, Empedocles and Anaximenes both taught that air was the cardinal element. Heraclitus cast his vote for fire, while Thales advocated that water underpinned the universe. Later, Aristotle enlarged the debate by nominating a new, invisible element, *aether*.

In this way, one could add to the authority of one's interpretations and prescriptions regarding nature, mankind, society and the individual by linking it all the way back to a specific cosmology.

A very old and widespread habit, the inclination to place ideas about the human world within the context of universal first principles still persists. We can see it, for example, in the way that Karl Marx's economic and political prescriptions are based on a dialectical materialism that, in turn, is heavily indebted to Hegel's system of logic (such as his idea of the interplay between thesis, antithesis and synthesis), his philosophy of history, and beyond that to certain Greek insights.

For their part, Nazi ideologues and apologists drew selectively and mostly erroneously upon Victorian evolutionist pioneers like Charles Darwin and Sir Joseph Dalton Hooker.

However, this tendency should always be looked at with a sceptical eye. Indeed, the fallaciousness of such thinking was emphasised by the philosopher-mathematician, Bertrand Russell (1872-1970), towards the end of his *'A History of Western Thought'*:

'Philosophy, throughout its history, has consisted of two parts inharmoniously blended: on the one hand a theory as to the nature of the world, on the other an ethical or political doctrine as to the best way of living. The failure to separate these two with sufficient clarity has been a source of much confused thinking. Philosophers from Plato to William James, have allowed their opinions as to the constitution of the universe to be influenced by the desire for edification: knowing, as they supposed, what beliefs would make men more virtuous, they have invented arguments, often very sophistical, to prove that these beliefs are true.'

Mindful of Russell's admonition, I should hesitate to propose the Ocean of All Possibilities as a philosophical or ethical compass for humankind. However, we cannot avoid recognising that its perspectives do suggest (compel?) a radically new way of viewing our selves, our destiny, values and behaviour.

Such a change has happened before, as we have seen. Copernicus' challenge to the earth-centred Ptolemaic universe certainly amounted to more than merely a revised astronomical model. Once our Earth had lost its privileged position in the universe, thinking people were forced to see *themselves* differently: no longer at the cosmic epicentre, they took greater account of other worlds. Spurred along by Europe's rediscovery of Aristotle, curiosity was emboldened and extended by the Renaissance, the Enlightenment and the scientific and the industrial revolutions that followed.

Of course, as we know, this was a Faustian compact whose price was that, as we learnt ever more about the cosmos, we became increasingly mindful of our own vanishing significance. Having long been nurtured on the rich milk of self-esteem, Mankind found itself tumbling into cosmic negligibility in an unfathomed fall steeper than anything Milton could have imagined for proud Lucifer.

Now, with the suggestion that the scale of creation has moved to the infinite and eternal, our own relative physical significance would seem to have collapsed from the utterly miniscule to nothing, and so we must struggle to find any slightest meaning to our existence. In the light of these appalling revelations, how are we to find any place for our selves? Once again, we can start by looking skyward.

The Immortal Self
In Chapter 8 we considered how eternal recurrence, the Ocean of All Possibilities, might just deliver some form of immortality that could be thought plausible, even logical.

But, as I noted before, the prospect of one round of life retracing another, unceasingly through all eternity, would seem wearisome, if not horrifying, to many. Certainly, these would number devout Hindus and Buddhists, for whom salvation itself is defined as the final release from rebirth. In this context, many of us will have been impressed by how calmly the elderly and afflicted often face approaching death, obviously seeing in it a welcome, or at least timely, release from this one life alone.

However, I suggest that eternal recurrence could simultaneously liberate us from the fear of complete annihilation and, on the other hand, the awful burden of an endless continuum of consciously linked, identical experiences.

Instead, in the Multiverse, or Block Time, innumerable other different fates would also be explored by our 'selves' and by all those we know. Every sort of variation will be encountered, but the particular thread of consciousness within one life does not, apparently, connect with any of the myriad of your 'selves' following other life-pathways. That, surely, is a relief.

So, that flashing moment, the sideways look or the unknown face in a passing train window, the lover's bedroom fragrant with summer's night air: might those lace-delicate memories really be embedded in eternity, after all? Yes, and that long-ago day when a child looked out white-framed bay windows traced by rivulets of soft rain, and gazed at the gently waving cypresses: that, too, is being rediscovered endlessly in infinitely distant worlds.

And with all these, remember, are also to be found the slurry of day-to-day impressions and experiences, the ennui, the yearning, the arguments and every other tiresome component of a life being lived. Yes, all that, too, is preserved like a mayfly in amber, to be seen and experienced over and over forever.

So then, whether now remembered or forgotten, your whole life is clasped in eternity, ever to be relived as a unique, first-time experience. If this is so, how then can the old envy the young, or the young be dismissive of the old when, at one remove, our entire lives - from birth to death - are a single tapestry in the hall of timelessness? Think again of that fleeting moment, two millennia ago when Cicero paused to look across the blue waters of the Bay of Naples, contemplating the possibility that this scene might be mirrored again and again in a limitless cosmos? Captured in timeless eternity, is Cicero's unblinking gaze forever fixed on distant Puteoli?

Our Cosmic Interconnectedness

The renowned astronomer, Carl Sagan wrote and said much about our physical insignificance in a cosmos whose incalculable immensity is beyond any merely human frame of reference. It was clearly a preoccupying question for this thoughtful man.

The idea occurred to him that, for all our microbial inconsequence, what sets us apart and makes us rare and valuable is that *we are thinking and observing creatures* in what, as far as we yet know, could be an otherwise inanimate and insentient universe. Perhaps, as some suggest, our role really is central because we are the Universe contemplating itself, no less. Given that quantum mechanics long ago established that the act of observation imposes a physical effect upon the subatomic world, perhaps it may not be impossible that sentient beings like our selves likewise leave our imprint upon what we perceive on the much larger, cosmic scale?

This possibility, remote as it might seem, may hearten a scientist or a philosopher, but would hardly offer more than scant comfort to most existentially marooned individuals. We are all of us much more likely to warm to this other insight of Carl Sagan:

'For small creatures such as we, the vastness is bearable only through love.'

But what love? Love for whom - or for what? *'The love of all for all'*, is the reply we would hear from the greatest moral teachers of all ages, because love that is conditional, filtered or constrained within a silo is no love at all; it is *partiality*.

To me, the most fundamental divide in the way different individuals understand and relate to the world is not the separation between religious believers and non-believers. It is, I have long believed, the profound gulf between those who see themselves as part of a vast community of inter-related beings and phenomena and, on the other hand, those who see each individual as standing separate, even opposed, to everything outside self.

In the world of the disconnected individual, life is thinly supplied with universal values, meaning or overall context. They may find some satisfaction in narrow scriptural interpretations that are forever separating goats from the sheep, thus cleaving the world into the elect and, on the other side, the heathens, hell-deserving sinners, apostates and unbelievers.

And what about those who measure self-worth through the heaping up of material, and therefore transient, prizes or the equally ephemeral pursuits of celebrity or power? Almost always, this is a race in which there will always be someone ahead of you and where there is no finish line: and, in any case, of what value is the esteem of strangers? In short, here is a solipsistic limbo where everyone is at constant war with his fellow man and all this played out before an indifferent, or even seemingly hostile, cosmos. You are locked into a Manichean universe of unremitting struggle between two forever-irreconcilable forces: in this case, Self and All Else.

Then there are those who embrace, a sense of connection and unity with the world around them. Often realistic and tough-minded, they still accept that we live in a universe in which, ultimately, all phenomena and events are interwoven, and all minds and lives are part of a complete whole.

If my description of the Ocean of All Possibilities has any single effect on the imagination, it must surely be to open the window to a Multiverse in which even the least significant particle is linked eternally with everything and everyone else. With existence ever piling up on existence, the innumerable threads of individuation must finally be seen to weave into an infinite and seamless continuum of possibilities and existences, including like and dissimilar, opposites and contradictions. We - and everything - are linked to the great oneness; what the devotees of Hermes so many centuries ago called 'The Great Chain of Creation'.

Circles of Affinity

As our sense of shared community reaches, however erratically, farther into the outside world, we should discover that more and more entities are swept into the orbit of our care and concern. I use the term *Expanding Circles of Affinity* to describe the process of moving from infantile self-preoccupation to, by degrees, an identification with family or clan, through to nation, religious community and ethnicity, and beyond that to all humankind, then on to every living thing and, finally, to caring for *all* of creation, both animate *and* inanimate.

To go the other way is unthinkable. By way of example we could turn to Mario Puzo's epic story, *'The Godfather'*. This introduces us to an extended Mafia family whose moral horizon begins and ends with their own tight clan. With few exceptions, they treated those outside their Sicilian village of Corleone as either potential enemies or potential victims or both, typifying a Hobbesian culture that the political scientist, Edward C. Banfield (1916-1999) defined as 'amoral familism' in his book profiling a post-War Sicilian village, *'The Moral Basis of a Backward Society'*. At the other polarity is the archetypal example of Saint Francis, who saw the whole world and its creatures united and lovingly enveloped by God's benevolence.

As we grow away from infantile egocentricity, our gaze reaches out to ever more distant horizons and seeks insights into the greater and wider mysteries. In time, the tight readings of ancient and long-closed-off testimonies will surely become ever less satisfying or relevant.

Yet we must acknowledge that many lives have been inspired by religion, especially where they found a universalist and open pathway towards spiritual and mystical enrichment. Despite significant differences at their respective doctrinal starting places, those following these routes seem to converge with other seekers as they, too, approach their promised spiritual insights. As was said earlier, this is most evident in the remarkably similar ecstatic language and images they employ to describe what are clearly very similar experiences. For all the long and sorry history of religious cruelty and intolerance, these elevating epiphanies and the saintly benevolence they can inspire represent the most redeeming face of faith.

However, we ought not forget that a sense of oneness with all, 'cosmic consciousness' if you like, is also to be found among non-believers. For them it is a sense of community with all things, of marvelling wonder and open curiosity about all that surrounds them. Once again, Carl Sagan, always comes first to my mind when I think of how spiritual, and spiritually inspiring, an avowed atheist can be. Scientists and lovers of nature, but also artists, poets, painters, musicians, writers and ordinary, thoughtful individuals can share such insights and find their lives transformed accordingly.

Although I subscribe to no religion, I will always find more uplift in the rapturously mystical verses of the great Persian Sufi poet, Jalāl ad-Dīn Muhammad Rūmī, in Tchaikovsky's intensely moving Orthodox vespers and the marmoreal transcendence of Michelangelo's *Pieta* than I ever gain from the arid fixations of relentlessly pragmatic and earth-bound reductionists.

Open your eyes to the universal kinship that reaches across a world of apparent differences and you will discover that compassion and empathy flow inevitably. Once you intuitively grasp the ultimate oneness of all, everything becomes clear, particularly how you should behave to others. Formal rules are necessary, of course, but read only on their own they condense down to narrow, segmented and legalistic thinking that encourages, or at least, sustains, attitudes of 'us and the other' between individuals and communities - and that sad attitude is usually applied with even less compassion to the other creatures who share our planet.

By contrast, the ultimate spiritual aspiration - selflessness - frees us finally from egotism's circumscriptions and gives us our best chance of finding serenity. This is what great moral teachers have been telling us over long ages.

As Saint Francis of Assisi urged in his *'Canticle of the Creatures'*, we should extend our tender concern to our brothers and sisters, the birds in the air and all creatures on the land and in the sea. And then we embrace the rolling plains, the mountains, the sea, the Moon, the Sun and all the myriad stars of our vast Cosmos and everything beyond.

This is perfect, immersive love and it both creates, and is nourished by, all wisdom and all goodness. It brings joy and the deepest peace and it is the greatest fulfillment of one's humanity.

Remember, we were never truly separate and autonomous creatures: we are intimately bound to our universe in a very *physical* sense. To begin with, any atomic structure more complicated than the simplest of atoms (hydrogen and helium), was formed from those basic building blocks during titanic fusion processes. In the unimaginable heat deep within the bowels of each star, the energy and light generated from primordial atoms transformed them into ever-more complex atomic structures - or, in the case of heavier elements like uranium, during the cataclysmic death of a star in its supernova explosion. Thus, every atom in your body was created eons ago by a far distant, now long-dead sun: we are in the beautiful phrase of the astronomer, Carl Sagan, 'made of star-stuff.'

(Indeed, recent research suggests that up to half the material making up each individual originated in other, far-flung galaxies. Supercomputer simulations by a team of astrophysicists at Northwestern University, Illinois, suggest that over billions of years this material was blown into our cosmic neighbourhood by ancient supernova explosions and cosmic winds. Published recently as a full study by the UK's Royal Astronomical Society, these findings draw upon extensive earlier work on galaxy formation and it is hoped that they will be corroborated by planned Hubble Space Telescope and earth-based observations.)

Here, then, we turn again to W. Macneile Dixon's *'The Human Situation'*:

'We must rid ourselves of the notion that the universe is something outside ourselves, to which we accidentally belong. We are the universe, in every fibre of our body and being, nerve and thought, as are all other souls, each a microcosm of that macrocosm. There is a saying attributed to Hippocrates and quoted by Leibniz, that "animals are not born and do not die, and that the things which we suppose to come into Being merely appear and disappear". And with this opinion we are in agreement.'

Handling Good & Evil

For the philosopher and the person in the street, the matter of ethics is always a big question; how are we to live within the eternal interplay between good and evil? Above all, how are we to reconcile that good and innocent people can be buffeted by one affliction after another, while habitual wrongdoers reach comfortable old age without ever being brought to account?

Most religions assure us that every wrong and inequity suffered will be recompensed for in the next life, yet even so their most unquestioning votaries still cannot look upon gross injustice in *this* life with any equanimity.

On the other hand, the hard rationalist may argue bluntly that this is how it is, and how it must be, in a universe in which life, including that of reflective beings, is no more than a very rare and interesting phenomenon. It is a fortuitous and accidental occurrence for which we must unquestioningly give thanks... and then get on with things as best we can.

With our lives so fleeting and insignificant, such a person would say, it hardly matters what occurs during our fistful of days, especially as to whether we are happy or miserable. After all, how little do we worry about the tribulations faced by a cockroach? The individual brave enough to accept this meagre view of our utter negligibility in the cosmic scheme is only lightly armed to contend with the inescapable turmoil of life, and has little consolation to offer any one else.

Within a Multiverse, however, it is possible to imagine a justice of sorts. In our eternal passage of lives we will encounter every dilemma and setback, cruel ailments and loss, but we will also enjoy every species of success; here and there, we will win great prizes and be garlanded by fame, fortune and acclaim. Every one of us!

Gauged in this way, good or bad luck now seem much less arbitrary when our fortunes are set against eternity. In fact, charting fate's vagaries soon settles down into an utterly predictable, actuarial exercise as we scan across more and more of our lives. Added together, the ups and downs of all these many narratives start to average out into a profile that matches exactly the balance of good and bad seen in the mean profile for the life of an individual such as oneself.

To put it more directly, while it is easy to imagine going into a casino on a very lucky night and coming out flush with winnings, the odds of enjoying such a winning streak every night over, say, a month quickly become vanishingly small. Pretty soon, the house odds will have become as inescapably intrusive as a fundamental law of nature. I have gambled modestly in three casinos in my life - on the island of Malta, in the Chinese city of Macau and in Australia's Sydney - and on each occasion managed to emerge with useful winnings from the roulette table, of all things.

Nonetheless, I knew that the more one plays, the more unrelentingly and brutally the house odds intrude - and the less sustainable a lucky run becomes. So, determined to protect my status as 'the one who got away', I vowed never to approach the green baize table ever again.

The point is that the bigger the sample or the longer the play, the more predictably do the results match the statistical average – and eternity, being a very large and long sample, will see that not the slightest deviation to that rule is tolerated! Thus we can be sure that, whatever their individual fates, our many-mirrored selves will collectively reap an equal and exact dispensation of karmic justice.

Perhaps this is our answer, after all. Assured of an equal and impartial balance between good and bad in the long run of countless lives, should we not temper any envy for those lucky in *this* life, yet also remain mindful of the plight of those who struggle in the present round of existence?

Perhaps the Stoics do have something important to pass on to this age, after all. They proclaimed, and tried to live by, a life-philosophy that was serenely indifferent to life's unpredictable vagaries, regarding both good and bad fortune as relative and transient. They saw the accumulation of petty advantage as a distraction and an imposition. Your charge, they would say, is to live in accord with Nature and a good society and to guard your honour and virtue as the *real* attainments of a laudable life. All of us have a worthy role to play, big or small, and we should each carry it out as well as we can, trying always to live in accord with the larger world as it is.

Whether these insights really can offer much cheer to most of us in *this* world, I cannot say. But, to those who understand *amor fati*, the love of one's fate, I suggest an intriguing thought. Imagining your numberless lives and fates, all utterly unknown and unknowable each to the other, are you not curious about all the astonishing experiences you are destined to encounter out in your there-now, even if so few are ever to be found in *this* here-now?

Quantum Karma

If limitless life-lines permit one to act in all sorts of ways, seeking out every possible situation leading to every possible experience or outcome, does this not grant license to behave just as we please in *this* existence?

What, after all, is the significance of a moral transgression in this life if we can yet make good in the course of countless other existences?

Remember, this was the very opportunity explored by Bill Murray's Weatherman in the film *'Groundhog Day'*, when he discovered the same day endlessly repeating itself.

To this, I would offer the following answer: according to Dr Hugh Everett's 'Many Worlds' theory, new universes continue to split off with every action at every instant of your life. Up to the point of each hiving off, the two potential versions of you and the world around you were identical, but what happens thereafter in each case follows its own different trajectory.

Consider then that, if you are doing something wrong, that will be the legacy carried on into all those other self-manifestations, on and on, constantly bifurcating through eternity. Conversely, all your good thoughts, behaviours and actions will also be relayed across countless lives, providing launch-pads that will benignly direct your uncountable future narratives, including those of the other innumerable beings you touch across the Multiverse.

This thought echoes the Hindu and Buddhist doctrine of Karma, which says that even your smallest act spreads out like a ripple on a pond to project influence near and far - and, eventually touching a faraway bank, will then return to you once more. That everything we do has far-reaching consequences for ourselves and countless others is an idea that links with, and reinforces, the cosmic interconnectedness talked about earlier. Thus, if we are an individual part of the great Ocean of All Possibilities, should we then not conduct ourselves in a way that best protects the interests of all and everything?

In the Multiverse, I believe, we each carry a big responsibility to live our lives thoughtfully and well.

However, if we look at the Block Time-Multiverse model, as opposed to Everett's unadorned Many Worlds proposition, then we cannot be seen to be authoring different starting points for particular trajectories: they already exist anyway, waiting for a conscious mind to explore them. But the fact that one direction is taken more frequently than another, may well reinforce the Sum-Over-All-Histories bias described by the physicist Richard Feynman. This suggests that the frequency with which one choice (or event collapse) is made affects the likelihood of future similar choices being preferred. In this case, we are looking at swinging more pathways towards virtuous or kindly behavior, rather than towards bad or selfish conduct.

The Boundless Self

How can one see oneself as an integral and eternal (albeit miniscule) part of the Cosmos without also sloughing off narrow egotism and selfish striving? In that process we are lifted above the countless small anxieties and aggravations that daily assail us: our reflex will be to see them, not in terms of how they afflict our personal well-being, but rather their inconsequence within an infinitely wider context. At this level of enlightenment, even one's own mortality may be regarded with serenity.

On this, I can think of nothing better than this passage from Leo Tolstoy's masterpiece, *'War and Peace'*. Here the introspective Russian aristocrat, Pierre, Count Bezukhov, was a captive of Napoleon's invading soldiery and, along with a group of fellow prisoners, was awaiting execution.

'The sun had set long since. Bright stars shone out here and there in the sky. A red glow as of a conflagration spread above the horizon from the rising full moon, and that vast red ball swayed strangely in the gray haze. It grew light. The evening was ending, but the night had not yet come. Pierre got up and left his new companions, crossing between the campfires to the other side of the road where he had been told the common soldier prisoners were stationed. He wanted to talk to them. On the road he was stopped by a French sentinel who ordered him back.

Pierre turned back, not to his companions by the campfire, but to an unharnessed cart where there was nobody. Tucking his legs under him and dropping his head he sat down on the cold ground by the wheel of the cart and remained motionless a long while sunk in thought. Suddenly he burst out into a fit of his broad, good-natured laughter, so loud that men from various sides turned with surprise to see what this strange and evidently solitary laughter could mean.

"Ha-ha-ha!" laughed Pierre. And he said aloud to himself: "The soldier did not let me pass. They took me and shut me up. They hold me captive. What, me? Me? My immortal soul? Ha-ha-ha! Ha-ha-ha!..." and he laughed till tears started to his eyes.

A man got up and came to see what this queer big fellow was laughing at all by himself. Pierre stopped laughing, got up, went farther away from the inquisitive man, and looked around him.

The huge, endless bivouac that had previously resounded with the crackling of campfires and the voices of many men had *grown quiet, the red campfires were growing paler and dying down. High up in the light sky hung the full moon. Forests and fields beyond the camp, unseen before, were now visible in the distance. And farther still, beyond those forests and fields, the bright, oscillating, limitless distance lured one to itself. Pierre glanced up at the sky and the twinkling stars in its faraway depths. "And all that is me, all that is within me, and it is all I!" thought Pierre. "And they caught all that and put it into a shed boarded up with planks!" He smiled, and went and lay down to sleep beside his companions.'*

Finding Mindfulness

In our day-to-day lives we are preoccupied with furthering our self-regarding interests. Within limits, of course, that is how it should be, for life would soon trample us underfoot if we did not adequately shift for ourselves. Nonetheless, every reflective individual must occasionally rise above the daily tumult to look at life in its much wider context - and, once in a while, reflect that he or she has a valued place in the wider scheme of things.

Should one grasp, rationally *and* intuitively, that the Ocean of All Possibilities is an undifferentiated, single entity, surely one must be close to attaining 'Cosmic Consciousness'. This term was developed in the 19th century by a Canadian psychiatrist called Richard M. Bucke (1837-1902) to describe a direct, personal *experience* of the essential unity of the cosmos. His book, *'Cosmic Consciousness: A Study in the Evolution of the Human Mind'* (1901), was a classic account of the mystical state that drew upon his own experience and the accounts of many individuals throughout history who, he believed, had reached this higher state of consciousness. Among these was his close friend, the poet Walt Whitman. According to Bucke, cosmic consciousness represents the most evolved level of human mental and spiritual development.

When we look at how he describes the lives and utterances of individuals who likely possessed this attribute, we can see they intellectually grasp that, behind the mere appearances of difference, there is the reality of indivisible unity. But more than that, they also seem to have an intuitive grasp of this ineffable truth; they know it as a personally experienced encounter.

So how then, one wonders, is the unenlightened searcher to attain such an insight? Especially, is it even possible to attain the slightest acquaintance with a reality outside linear time, when everything we know and see seems to testify against it?

In a way, most of us have already had a foretaste of such an ego-transcending state of mind. Have you ever been transfixed by indescribable beauty or touched by an epiphany that, momentarily, sends you soaring above selfhood, time and place? For me, a great symphony will do that - or a magnificently primordial natural vista, a diamond-spangled sky, or the ageless, shoreward march of serried waves. In such special moments we may be brushed, however lightly, by the ageless and the numinous.

Beyond these, often serendipitous, encounters, can one learn to see the world in this way, all the time? I believe, yes, one can – and it is through the time-honoured practice of meditation.

I was privileged to study and practise under the instruction of a Zen teacher for some eight years, until his retirement. Bill Rait, a Scot, taught in the Soto Zen tradition, which is very much focused on *zazen*, or sitting meditation. I appreciated his austere approach that relied very little on ritual and devotional activity: all very much in keeping with the Caledonian Calvinism of his upbringing! The ego-constrained mindfulness cultivated during regular meditation sessions eventually spills over into one's everyday life, to a greater or lesser extent. This is not only calming and psychologically enriching, but it may also make one receptive to the idea, and the intuitive experience, of a world of non-duality and non-linear time, and with that, the sense of being unbounded... and deathless.

Inspiring This Life

Among your innumerable Multiversal selves you are inescapably predestined to confront all that can be experienced, and it has been thus throughout all time. Surely, this thought must temper wild exultation or deep despair at what happens in this world? But this is no invitation to passive fatalism: after all, if every possible achievement is to be attained somewhere among your ensemble of numberless lives, why should you not also make something positive and special happen along *this* life-path?

T. S. Eliot's poem *'Burnt Norton'*, tells of the unfulfilled possibilities we all pass by in life, whether through choice, neglect or necessity:

'Footfalls echo in the memory
Down the passage which we did not take

Towards the door we never opened
Into the rose-garden.'

Hinduism and Buddhism, with their belief in endless cycles of rebirth, are commonly thought in the West to engender a passive fatalism. While this shallow assumption may not survive a close-up encounter with the frenetic energy of an Asian city, for some the prospect of recurring lives, each offering the chance to revisit what one did or did not do in a previous existence, might *possibly* take the urgency out of one's present striving.

If death no longer imposes the ultimate deadline, but merely ushers in a sabbatical break, why not defer that challenging enterprise to another life? Considering the infinite iterations of your life promised by the Ocean of All Possibilities, well, why not let this existence be the one in which I ease my foot off the accelerator? What is the rush, after all? I write this wondering if I might succumb to competing distractions, or to just plain procrastination, that could rob me of a completed book: but what of that? Absolutely certainly, my book will be published - is published - in countless other universes and, if excoriated in some, ignored in yet others, it will as certainly be received well somewhere else. So, need I drive myself so hard when surely, after all my labours, I have earned a little respite?

No, I say! Of course I will achieve, and have achieved, great, ambitious enterprises in elsetimes, even against crushing odds and have succeeded beyond my most extravagant dreams. But then I must ask: why not in *this* existence, too?

For me, the near-certain knowledge that a possibility must become a reality somewhere is a sharp spur to action - and leaves no excuse for dreamy indolence! Can you leave to your other selves, or to some almost identical you, a task that you could have achieved in this here and now? So then, let us give things that 'red-hot go' in *this* lifetime!

As Tycho Brahe would surely exhort us: "May you not seem to have lived in vain!'.

A Consolation

The strand of each life must find its end eventually, yet every experience it encounters is immortal - and so also is everyone you have ever known or everything you ever treasured. Is this a thought to turn to when afflicted by sorrow or setback? Would the loss of a loved one be made a little more bearable if you could hope that he or she - and every smallest moment of the life you had shared - might be living on elsewhere, and forever? That all those you ever cared for, and you with them, yet exist in other worlds just like this one, even if beyond your present purview?

Contemplating a young life, full of bloom and promise, and cut down tragically short of its natural season, we are engulfed by what must seem beyond consolation or, even, comprehension. But there may be some balm in the hope that, in the endless round we are all fated to travel, some lives will be short and unfulfilled, just as in others we will look back over many rich and fulfilled years. In the bowl of eternity, you can be sure that the one you cherished lives still and, somewhere, enjoys what they might have been robbed of here.

This was the consoling thought that inspired a grieving French professor of mathematics to record his meditations upon the loss of his wife. Acclaimed author Jacques Roubard's collection of poems and prose - *'The Plurality of Worlds of Lewis'* - was an eloquent elegy for his late, young wife in which he explored the possibility that she might yet be living and loving him in another, parallel world.

Translated into English by Rosmarie Waldrop, the title was inspired by the previously mentioned book by philosopher David Kellogg Lewis, *'On the Plurality of Worlds'* which outlined his theory of modal reality.

In this poem, *'Division of Worlds'*, Roubard spoke of a longing to join his wife in that other, unreachable world in which she still lives:

'This world: split into two irreducible, unconnected space-times.

In one of the two halves, all points are joined from arc to arc; in the other, likewise.

But between them nothing, not even arrow: impassable space.

One cannot cross from one sub-world to another, one cannot cross alive. Or dead.

Me here, you there. Not together. Over there I'm dead

Over there no more than here, we are no longer in the world together

(You will die there, I here)

In return you are, are there, still. It is the only consolation. Survival is too big a word.'

In the Plurality of Worlds, every destiny is yours. Right now, in some universe and in some other timeline, you are holding a lottery ticket in your shaking hands – and trying to comprehend that you have just secured a life of security and almost boundlessly open possibilities. You are also, somewhere, sitting in a quiet room and noticing the deepening lines on a loved parent's face. And elsewhere, you are turning to wave goodbye to your misty-eyed mother as you start your first day at school.

This exact life of yours is being re-enacted endlessly, not one cycle after another, but simultaneously across the Multiverse. This very day, this very minute, is replicated down a double-mirrored corridor stretching into infinity and, as well, so is every other day of this life of yours, past and future. In fact, the whole span of your whole life, including every detail and every small event, exists right now in the Multiverse, and it will always so exist, just as it always has. Among all these parallel existences you are finding every longed for thing that was denied you in this life, or the things that you feared or that you might never even have dared imagine. But do you say:

'None of these other 'selves' are really me - they are simulacra, avatars or, at best, simply versions of me that happen to share all or most of my characteristics - but otherwise are other people still, even if my doppelgangers.'

Then reflect on this question: are you really the same person you were a decade ago, or even yesterday? Buddhist teaching says that you are not. It tells us that there is no fixed self and that we are in a continuing state of change. Psychologists also concur with the idea that the brain is subject to subtle but continuing change over the years.

'But, we have no memory or knowledge of these other lives - so how could they still be me?'

Consider: every night most of us dream, yet apart from faint echoes, we wake to recall little of that phantom life we lead in our sleep. Yet is not that dreamer still the very same person as the conscious you, awake and here?

You Forge Your Own Universe

Finally, consider this: what if, together with every other sentient being, you really do cause a new world to spin into life with every action and every choice you make? Remember, this is the central premise of the Many Worlds model, which simply applies the 'event-collapse' mechanism on a cosmic scale, in the way that laboratory experiments show it operating at the sub-atomic level. Remarkably, this would make you the author of a unique reality that, by your own individual action, you pull out of the tangled skein of possibilities contained within Multiverse-Block Time. Others have pondered over the implications of this astonishing possibility - and have written on it. Professor M.R. Franks put it this way in his book, *'The Universe and Multiple Reality'*:

'There is no one reality. Each of us lives in a separate universe. That's not speaking metaphorically. This is the hypothesis of the stark nature of reality suggested by recent developments in quantum physics. Reality in a dynamic universe is non-objective. Consciousness is the only reality.'

To create your own very real universe, as quantum theory suggests: does that not tell of god-like power? And does it not make your life significant?

13. A Compass For Our Time

A Perspective for Living

We live in remarkable times.

We now know so much more about ourselves, our world and the Cosmos. Mysteries long thought unfathomable are explicable, and most of what is not yet fully understood will be clarified sooner or later, we confidently expect. Indeed, the physicist Stephen Hawking and many of his colleagues believed that the holy grail of physics, the so-called Theory of Everything, is now almost within our grasp and then we shall have an account of all creation: the nature of matter, the origin of our universe, everything.

Our field of vision and depth of understanding have changed considerably, and surprisingly rapidly, too. And every time we rolled back the unknown, we not only saw our world in a slightly different way, but ourselves also.

We hardly appreciate just how unsettling some of today's foundation ideas once were. Yet if a transformative revelation arrives with a seismic shock, it soon becomes uncontested orthodoxy. Consider what imagination, even intellectual bravery, was needed to let go of a familiar world, so obviously flat, for the preposterous idea of a globe floating unsupported in empty space! Yet, in time our early astronomers and navigators came to accept this idea comfortably. And in our own age intelligent people are just starting to accept the counterintuitive, yet demonstrable, fact that subatomic particles can occupy two places at once. Again and again, our 'commonsense' view of the world is brusquely shoulder-charged to one side by science!

So, despite that most of us seem prewired with a strong Newtonian bias, one day the Multiverse - a surreal proposition that could have been penned by Lewis Carroll - might also become an unremarkable, even conventional, notion.

Unforeseen Transformations

When they first appear, few breakthroughs signal where they might lead once their full potential is realised. Faraday's discoveries about electricity aroused little interest among his contemporaries, outside of a small scientific circle. At that time, not even the most inquisitive and unfettered minds could guess how radically his new insights would transform the human condition; that his table-top experiments in a small workshop would herald in an entirely new civilisation in which ordinary men and women could command powers far beyond Prospero's magical gifts.

This continued to be true of many other scientific and technological advances since. In fact, not even the optimistic visionaries driving these innovations had the slightest inkling of where they would all lead.

Let us take the case of Charles Darwin. As soon as his *'The Origin of the Species'* came off the presses in 1859, it was snapped up by naturalists and biologists, as he had hoped. But Darwin had not guessed that most sales of his book would be to laypeople acting only on the rumour that his revelations were about to jolt the intellectual landscape of their time. Here was no mere dissertation on the adaptation of finches to the environments of isolated islands, but an idea that must collide head-on with the scripture-buttressed orthodoxy of the day. And that was exactly what was to happen, and much more besides.

Little wonder that the entire first edition of *'The Origin of the Species'* was sold out on its first day of publication.

It was Darwinism, far above the Enlightenment's undirected sentiments, which drove the notion of man's perfectibility: a complete heresy to those religionists who preached the innate sinfulness and *imperfection* of man.

After all, the reasoning went, if evolution were an established fact, then all species, humankind included, could be regarded as works in progress. With conscious effort, guided by science's sure hand, might we improve our stock infinitely faster and more purposefully than blind nature? Abetted by a torrent of wondrous new technologies, here was our chance to transform ourselves, physically, mentally, morally, culturally and socially!

That impulse propelled much of the idealism and progress of the nineteenth and twentieth centuries, as it still does today. It convinced multitudes that they could challenge the fate allotted to them and forge a better destiny; and that their continued passivity and fatalism could be questioned.

Then there was the other side of the coin. The notion of the perfectibility of man, as consciously articulated Darwinism, also created monsters that were to configure the twentieth century as profoundly as technology's positive achievements. National Socialism's drive to create the Aryan ideal man, a racially-cleansed *Übermensch* imbued with unsentimental hardness and indomitable will, was, in terms of lives lost, as cruel and costly as the mad commitment to incarnate the New Soviet Man out of unremitting class struggle and Stalin's gulags.

Despite those failed dystopias built on perverted ideologies, and despite the social and economic cost of other man-made 'paradises', we remain deeply attached to the idea that we are moving towards a better world. Since Darwin, it has been widely assumed that evolution leads us inexorably towards a secular Eden where we will find ourselves more intelligent and moral, and more artful custodians of our planet.

As it happened, Darwin never subscribed to such a teleological interpretation of his theory: he simply stated that the best adapted to a particular environment would outbreed those less well adapted. There is no over-spanning imperative that impels life along a pre-ordained pathway, and we certainly have no reason to flatter ourselves that human intelligence was ever the manifest goal of 3.8 billion years of biological evolution. It has been stated that our superior intelligence is merely an adaptive feature, albeit a superbly versatile tool.

(It took more than 2.9 billion of those 3.8 billion years for single-celled life to make room for multicellular organisms. After that hiatus, vertebrates appeared in the sea 540 million years ago, with amphibians migrating to the land around 150 million years later. Since then, all kinds of land creatures have appeared and disappeared, with our ancestors coming on the scene only two million years ago. Evidently, what some see as evolution's end goal – producing human intelligence - was not a pressing or urgent priority.)

Now we come to the question: 'Does the Multiverse itself have any evolutionary direction? Does the endlessly churning matrix of the Multiverse lead to 'better' universes, such as those increasingly friendly to the development of conscious life?'

It is hard to think so. Otherwise we would have already arrived at this absolute perfection. An eternity ago, we would have fetched up at the Panglossian paradise, 'the best of all possible worlds' described by Liebniz. In any case, the idea of such progress first requires us to accept that the Multiverse is guided by a teleological, directed purpose operating on a cosmic level, despite there being no evidence for it at the level of our own biological existence.

Searching for Our Compass Bearing

At the very time when we understand so much more about our physical world, many in the increasingly secular western world are less certain about who they are and where they fit into the scheme of things. Science tells us much, but it does not give us a fully coherent narrative about the overall human condition itself.

This is an uncomfortable position to be in. After all, few past societies got by without a clear religious or philosophical route-map. Whether we look at primitive cultures or sophisticated civilisations, a shared belief system has an important role in binding a community together, for giving context and meaning to our activities, providing consolation and above all, for helping us define a set of ethical values that we can all live by or, at least, understand.

This age offers us little in the way of real choice. Unquestioned and exclusive Church authority has been in retreat ever since the new printing presses and the rediscovery of the Greek thinkers launched the Renaissance and, with it, an unstoppable surge of febrile curiosity and intrepid speculation. Peering up to the heavens, astronomers mustered the evidence that eventually challenged the Church's standing as the sole commentator not only on the spiritual realm, but on the physical world as well. The scepticism and rationality of the Enlightenment continued the advance and then in the nineteenth century began a still-accelerating process of scientific discovery.

All this left a void that many sought to fill with the quasi-religion of Communism and then, later, by the several versions of fascism and nation-worship. In turn, these discredited belief systems gave way to a vague set of humanistic beliefs that, while worthy enough, still fall well short of defining a universal ethos.

Thus, while most get by with little more than a vague scepticism, others avidly explore all sorts of New Age exotica: ancient beliefs brought back from obscurity and newly coined cults framed upon science fiction fantasies. Then there are the fundamentalist and illiberal reinterpretations of established religions that present a direct, atavistic attack on modernism and civilised tolerance. Vulnerable or alienated individuals, struggling in a confusing and rapidly changing world, too easily read their vehemence and conviction as credibility and clarity.

At the other end, some see in science an alternative to religion or philosophy, but here the problem is that science in itself is not a *belief* system. Quite the opposite: science is a mode of enquiry that is largely about provisional positions on specific questions that always remain challengeable. The eminent philosopher of science, Karl Popper, bluntly stated that anything that is not capable of being put to the test of falsification is, pure and simple, not scientifically valid. That, it has to be said quite clearly, should also apply to the Multiverse, Block Time, and so on. Scepticism, resolute and persistent and not absolute belief or faith, is what drives science and, it has to be said, should drive all scientists.

Most people face a choice between, on one hand, the creeds that conflict with science and any rational interpretation of the world, and, on the other, a coldly logical world-view that inadequately addresses those perennial questions that most concern us at psychological or spiritual levels. Fortunately, we generally are guided by a wired-in inclination to goodness and altruism, yet it makes a big difference that these virtues are also defined, endorsed and reinforced by a code of values, practices and language shared by our wider society. Indeed, it is almost impossible to point to any culture or or era where this has not been found to be so. Quite plausibly, some scientists suspect that human evolution acknowledges the advantages of an embedded group-binding system of shared beliefs, behaviours and rituals.

In the absence of a relevant and commonly shared belief system or world-view, what the philosophers describe with the German term *weltanschauung*, a society lacks a reliable compass direction. One consequence of this may be rising moral relativism or even nihilism. Unguided by a reliable bearing, some warn us, individuals may feel less connected to each other and the wider world, and could sink into narcissistic materialism and self-preoccupation or, too often, destructive behaviour.

The Roman Experience

The situation in today's developed world is not unique. In fact, we have the detailed account of an advanced society that similarly found itself adrift, with almost nothing adequate to offer the dispossessed and spiritually hungry. It was incomparably the greatest power the world had ever seen and, in one form or another, it lasted more than a millennium before falling, it is said, as much from its own internal dissolution as from external shocks.

Rome's state religion was an untidy wicker-basket of gods inherited from the Etruscans, some 'rebadged' Greek deities and not a few accretions from other Mediterranean societies. To this burgeoning pantheon Rome would begin adding deified emperors, such as Augustus. There soon came a time when all emperors were deemed to be divine and the refusal to respectfully – and publicly - accept this by any Roman subject was seen as treason: an issue of great difficulty for the rigorously monotheistic Jews.

The Roman religion's essential purpose was simply to keep the wheels of state turning smoothly: to ensure bountiful harvests, military success and the avoidance of plagues and natural and civil calamities. Helping bind together the various levels of a very stratified society, its public rituals were very much central to the state apparatus, with the emperor of the day holding the position of the head priest, or *pontifex maximus* (greatest bridge-builder, a title inherited and retained by the Christian popes to this day). Thus, Roman religious practices were largely civic functions at which the great masses' only real role was that of spectator.

The fate of ordinary folk in this life, much less the next, was of little consequence to the gods: the plebs had to get by on their own resources, aided by charms, spells and a little luck. The jostling pantheon on Mount Olympus in Thessaly, home to both Greek and Roman gods, offered the individual little promise of a better lot in the afterlife, any reward for virtue or redress for wrongdoing. Indeed, the accounts of the hereafter were generally very vague, and where at all specific, not in the least appetising. The emperor was assured of divine status, but little was held out for anyone else beyond a half-existence as a wandering shade pining for the material world they had left behind.

In a teeming city of a million, often rootless and alienated, inhabitants, beset on all sides by danger and uncertainty, there must have been an enormous spiritual vacuum. Slave and senator alike, they needed only look around them to understand well what Virgil meant in his *'Aeneid'*:

'Sunt lacrimae rerum et mentem mortalia tangent.'
(There are tears in things and the mind is touched by mortality.)

Not surprisingly, the educated classes sought refuge in philosophy. As we read earlier, the two main Greek schools, Epicureanism and Stoicism, were much more than what we today understand a philosophy to be. They were, in fact, comprehensive belief systems that started with their own explanations for the physical world and human society and then proceeded to prescribe a full set of guidelines for the inner, and the public, person.

Stoicism's stronger following meant its covert influence continued through the Christian era, enjoying a revival during the Renaissance, and still having its adherents and admirers to this very day.

With its rationality, indifference to worldliness and a firm commitment to good, Stoicism made much of the equal brotherhood of man, an ideal underlined by the fact, mentioned before, that the two best-read Stoic writers were - and still are - the slave Epictetus and the Emperor Marcus Aurelius.

However, such an austere credo found few adherents among the masses. Instead, their thirst for religious meaning and comfort was slaked by an array of exotic gods and cults drawn from across the Empire's vast reaches. The cosmopolitan inflow into Rome was considerable and, unsurprisingly, the new arrivals brought their various beliefs with them. Noting the influx of Asians and their alien ways, the first century A.D. poet, Juvenal, quoted an acquaintance's fear that 'the Orontes was emptying itself into the Tiber'.

Roman legionaries returned from their distant postings with all sorts of new beliefs and superstitions in their backpacks, usually monotheistic. These were more accessible and, it was thought, more helpful than the native Roman gods, and, above all, they offered their devotees a guaranteed afterlife. Usually, their rites were more directly participatory, theatrical and emotionally satisfying than the measured pomp of the state religion.

From Egypt came the worship of the Egyptian goddess Isis, who soon became so popular that she elbowed her way into the main Roman pantheon. Among the many other new beliefs was the cult of the goddess Cybele, then came the worship of the Persian Mithra (taken by Roman soldiery as far as Britain) and, of course, Christianity itself.

If a second century citizen had been asked to pick the religion most likely to succeed, Christianity would have seemed an unlikely contender. The followers of 'Chrestus' represented the lowest stratum of the Eternal City's underclass and operated like a secret society that was, for a while, regarded by many as no more than an unusually aberrant Jewish sect.

Yet Christianity offered what the others could not match. It was a universal religion that held out the promise of salvation to even the lowliest slave, and its guarantor was a personal deity who had sent a human-divine intercessor to this world. Moreover, Christianity taught a universal compassion that hitherto was quite foreign to the hardened Roman mind.

Because its messages were what the times hungered for, Christianity (with the help of the Emperor Constantine) killed off the old gods and conquered the Empire, irreversibly shaping all of Europe and many lands beyond.

Where Are We Now?

Two millennia after the birth of Christ, many in the West now stand where late pagan Romans stood... ready and hungry for a new explanation and inspiration.

As I said, many Western societies are described as essentially 'post-Christian'. Whatever nominal allegiances might be admitted to, only a very small minority in most European and Australasian countries, and a declining majority in North America, go inside a church even once a year. And the children brought up in this cheerful semi-paganism are hardly likely to reverse the process *en masse*.

For most mainstream Western religions, the bothersome issue of science is now largely out of the way: in the face of overwhelming evidence, science's tenets are generally accepted by most religious authorities, rather than scripture's literal explanations. The long retreat of revelation from where it adjudicated on the detail of our world continues. But what do we now have in its stead?

As in the later Roman Empire, we see people turning from the old verities to dabble with arcane cults, faddish beliefs and esoteric superstitions of old and new provenance. Today's emporium of beliefs is a sellers' market in which the most bizarre and fantastical creed will find its eager devotees. Bookshelves are stacked high with a choice of titles on esoteric beliefs that rivals fad diet books!

If they are answerable to no god or higher authority, such as a set of distinct and venerated cultural values, there is the danger that some may decide they are answerable only to themselves – and we all know how exculpatory our judgments are when it comes to marking down self-interest!

From a socio-evolutionary perspective, the role of religion is not primarily to explain the world, but to rein in anti-social behaviour and to employ something more effective than brawn and weapons to curtail some individuals' wilder impulses. Wouldn't a tribal chieftain feel more secure with an omnipotent god or priesthood backing up his authority, rather than his own inattentive men-at-arms only? Especially if that god could keep a watchful eye on wavering individuals when no mortal warden was about!

Likewise, in our times, we generally feel more comfortable under the umbrella of values broadly shared across our community. Fast communitarian bonds require not only the assent of the moral elite and the educated, but also that those at the outer margins embrace these values, including the ethics, laws, civilities, rituals and the courtesies that follow from them. Remember, it is not enough that such values are widely understood: they must be recognised as relevant and valuable. That is how traffic rules, anti-litter laws and ethical norms work.

A Guide for Living?

Looking at the evening television current affairs, a sceptic might think that if humanity walked away from all religion our planet would be afflicted by much less strife. Muslim sect against Muslim sect, discord between Muslims and Jews, Christians against Muslims, Hindus fighting Muslims, Buddhists against Hindus and Muslims: this sorry catalogue covers many disgraceful pages.

Nowhere was the contest between people of faith as protracted or sanguinary as the holocaust carried out in Christ's name in Europe only a few centuries ago. But if one imagines that conflicts between Catholics and Protestants had all mercifully ended in the 15th century, I can vouch from personal experience that this is not entirely so. As a journalist in Northern Ireland in the late 1960s, I witnessed violent tribal hatred in that small Province's protracted civil war, euphemistically described as 'The Troubles'. True, there were also many historical, ethnic and cultural factors behind this antagonism, but I am convinced that religious sectarianism was its mainspring. Certainly, had there been even a little interdenominational mingling over generations, it is unlikely things would have come to such a tragic pass.

The problem with most rigidly prescriptive belief systems is that they claim to speak with the assured authority of God or a god-like secular authority, and their doctrines are encased in closed and unchallengeable books. But worst of all, they are exclusivist: uncompromisingly, they set apart their faithful believers from the infidels and apostates.

In a shrinking world in which we are so interdependent for our security and prosperity, and in which the devastation of conflict and war has been so extended by technology, we simply cannot sustain any creed that proclaims anything less than the universal sisterhood and brotherhood of humankind.

We need to clearly define such an ethic, and then begin to actively promulgate it everywhere. Many recall when, some years ago, an outward-bound spacecraft on the edge of the outer solar system swung its camera homeward and sent us a fuzzy dot of several pixels of blue light. That image of our small and lonely Earth, sent over many billions of kilometres, should be enough to convince us to live in amity and to work together as one, if only to nurture and protect our vulnerable little world, drifting so alone in an incomprehensibly vast blackness.

Yes, images are powerful, and so are the rituals that bring people together to express and share their common beliefs. Could a deep reading of Thomas Aquinas' neat theological arguments have ever brought so many to the experience of their God as the transcendental sensuousness of a high mass said in a great cathedral? The ethereal purity of Mozart's 'Ave Verum Corpus', the many-coloured shafts of light slanting down through curling clouds of sacred incense: is this not sublimity enough to cause even the convinced atheist to pause momentarily? This grand and voluptuous theatre, playing so powerfully on all one's senses, is what most directly reaches into the souls of so many.

The philosophical precepts we are talking of are already well known and have been spoken of often, just as they have also been disregarded for as long. Drawing together wisdom both modern and ancient, the guide for our era must promise a radical reshaping of how we see ourselves and the wider creation. And to make any sense to this age, it must reconcile the insights of both the scientific and spiritual quests.

As to how we, individually, conduct ourselves, I believe that a good and wise life is one in comfortable accord with nature and also with the best interests of human society. All else follows from this. When confronted by a moral question, we need simply reflect on the transience of forms and the eternal nature of existence, and meditate on the underlying unity of all things and our fellowship with all creatures. Only then will we surely make the best choice for ourselves, and for others.

This is affirmed by one of the great Christian mystics, the 13th century Dominican monk, Eckhart von Hochheim, better known as Meister Eckhart:

'People should not worry as much about what they do but rather about what they are. If they and their ways are good, then their deeds are radiant. If you are righteous, then what

you do will also be righteous. We should not think that holiness is based on what we do but rather on what we are, for it is not our works which sanctify us but we who sanctify our works.'

Where now? We must stand firmly for what we have discovered thus far, confident that right intentions and commitments will take us farther down the paths to yet greater insights and understanding. Along the way, our continuing task is to align our own evolving human needs with our deepening understanding of the cosmos. Inevitably, in my view, the majestic sweep of this great enterprise will take in many of the insights I ascribe to the Ocean of All Possibilities.

Perhaps, this vision seems too abstract and remote for most people - and provides no compelling reason to change familiar outlooks and behaviors. Most likely, I concede; but has such not always been the case? In Greece and Rome only few inquiring and reflective individuals ventured down the Stoic's road, drawn by its coolly rational and unsentimental vision of life as it is. No, what most folk looked for - then, as now - was ready consolation and reward and, above all, the firm promise of paradise, quite undiluted by philosophical reservation or speculation. And yet, if is true that only few had ever listened directly to its gentle counsel, there were many more whose lives came to be indirectly touched by what had once illumined the Stoa. What is more, that continues to our own age.

14. The Celestial Revolutionary

The Heroic Quest Continues

As he had done for many long nights, the gaunt prisoner peered out the cell window, his deep-set eyes intently fastened on the vista arcing across the black sky, untold billions of kilometres distant.

Auguste Blanqui, born in 1805, had been entombed within prison walls for most of his adult years, starting from when he was a young man and, now with hair and beard silvered by age, he was still not free.

A charismatic individual with an intellectual's high forehead, strong cheekbones and piercing gaze, Blanqui was a life-long revolutionary fanatically devoted to the violent overthrow of French monarchism, particularly as represented by the odious King Louis Philippe. Yet, again and again, his untiring struggles had only ever been rewarded by one setback after another. In that time he had received numerous jail terms, one of which was a death sentence commuted to life imprisonment, altogether accounting for 30 years of his 76-year lifetime.

Even now, Blanqui was as impossibly far as ever from his dream of leading a socialist insurrection. Little wonder that

Karl Marx, himself an early sympathiser, had finally dismissed Blanqui as a hopeless revolutionary.

So, one can easily imagine Blanqui staring out that cell window, night after long and solitary night, desperate to find momentary escape from his cramped confinement by contemplating the majestic heavens.

Despairing at the wreckage of all his hopes and plans, Blanqui's restless mind turned to another far-reaching enterprise. Gradually, we are told, an idea seized him that would inspire a remarkable book, *'Eternity by the Stars'* (1872). His nightly vigils had gifted him with an epiphany: the realisation that our little world floats in a Cosmos that *must* be both infinite and eternal.

As he wrote: *'Of course, the limitless universe is incomprehensible, but the limited universe is absurd.'*

If this is so, he reasoned, an unbounded plenitude would surely encompass everything that could ever happen, had happened - and was fated to happen yet again, endlessly. Worlds would follow worlds, as he described it, in the monotonous flow of an hourglass eternally turning itself over and emptying itself.

'What we have is ever-old newness and ever-new oldness.'

While our vast universe might encompass an incalculable variety of phenomena and interactions, the number of possibilities is not infinite, and as Blanqui declared:

'Such is our basis for affirming the limitation of differentiated combinations of matter and, consequently, their inability to sow celestial bodies throughout the fields of space. In spite of their multitude, these combinations are limited and, therefore, they must repeat themselves in order to attain the infinite. Nature prints a billion copies of each of its works. In the texture of the stars, similarity and repetition are the rule, dissimilarity and diversity, the exception.

Once we come to grips with such numbers, how are we to formulate them except by way of figures, their only interpreters? However, these interpreters by default are unfaithful and powerless; unfaithful, when it comes to the type-combinations whose number is limited; powerless and vacuous, as soon as we talk about the infinite repetitions of these combinations.'

He accepted that, in his words, *'One may come across a billion such earths before they encounter perfect resemblance'.* Nonetheless, across the tracts of eternity, there will be encountered our exact and near-exact twin-worlds – and more, our own selves:

'Each of our body-doubles is the child of an earth and each earth is the body-double of the actual earth. We are part of the copy. The lookalike-earth reproduces exactly everything that is found on ours and, consequently, it reproduces each individual, with its family, its house (for those who have one), and all the events of its life. It is a duplicate of our globe, both as content and as container. Nothing is missing.'

However, there will be those lives in which the smallest nudge by fickle chance would be enough to create a very divergent destiny:

'Show me a man who is not at one point in his life before two possible career paths. Although his individuality would remain unchanged the one he leaves aside would make his life very different. One career leads to misery, shame, and slavery. The other leads to glory, to freedom. Here, a charming wife and happiness all around; there a shrew and a life of desolation. I speak for both sexes. We take such and such option by chance or by choice; no matter: no one escapes fatality. On the other hand, fate has no grip on the infinite, for the infinite knows no alternatives and has room for everything.'

Unfortunately for Blanqui and the rest of us, we are doomed to retrace anew the steps of all our fates without any benefit of foresight or hindsight from our other lives:

'No one can warn anyone else. If only it were permitted to provide access to the history of our life, complete with a few good tips, to the doubles we have in space, we would spare them a lot of foolishness and sorrow...'

And, so:

'On billions of earths, the future will witness the very same ignorance, the very same foolishness, and the very same cruelties of our old ages!'

In a remarkable insight, Blanqui saw that within the Multiverse, every second of this version of our life has innumerable twin experiences.

'Every man is infinite and eternal through the being of other himselves, who are not only of his actual age, but also of all his ages. At every second, simultaneously, he has billions of body-doubles who are being born, others who are dying, others whose ages range, from second to second, from his birth to the age of his death.'

And again,

'Therefore, every one of us who has lived, lives, and shall live endlessly, under the form of billions of alter egos. Whatever we are at every second of our life is how we will be stereotyped to a billion copies in eternity.'

Thus, every being great or small, alive or inert, shares the privilege of this immortality, observed Blanqui, and with this comes a great solace:

'But is it not a consolation to know that at every moment, on billions of earths, we are in the company of beloved people, people who are now only a memory for us? Is it not another consolation, however, to think, that we have tasted this happiness and that we shall taste it eternally, under the guise of a body-double, of billions of body-doubles? It is truly ourselves.'

Blanqui would count off the creeping years in his dank cell alone and disavowed by the society he sought to save. But he would also live in other universes, possibly many more universes, where his dream of overturning tyrannical rule would be amply fulfilled and where ordinary men and women were enjoying the fruits of liberation and equality.

'Let us not forget that everything we could have been on this earth, we are it somewhere else.'

Dismissed as the flimsy, metaphysical fantasy of a failed revolutionary, Blanqui's book was to remain largely unknown for generations after his death. Even though we know from his own pen that Nietzsche was aware of *'Eternity by the Stars'*, we can only guess at the impact, if any, it had upon his own, more limited, notion of the Eternal Return. What little comment Blanqui's book attracted among his contemporaries largely focused on some astronomical errors: hardly surprising, given that he was an autodidact able to draw upon only very limited resources while writing in prison.

Later, of course, even some of his astronomical assertions deemed to be orthodox in his day were overtaken by new scientific discoveries. For example, in *'Eternity by the Stars'* he talked of the Sun's radiation being generated by the combustion of its hydrogen: physicists soon worked out that the solar stock of hydrogen, vast as it is, still could not possibly support a steady output of heat long enough to match the known geological ages on Earth. Only in the early 20th century did we learn that our sunshine comes from nuclear fusion in which hydrogen atoms are converted to helium, releasing a prodigious and sustained output of energy. For all these criticisms, which also apply to Poe's *'Eureka'*, they do not in any real way lessen the importance and originality - even from today's perspective - of Blanqui's central insights written back in the 19th century.

In any case, for generations Blanqui himself was remembered, if at all, only for the almost insanely dogged way in which he had clung to his violent brand of utopianism, despite all setbacks. (Even during the brief life of the left-wing Paris Commune insurrection, Blanqui was, inevitably, still mouldering in prison).

Rediscovering Blanqui

Luckily for us, the German-Jewish cultural historian, Walter Benjamin (1892-1940), chanced upon *'Eternity by the Stars'* and was struck by the similarities between Nietzsche's ideas on the Eternal Return and Blanqui's own earlier conclusions. Writing in 1938 of Blanqui's 'final phantasmagoria', Benjamin said of *'Eternity by the Stars'* that:

'...The book proclaims the idea of the eternal return ten years before Nietzsche's "Zarathustra", with hardly less pathos and with truly hallucinatory power.'

In an essay on the subject of recurrence, he explored the different ways it had been interpreted by Blanqui, Nietzsche and also by the French poet, Charles Baudelaire, another who subscribed to the idea and who was also an admirer, and translator, of Edgar Allen Poe's works.

Unfortunately, Benjamin died from his own hand while fleeing the Nazis only two years after that essay, but his support was enough to keep Blanqui's book in the view of a small number of thinkers and writers.

Borges & Blanqui

Among these, for example, was the famous Argentinian writer Jorge Luis Borges, who read *'Eternity by the Stars'* with great interest and referred to it in his 1936 essay, *'A History for Eternity'*. Here he noted the plurality, not only of worlds, but eternities:

'I will pause to consider this eternity from which the subsequent ones derive.'

It is easy to see how the concept of infinite possibilities inspired much of Borges' writing. Stories such as *'Tlön, Uqbar, Orbis Tertius'*, and many others, are threaded with themes of limitless multiplicity, parallel realities and other echoes of the infinite cosmos. In *'The Library of Babel'* short story of 1941, Borges imagines a library that contains not merely every book ever written, but every book that could possibly be written, with texts being generated randomly and ceaselessly. Churning out such an endless torrent of books might be a challenge even for the vaunted new quantum super-computer!

Borges' collection, *'Ficciones'* (1944) contains the short story, *'The Garden of Forking Paths'* ('El jardín de senderos que se bifurcan'), which looks at the coexistence of every possible narrative and fate, thus anticipating Hugh Everett by years:

'In the work of Ts'ui Pên, all possible outcomes occur; each one is the point of departure for other forkings. Sometimes, the paths of this labyrinth converge: for example, you arrive at this house, but in one of the possible pasts you are my enemy, in another, my friend.

This network of times which approached one another, forked, broke off, or were unaware of one another for centuries, embraces all possibilities of time.'

And, again:

'In contrast to Newton and Schopenhauer, your ancestor did not believe in a uniform, absolute time. He believed in an infinite series of times, in a growing, dizzying net of divergent, convergent and parallel times. This network of times which approached one another, forked, broke off, or were unaware of one another for centuries, embraces all possibilities of time. We do not exist in the majority of these times; in some you exist, and not I; in others I, and not you; in others, both of us.'

He ends with a thought that seems to anticipate the Many Worlds paper written by the young physicist, Dr. Hugh Everett, more than a decade later:

'Time forks perpetually toward innumerable futures. In one of them I am your enemy.'

Borges pays Blanqui the compliment of various allusions to his name, such as by giving a colour the name 'blanqiceleste' in his tale, 'El Aleph'.

The Bequest

Today, there is renewed interest in Blanqui's ideas about eternal recurrence - much more so than his plots against the now long-dethroned Bourbons. Like Edgar Allen Poe's earlier speculations on an infinite and expanding cosmos, Blanqui's speculations are now receiving their merited attention.

When I became aware of Blanqui's book I was disappointed to discover that, although published in French in 1872, it was, apparently, not available in an English translation. Deeming it importantly relevant to this book, I laboriously translated it, driving my imperfect French and translation software to the limits. Imagine my frustration, mixed with relief, when I learnt that just three weeks after completing my arduous task, it was announced that Blanqui's book had just been released in an English language edition, translated by Assistant Professor Frank Chouraqui. Not surprisingly, it presented a far more felicitous translation than my own effort. (That such an inconveniently mistimed coincidence could occur somewhere in the Multiverse was no wonder to me - but did it have to be in *this* universe?)

Occasionally I reflect upon the image of Blanqui, suffocatingly enclosed in his cell and peering through the bars up to the vast night sky. Were his feelings similar to those of Tolstoy's imprisoned Count Pierre Bezukhov, looking heavenwards and contemplating his death by firing squad:

'And all that is me, all that is within me, and it is all I!'

Fearing that he might never taste freedom again, Blanqui must surely have been consoled by the thought that in countless other worlds his life-long strivings would have been rewarded with success. Yes, there he would have been acclaimed by a grateful nation as the leader of the glorious insurrection that had finally overthrown the detested royalist reactionaries! But he also knew well that across eternity, his present bitter fate would also be revisited, again and again, time without number.

Finally released on account of ill health, Blanqui - all too predictably immediately resumed his tireless activism. Three years later, having just delivered an impassioned speech at a political meeting, the weakened revolutionary suffered a stroke and he died on the 1st of January, 1881. He rests among many giants of French civilisation in Paris' largest cemetery, the Cimetière du Père-Lachaise, in a tomb designed by the leading French sculptor of that age, Jules Dalou. Atop the tomb is a realistic and life-sized bronze sculpture of Auguste Blanqui, half-shrouded and lying like a fallen warrior, with garlands at his feet.

In Blanqui's indomitable striving do we see a metaphor for humanity's own condition? Staring into Eternity's black maw, we are groundlings of vanishingly small significance, yet some can find meaning to existence by reaching out to the ever-receding horizon of the Ocean of All Possibilities.

Printed in the United States
by Baker & Taylor Publisher Services